Expository
Commentary on
ACTS

Expository
Commentary on
ACTS

J.C. Macaulay

MOODY PRESS

CHICAGO

Formerly entitled *A Devotional Commentary on the Acts of the Apostles*

Copyright, 1946, by J. C. Macaulay

MOODY PRESS EDITION 1978

Library of Congress Cataloging in Publication Data

Macaulay, Joseph Cordner, 1900-
    Expository commentary on Acts.

    1. Bible. N.T. Acts—Commentaries. I. Title.

BS2625.3.M25   226'.6'07   78-9113

ISBN 0-8024-2421-X

Printed in the United States of America

TO MY WIFE,
who by her constant encouragements, kindly
criticisms, steadfast love, and unceasing prayer,
has proven herself a minister's true helpmeet,
I gratefully and affectionately
inscribe this work.

CONTENTS

PART THREE—INTO ALL THE WORLD

PART FOUR—THE MARCH ON ROME

FOREWORD

All true Christians would like to have apostolic results in their work for Christ. They would like to see large numbers of men and women brought into the Kingdom, every believer grow in grace and in the knowledge of our Lord and Saviour, and all church members active in the service of Christ; they would like to see the gospel sweep like a great fire over the whole world in this generation. In many hearts the conviction is deepening that now the times are auspicious for the launching of a great forward movement for Christ, both at home and abroad.

But many Christians forget that apostolic results are possible only on the basis of apostolic beliefs, experiences, and practices. We turn to the epistles for a formal exposition of those beliefs, for systematic teaching concerning the nature of Christian experience, and for authoritative instructions as to proper church polity. But we go to the book of Acts for a practical application of those doctrines to life, for concrete illustrations of the power of the Holy Spirit in the lives of the early believers, and for specific examples of apostolic church practice. In other words, we turn to the latter for an explanation of the marvelous power and growth of early Christianity.

Acts is, therefore, perpetually significant for the Christian church. Pastor Macaulay recognizes that fact and makes the most of it in this book. He shows that although some of the early practices are not to be regarded as precedents for all time (for instance, the practice of the community of goods), the book as a whole is intended to teach us what are the beliefs, experiences, and practices essential to success in every period of the church's history, including our own.

The author does not merely adhere loyally to Christ and the Scriptures, but also shows a deep personal acquaintance with both of them. His expositions are, therefore, no mere abstract analyses of the text, but living insights gained in the school of experience. In addition to those insights into the teaching of Scripture, the author displays a profound understanding of human nature and of the workings of the human mind. Since he writes in a charming style and enlivens his expositions with many an apt illustration and with choice bits of verse, these studies are bound to bring great blessings to all who may read them.

I heartily recommend this volume to all who desire to recapture for themselves and their congregations the enthusiasm of the early church, an absolute confidence in the power of the Christian message, and the secret of a Spirit-filled life.

HENRY C. THIESSEN

PREFACE

This work is not offered as a critical commentary. The devotional studies were prepared for my own people in line with the expository ministry which I seek to maintain. I offer them in this form, as a companion volume to my previous work on John's gospel, in the hope that a wider constituency may share the refreshing.

Need I throw out the suggestion that a reading of the text of Scripture will greatly add to the understanding of the studies, and so to the spiritual profit? The text has been omitted to save space, and to hold down the cost of the book. That should not be a great loss, since all who read this volume will doubtless have a copy of the Holy Scriptures to which they may conveniently turn.

I have not bound myself to the use of one version of the Bible. Where there was no special reason to do otherwise, I have in general followed the King James Version, but I have made free use of the American Standard Version also, which frequently makes the sense of a passage clearer. At times I have made bold to offer a rendering directly from the Greek, where I wished to lay special emphasis on a shade of thought not clearly brought out in the standard versions. At all times, both in quotation and in exposition, I have tried to be faithful to the original text.

As a record of action and experience, Acts is vibrant with interest, and one becomes more and more aware of the up-to-dateness of this ancient document. Its applicability to modern life, both for the individual and for the church, lends it perennial freshness. May the blessed Holy Spirit make His own applications to all our hearts, to the glory of the great Head of the church, our Lord and Saviour Jesus Christ.

PART ONE

Pentecost—and After

1

THE UNFINISHED WORK OF CHRIST

ACTS 1:1-5

In this first chapter we learn of:

1. The incomplete record (v. 1)
2. The infallible proof (vv. 2-3)
3. The indispensable equipment (vv. 4-5)

THE ANCIENTS frequently marked the graves of their dead with the symbol of a broken pillar. They thus expressed their sense of the incompleteness of this life. Such a symbol would be most inappropriate to the life of our blessed Lord, who came to His last hours with full consciousness of the task accomplished, and cried from the cross, "It is finished!" (John 19:30).

Yet the records of the gospel refuse to write finis at the end of their story of the life of Jesus. They have a strange new title covering His whole earthly sojourn—*Initia*. Mark affirms that his account is "the *beginning* of the gospel of Jesus Christ, the Son of God" (Mark 1:1, italics added), while Luke refers to the content of his gospel as "all that Jesus *began* both to do and teach" (Acts 1:1, italics added).

When a biography ends at a tomb, we may write finis and erect our broken pillar, but a story that ends with, "He was received up into heaven, and sat on the right hand of God" (Mark 16:19), is a first chapter only, not a complete record.

Winston Churchill, speaking in the British House of Commons on the North African victory, sought to curb the too easy optimism of the hour by saying, "This is not the end; it is not even the beginning of the end: it may be the end of the beginning." That is what the cross was—"The end of the beginning," a completion that opened the way

15

for vast operations, a work of provision that began the long labor of
application and realization. The divine processes of these two thousand years have been built upon the finished work of the cross. The
finished sacrifice is the material of the finished mystery. The new
heaven and the new earth are the end of that so dark beginning.

What is true cosmically is equally true in the individual. Calvary is
such an end as sends out "bright shootes of everlastingenesse" in the
souls of men. This book of the Acts of the apostles, the first published
volume of church history, relates the beginnings of these "bright
shootes." As we stand in the beam of them, may our own souls be
lightened from that seat at "the right hand of the throne of the
Majesty in the heavens" (Heb 8:1*b*, ASV) , where sits our risen, living,
glorified Lord, gathering the spoil of His work on the cross for the
final triumph.

The disciples learned that that day of sad ending was in reality a
most blessed beginning when "he shewed himself alive after his passion by many infallible proofs" (Acts 1:3*a*) . Their hopes had been
buried with Jesus in Joseph's new tomb. They "trusted that it was
he that should have redeemed Israel" (Luke 24:21, author's trans.) .
But that was a thing of the past, and they were engaged in the doleful
discipline of adjustment to a life wounded and scarred by the blasting
of their high and holy anticipations, when He broke in upon their
frustrations with His gentle reproofs and glad assurances; till they
could utter scarcely a word to each other except, "He is alive!" Now
they found themselves wrestling with another sort of adjustment—
adjustment to a joy and certainty that were almost as overwhelming
as the previous sorrow and darkness.

"In many indisputable evidences" (Acts 1:3*a*, author's trans.) , says
the sacred historian. After all, the supreme evidence was Himself,
standing before them alive. But the manner and the settings and the
accomplishments of those presentations of Himself were such as to add
proof to evidence. There was no place for hypnotic suggestions, for
the fancies of overwrought minds, for the play of vivid imagination or
wishful thinking. The appearings were not in keeping with previous
expectation, for despite His declarations that He would rise, they did
not expect Him. His enemies had given more heed to the promise of
resurrection than His friends! The "lines" of the incidents were too

clear for an apparition. "It is I myself" (Luke 24:39) was His constant assurance as he heaped evidence upon evidence to convince their questioning hearts.

The disappearings were as important as the appearings, for the Lord had the double task of establishing the disciples in the faith that He was alive, and teaching them to live in that faith when He was absent from view. Till at last, when He went up from them into heaven and they knew they would see Him no more as formerly, they departed from the scene of the ascension, not in deep mourning as from a tomb, but with great joy. His blessed presence was as real to them unseen as seen. The "infallible proofs" had worked.

All the days of His flesh the Lord had been "grooming" His followers for a great undertaking: the heralding of His name abroad. Those precious forty days constituted the graduate course for His disciples. "The things concerning the kingdom of God" (Acts 8:12) were the topic of His lessons. "Moses and all the prophets" (Luke 24:27) were His textbook. It was an intensive course. We have listened to sermons and read books setting forth Christ in the Old Testament. How we should have loved to listen in with the apostolic band as our Lord Himself handled that vast subject! But, then, He has given us the Holy Spirit to dwell in us, with the promise, "He shall take of the things of mine and shall reveal them unto you" (John 16:14, author's trans.). If only the Holy Spirit can command our ear, our mind, our heart, we too shall see our Lord drawn full stature "in the volume of the book" (Heb 10:7).

One would think that after all the training they had received under such a Teacher, both before His death and after His resurrection, the apostles would be fully prepared for the work of the ministry. Yet the Lord bade them tarry at Jerusalem until an event should transpire that would bring them the indispensable and invincible equipment. For all their understanding of the Scriptures, they were totally inadequate to the task before them until they should be endued with power from on high. That power was to come in a mighty, glorious baptism. "For John . . . baptized with water; but ye shall be baptized in the Holy Spirit not many days hence" (Acts 1:5, ASV).

This is not the place to discuss the various teachings in regard to the baptism of the Holy Spirit. Whatever else is involved in that

grand doctrine, it is clear that in His statement here our Lord linked
it with the thought of equipment for service, as the parallel passage
in Luke's gospel indicates. "Ye shall be baptized" means, among other
things, "ye [shall] be endued with power" (Luke 24:49*b*). If, then,
the apostles, after three years of training under the Lord Himself, followed by these forty marvelous days of communion with the risen
One, still required the Pentecostal effusion to fit them for the work of
the ministry, it is to be hoped that our young men will not make the
sad mistake of reckoning themselves fully equipped because they can
show diplomas bearing college and seminary degrees. We must bring
to the task such a submission of mind and heart to the blessed Holy
Spirit that He will have full control. Without it the training of the
schools is but ashes, while a man unlettered but filled with the Spirit
may be so used as to put to nought the wisdom of the wise. Scholarship is important, and to be sought after if the Lord permits, but the
Holy Spirit is the indispensable equipment of the servant of God. The
equipment is provided. We are not sent a-warring on our own charges.
Only in this case we do not use the equipment; the equipment uses us.

2

TIMES AND SEASONS

Acts 1:6-11

In this chapter we learn that this is the time to:

1. Witness with power (v. 8)
2. Walk by faith (v. 9)
3. Wait in hope (v. 11)

Dr. A. J. Gordon has reminded us that "Christianity is not a system of philosophy, but a revelation to faith." In that statement he is regarding philosophy as the attempt of the human mind to understand the mystery of the universe. It is the glory of man to search out a matter, but he has not progressed very far in the path of glory. Revelation is God's gracious gift to man, to save him from his groping and give him certainty where he most needs it.

If philosophy is bounded by the limits of human thought, revelation is limited only by the sovereign will of God. It is His glory to conceal or reveal at pleasure, and He does so according to His infinite wisdom and His purposes of grace. "It is given unto you to know the mysteries of the kingdom of heaven" (Matt 13:11), said our Lord to His little company of followers. Yet now the risen Lord declares to the same group, "It is not for you to know the times or the seasons, which the Father hath put in his own power" (Acts 1:7). So there are things which are "freely given to us of God" (1 Cor 2:12b) to know, while other matters are withheld.

That is a lesson that seems hard for us to receive, and in no department of revelation do we kick at the limitations more than in the prophetic sphere. We are intent on knowing the times and the seasons, so we build veritable pyramids of dogmatic interpretation, allowing no point to go unexplained. We had better be sure that our pyramids are not resting on their apex or buttressed with speculation rather than built of the granite of truth, lest they crash around us.

What could be more natural, or more legitimate, than the question of these disciples, in face of the renewal of their Messianic hopes by the resurrection of Christ from the dead? If their expectation of the revival of the Jewish kingdom had been keen in the days of our Lord's brief popularity, how much more sure were they now that the risen Lord would ride forth to conquest and a crown! But waving aside their question, He filled the season before them with holy occupation. "Ye shall receive power, after that the Holy Ghost is come upon you: and ye shall be witnesses unto me both in Jerusalem, and in all Judea, and in Samaria, and unto the uttermost part of the earth" (Acts 1:8).

"Ye shall be witnesses unto me." That is the grand occupation of the Christian church. Whenever the church has held undeviatingly to this holy task, she has gone forth "fair as the moon, clear as the sun, and terrible as an army with banners" (Song of Sol 6:10); but when she has deflected from her calling, she has brought herself into Philistian bondage. Too often evangelism has had to yield place to other emphases—learning, reform, ecclesiastical order, political power: and the church has invariably lost her luster by such perversion of accent, while salvation has always come with a renewal of the witnessing note. The great revivals that have brought new life to the church and saved nations have all been "reversions to type," a return to the original undertaking to make Christ known in the simplicity and power of the gospel.

Our task is no narrow one. It is first local, then provincial, then universal. "I believe in . . . the holy catholic church" is one phrase in the Apostles' Creed which many who parrot that magnificent statement have no right to utter. We are no true believers in "the holy catholic church" unless we are committed to holy catholic witnessing. When William Carey presented his question to a meeting of ministers in Northampton in 1786, "whether the command given to the apostles, to teach all nations, was not obligatory on all succeeding ministers to the end of the world," the chairman, Dr. Ryland, roundly reproved him: "You are a miserable enthusiast for asking such a question. Certainly nothing can be done before another Pentecost, when an effusion of miraculous gifts, including the gift of tongues, will give effect to the commission of Christ as at first." Carey's question will bear repeating, not just for ministers, but for all believers. Do we stand with Carey or Ryland? Is ours a personal Christ only, or a catholic Saviour?

"Not by might, nor by power, but by my spirit, saith the LORD of hosts" (Zech 4:6). The task is too much for us, for it is a divine work: but "ye shall receive power, the Holy Spirit coming upon you" (Acts 1:8, author's trans.). We cannot but deplore the manifest powerlessness of so much that goes by the name of ministry. We should not be judges of others, nor dictate the particular manifestations of the Holy Spirit; but we recall the power that lay on Charles G. Finney, as when the very sight of him on the street would bring great sinners to their knees in repentance; or when his passing through a factory so affected the men and women at their machines that the superintendent had all work stopped to give them an opportunity to get right with God. Such phenomenal power may not be the portion of all, but the essential power is promised, and each of us in his own sphere ought to be realizing it. There can be no excuse for a powerless testimony when the Holy Spirit has come to empower the witnesses.

"When he had spoken these things, while they beheld, he was taken up; and a cloud received him *out of their sight*" (Acts 1:9, italics added). Now "we walk by faith, not by sight" (2 Cor 5:7). And this also:"henceforth know we no man after the flesh: yea, though we have known Christ after the flesh, yet now . . . know we him no more [after the flesh]" (2 Cor 5:16). "Because thou hast seen me," said our Lord to humbled, convinced, penitent Thomas, "because thou hast seen me, thou hast believed: blessed are they that have not seen, and yet have believed" (John 20:29). Peter, beholding the blessedness of these, breaks out, "Whom having not seen, ye love; in whom, though now ye see him not, yet believing, ye rejoice with joy unspeakable and full of glory" (1 Pet 1:8).

Many a cloud hung low upon those disciples in the after days of their apostolic labors, seeming to blot out the light of His countenance. In such days they would remind each other: "Remember the cloud that received Him out of our sight that day on Olivet? That cloud did not rob us of our Lord! Did we not that day return to

Jerusalem with great joy? Then neither shall this take away our Lord from us. He Himself hath said, 'I will never leave thee, nor forsake thee.' "

Our clouds, too, will teach us the walk of faith. We sing:

> O may no earth-born cloud arise
> To hide Thee from Thy servant's eyes!

Sometimes the clouds come—from somewhere—and in the desolation of not seeing we think we are altogether forsaken. But it is not so. He has dropped these clouds upon us that we may learn a sturdier faith.

> When darkness hides His lovely face,
> I rest on His unchanging grace,

until we can truly say:

> I'd rather walk in the dark with God
> Than go alone in the light.

Then it is that we are enriched with "the treasures of darkness" (Isa 45:3).

One more thought. This time of witnessing with power and walking by faith is also a time of waiting in hope. "While they looked stedfastly toward heaven as he went up, behold, two men stood by them in white apparel; which also said, Ye men of Galilee, why stand ye gazing up into heaven? This same Jesus, which is taken up from you into heaven, shall so come in like manner as ye have seen him go into heaven" (Acts 1:10-11). "Ye turned to God from idols," wrote the apostle Paul to the Thessalonian believers, "to serve the living and the true God; and to wait for his Son from heaven" (1 Thess 1:9-10). Serving and waiting! The waiting will keep the serving from becoming drudgery, and the serving will keep the waiting from degenerating into luxury and idleness on the one hand, or disappointment and despair on the other hand. We need both. "We look for the Saviour" (Phil 3:20) while we labor for Him; and if the burden becomes heavier and the toil more arduous, if tribulation and distress and persecution and famine and nakedness and peril and sword fall to our lot, we shall but look more eagerly for Him, and the "blessed hope" (Titus 2:13) will flame more passionately in our breasts.

> So even I, and with a heart more burning,
> So even I, and with a hope more sweet,
> Groan for the hour, O Christ! of Thy returning,
> Faint for the flaming of Thine advent feet.

"In like manner!" We shall do well to exercise a becoming reserve in the interpretation of such a phrase. From other descriptions of His appearing we know there will be a very great difference between His ascension and that glorious event "to which the whole creation moves." Some things, however, we can say quite boldly, supported by the consistent testimony of Scripture.

The going was personal; so shall the coming be. "The Lord himself shall descend" (1 Thess 4:16).

The going was visible; so shall the coming be. "Every eye shall see him" (Rev 1:7b).

The going was physical; so shall the coming be. "We look for the Saviour, the Lord Jesus Christ: who shall change our vile body . . . like unto his own glorious body" (Phil 3:20-21).

He went in a cloud; He shall appear in the clouds of heaven. "Behold, he cometh with clouds" (Rev 1:7a).

He rose from Olivet; "His feet shall stand in that day upon the mount of Olive" (Zech 14:4).

He went last from the midst of His own; He shall, at His appearing, gather His own about Him. "So shall we ever be with the Lord" (1 Thess 4:17b).

And who is this that so cometh in like manner? It is "this same Jesus." Blessed assurance! "Jesus Christ the same yesterday, and to day, and for ever" (Heb 13:8). I need not wish that I had seen Him in the days of His humiliation, if when He comes arrayed in power and glory and majesty and splendor, He is "this same Jesus." Neither need I be in deadly fear of His dazzling presence if He is "this same Jesus." If it be "this same Jesus" who says, "Surely I come quickly" (Rev 22:20a), then my heart answers with my lips, "Even so, come, Lord Jesus!" (22:20b).

3

PENTECOST–PHENOMENA AND ESSENCE

ACTS 2:1-16

In this chapter we consider:

1. The phenomena of Pentecost and their symbolic significance
2. The essence of Pentecost in its dispensational and personal aspects

As SYMPTOMS and disease are related but not identical, so phenomena and essence are not to be confused. He is a poor physician who is content to alleviate symptoms instead of seeking out and treating the basic ailment. So he is inexpert in the holy things who mistakes manifestations for essential spiritual experience. Some appearances may indeed be uniform and necessary, but others will be dictated by time and circumstance. The experience of "falling in love" is quite elemental with our race, and certain manifestations we universally look for, while other phenomena of the new state of heart will vary with the occasion, determined by the age, disposition, background, and circumstances of the parties.

Pentecost had its phenomena, accompaniments of the coming of the Holy Spirit which appealed to the physical senses. These phenomena were three in number. There was the mysterious sound, as of a mighty rushing wind, which filled all the place where they were sitting. There were the strange tongues as of fire distributed upon them, sitting like a torch upon each head. There was the miraculous speech granted to the various members of the group, that they might speak the wonderful works of God in languages and dialects unknown to themselves but familiar to the hearers.

24

The question arises: Are these phenomena necessary to the essence, or do they belong to the occasion?

As for the first, it is rare, but not unique. A mighty work of the Holy Spirit was introduced in the Dutch Reformed Church of Worcester, South Africa, where Dr. Andrew Murray was pastor, in the year 1860, to the accompaniment of such a sound, increasing in intensity until it filled the building, and the whole congregation burst forth in prayer. But for the rare occasions when the phenomenon has been known, one could recite multitudes of remarkable visitations of the Holy Spirit not so signalized. This manifestation, then, must belong to the occasion, not to the essence.

I am not acquainted with any claim to a repetition of the "distributed tongues like as of fire" (Acts 2:3, author's trans.). So far as I know, that stands unique. Here also, then, is a phenomenon of the moment.

The presumption would be that the third phenomenon would share the nature of the others. Yet there is a widespread claim for the speaking in other tongues that it is the necessary evidence of the full blessing of the Holy Spirit. Without denying the possibility of tongues, it must be charged that many a Babel passes for a Pentecost. There are two other instances of speaking in tongues recorded in the Acts, while the apostle Paul warns a very unspiritual church to hold that particular manifestation in close check. Many notable movements of the Spirit, both in the New Testament and in the history of the church, have been without the accompaniment of tongues. They also have been in the control of the sovereign Spirit.

For all the occasional nature of these phenomena, they must carry some fundamental value. God is not a showman, making mere displays of fireworks. If God decreed certain phenomena to accompany the sending forth of His Spirit on an age-long mission, we can expect them to be symbolic of that mission in its several aspects.

What will the "sough" of the wind tell us? "The wind bloweth where it listeth, and thou hearest the sound thereof, but canst not tell whence it cometh, and whither it goeth: so is every one that is born of the Spirit" (John 3:8). To the spiritual ear that sound is articulate with the message of regeneration, telling of the new birth, the new life, the new freedom which the Holy Spirit gives. "Prophesy unto the wind, prophesy, son of man, and say to the wind, Thus saith the Lord GOD; Come from the four winds, O breath, and breathe upon these slain, that they may live. So I prophesied as he commanded me, and the breath came into them, and they lived, and stood up upon their feet, an exceeding great army" (Ezek 37:9-10).

> Breathe on me, breath of God:
>   Fill me with life anew,
> That I may love what Thou dost love,
>   And do what Thou wouldst do.
>   EDWIN HATCH

The "distributed tongues like as of fire" symbolize another operation of the Holy Spirit. The suggestion of fire, that deeply purifying substance, speaks of the work of sanctification. "Every thing that may abide the fire, ye shall make it go through the fire, and it shall be clean" (Num 31:23) was the command given to Israel concerning booty taken from the heathen. We who have been seized as spoil from the powers of darkness need the purging of fire. "He shall baptize you with the Holy Ghost and with fire" (Luke 3:16b), said the forerunner of Messiah, and a noted scholar, McNiele, comments, "Spirit and fire are coupled with one preposition as a double baptism." Indeed the baptism of fire is part of the Spirit baptism. The purification of Israel is to be effected, we are told, "by the spirit of judgment, and by the spirit of burning" (Isa 4:4b). "Unquenchable fire" (Matt 3:12b) is not only reserved for the final judgment of the impenitent, but is kindled in every redeemed heart for the continual burning out of impurities. Healing science practices burning for the removal of malignant matter, as in the use of radium. So the Holy Spirit is the Spirit of burning for the removal of defilements. By a live coal from off the altar were the lips of Isaiah purged for the ministry of the prophetic word. "Tongues like as of fire" symbolize the sanctifying of the chosen witnesses.

> So wash me Thou, without, within,
>   Or purge with fire if that must be:
> No matter how, if only sin
>   Die out in me, die out in me!

If the "tongues like as of fire" (Acts 2:3) speak of the purification of the witnesses, the "other tongues" in which they spoke "as the Spirit gave them utterance" (2:4) surely signify the witness itself. "Go ye into all the world, and preach the gospel to every creature" (Mark 16:15) was the Lord's command. "Ye shall be witnesses . . . unto the uttermost part of the earth" (Acts 1:8). The gospel to the whole world is the order of the new age introduced at Pentecost. Were not these "other tongues," then, symbolic and prophetic of the ever widening flow of the message; of our own day with its more than a thousand languages pressed into the service of the Word of God; and of a coming day when "a great multitude, which no man could number, of all nations, and kindreds, and people, and tongues" (Rev 7:9) shall echo back to witness in loud and harmonious praise, saying, "Salvation to our God which sitteth upon the throne, and unto the Lamb" (7:10)?

So the Holy Spirit came, in such manner as to present His mission—to regenerate, to sanctify, and to bear universal witness.

The essence of Pentecost must be regarded in two aspects—dispensational and personal.

Dispensationally, it marked the inauguration of the Spirit and the institution of the church.

"This is that" (Acts 2:16), said Peter, pointing back to the old prophecy of Joel concerning the pouring out of the Holy Spirit in measure unknown under the old covenant. Commentators have been eager to emphasize that Peter did not say, "This is the fulfillment of that which was spoken by the prophet Joel," but in more guarded terms, "This is that." On that ground the Pentecost effusion has been reduced to a kind of token payment, a sort of shadow fulfillment, of something reserved for a still future dispensation. Some scale it down to the point where one begins to wonder if Peter was quite honest in applying Joel's prophecy to the occasion at all! Actually, the phrase "this is that" is as strong a term of identification as he could have used. It does not indicate, indeed, that the thing prophesied was exhausted in that one day's experience; but it had arrived and would continue to operate to the consummation. The prophecy had looked for the age of the Spirit; Pentecost introduced it.

Whatever that baptism means in personal experience and realization, it has also corporate significance. The disciples were that day
made one body, and ideally every believer was caught up by that
baptism into that one body. "For in one Spirit were we all baptized
into one body" (1 Cor 12:13*a*, ASV). So the age of the Spirit is also
the age of "the church, which is his body, the fulness of him that
filleth all in all" (Eph 1:22-23). So also the Spirit and the Body began
together their evangelical mission, not merely in cooperation, but in
living union.

In the personal aspect, the essence of Pentecost is summed up in
the phrase, "They were all filled with the Holy Spirit" (Acts 2:4,
ASV). That is the norm of Christian experience. "Be filled with the
Spirit" (Eph 5:18*b*), says the apostle. It is both an invitation to
realize a blessed privilege and a command to fulfill a holy obligation.
This normal state will express itself in joyous fellowship among the
saints, a constant lifting up of the heart in praise to God, and an attitude of humility and meekness in our several relations. "By their
fruits ye shall know them" (Matt 7:20). The Spirit-filled life is one
producing the fruit of the Spirit: "love, joy, peace, long-suffering,
gentleness, goodness, faith, meekness, self-control" (Gal 5:22-23, author's trans.).

The norm of experience and the experience of the norm are not
synonymous terms. It is our Christian obligation to see that we are
not falling short of our privileges. But how are we to attain to the
Spirit-filled life? One recommends tarrying after the order of the
primitive group's waiting in Jerusalem, for some unmistakable "experience." Another counsels a simple asking, accompanied by implicit faith. Another affirms we do not have to ask, but exercise only
the faith of appropriation. Now I suggest there may be some truth in
all of these. The "tarrying" will not be to induce the Holy Spirit to
come to us, but to allow Him to search the inner springs of our hearts
until the hindrances to His full control are removed; the asking will
be for a completeness of giving and receiving possible only when every
controversy has been settled; and the appropriation of faith is, of
course, the basic attitude of heart by which alone we possess our possessions in Christ, entering progressively into our inheritance as we
increase in knowledge of the ways of the Lord.

Those who seek to "experience the norm" of the Spirit's fullness should be warned against the dangerous perversion of looking for an "it," a "feeling," a "manifestation," an "experience." The sovereign Spirit may indeed grant some such accompaniment of His enthronement to some, whole others receive no such demonstration. It is all as He wills, who knows what is best for each. Nor should we mistake temperamental reactions for spiritual manifestations. The real test of our being "filled with the Spirit" is the measure in which the Lord Jesus is formed in us and glorified through us.

4

THE MANIFESTO OF A NEW AGE

ACTS 2:14-36

In this chapter we find that Peter preached a sermon on three pronouns:

1. An explanation concerning "This"
2. A proclamation concerning "Him"
3. An application concerning "You"

PETER'S MESSAGE on the day of Pentecost was homiletically correct as well as doctrinally sound. He had a theme that required skillful development. Before proceeding with it, he was under the necessity of adjusting the excited minds of the crowd to the sober, majestic topic of the hour. Then, too, his witness demanded a certain and definitive response from his hearers. The sermon, therefore, resolved itself into three distinct parts—the introduction, the development, and the application. Each of these parts carries a pronoun for its title. The introduction explains "this," the development proclaims "Him," and the application concerns "you."

We read of a certain Simon who threw his sermonic ditties down upon the heads of the amazed people from the top of a sixty-foot pillar. The Simon of Pentecost, for all the raptures of the recent effusion, had sense enough to begin his sermon on the level of his hearers. He took as his starting point their questioning amazement at the phenomena before them. "What meaneth this?" (Acts 2:12), they were asking, while some were advancing the thoughtless and utterly inadequate explanation, "These men are drunk" (see 2:13).

For two reasons Peter began with this ecstasy of the believers that was expressing itself in the testimony of the multitudinous but unconfused tongues. In the first place, it was hopeless to introduce his theme until some understanding of "this" was given to the assembly. Still more important, "this" had a definite relation to "Him." He will indicate that relation before he ends his sermon.

The apostle's explanation of "this" consists of a negation and an affirmation: "Not as you suppose are these drunk . . . but this is that which hath been spoken by the prophet Joel" (Acts 2:15-16, author's trans.) .

The form of the negation subtly admits a kind of intoxication, but a denial of the sort hinted. That is quite remarkable, for it suggests some likeness between inebriation and the fullness of the Holy Spirit. The same two conditions are thrown into juxtaposition in Paul's exhortation, "Be not drunk with wine . . . but be filled with the Spirit" (Eph 5:18) .

The likenesses are really contrasts. Wine affords an artificial exhilaration that simulates the holy elevation wrought by the Spirit of God. The stimulation of wine is toward evil, a quickening of the natural passions, while that of the Holy Spirit is in the realm of holiness. The momentary effect of wine recedes to leave a man weakened and debased, while the steady control of the Holy Spirit builds strength and nobility of character. Men "filled with new wine" (Acts 2:13, ASV) act in an exaggerated fashion, often ludicrous; men "filled with the Holy Spirit" (Acts 2:4, ASV) live above their natural selves, and "do exploits" (Dan 11:28) in the strength of the Lord God.

There is little danger of the world's accusing the average Christian of drunkenness. We are afraid of the holy intoxication, yet only as the church is lifted from the dead levels to an exuberant life will she command the notice of men for her message and mission. We are willing to bear, in some measure, the reproach of Christ. Is there not also a reproach of the Spirit?

The apostle's appeal to the prophetic Scriptures for an affirmative explanation of the remarkable phenomena of the hour was eminently satisfactory, for by it the preacher not only made a notable announcement of an epochal event, but incidently won his hearers' favorable attention for his main message.

The substance of Peter's statement concerning "Him" is contained in the designations at the beginning and the end of it: *Jesus of Naza-*

reth is *Lord and Christ.* This amazing leap of thought is made in three movements; and so skillful are the movements, and so deep the convincings of the Holy Spirit, that when the preacher arrives, three thousand people have arrived with him.

The first movement is factual and providential. The appeal is made to the life, the death, and the resurrection of Christ as facts which defy denial, and to the action of God in these events. The approval of God was on the life of this Jesus of Nazareth; the predestination of God was in His suffering and death; the mighty power of God was manifest in His resurrection. Are the marks of divine approval, divine purpose, and divine power seen in our ways?

The second movement is scriptural and dialectical. The great resurrection psalm is quoted. Then the argument follows that the inspired psalmist could not have written this about himself, as his tomb testified, so he must have been writing prophetically of the Christ "that his soul was not left in hell [sheol or hades], neither his flesh did see corruption" (Acts 2:31). One in whom these remarkable conditions are fulfilled can be none other than the Christ, and Peter stands supported by a goodly company in testifying that they have been fulfilled in "this Jesus" (2:32).

The third movement is experiential and dogmatic. The apostolic group and others with them have experienced this mighty effusion of the Holy Spirit, which is not only in keeping with the words of the prophets, but is in fulfillment of His own promise, and as such is full demonstration to them that Jesus has been received and exalted in heaven. Moreover, the senses of the hearers bear witness, for "this, which ye now see and hear" (2:33*b*), is a divinely suitable token of the enthronement of Messiah at the right hand of God. Thus, providentially ordered events, rightly divided Scriptures, and wholly unmistakable experiences give one voice to the dogmatic assertion that "God hath made that same Jesus, whom ye have crucified, both Lord and Christ" (2:36).

Preachers do not generally invite interruptions in their discourses, but any true herald of the gospel would welcome the sort of interruption that came at this point in Peter's sermon. Stirred with conviction of their sin and guilt, the hearers cried out, "Men and brethren, what shall we do?" (2:37*b*). The congregation asked for the application. A sermon without an application is an arrow shot at a venture, which may perchance reach the slit in some Ahab's armor, but which is more likely to be lost in the woods. The application is the sighting of the arrow on the bull's-eye of the target.

Peter's hearers perceived that if Jesus of Nazareth were indeed Lord and Christ, they were under obligation to do something about it. When His Royal Highness the Duke of York was crowned and enthroned on May 12, 1937, and received his regal title, it became necessary for certain representative personages to come forward and pay homage. These obligations affected only those within the British Commonwealth. That Albert Fredrick Arthur George, of the House of Windsor, became George the Sixth, by the Grace of God, of Great Britain, Ireland, and the British Dominions beyond the Seas, King, Defender of the Faith, Emperor of India was a matter of more or less passing interest to Americans, but there was nothing for them to do about it, no duty imposed on them with respect to it. But the elevation of Jesus of Nazareth to the "right hand of the throne of the Majesty in the heavens" (Heb 8:1) lays necessity upon every intelligent being in the universe, to neglect which is an act of high treason, punishable with "everlasting destruction from the presence of the Lord" (2 Thess 1:9). I do not wonder at the urgency of those awakened Jews on the day of Pentecost. Would that all were similarly eager to submit to the requirements of the exaltation of Christ Jesus our Lord!

"*What* shall we do? . . . Repent, and be baptized every one of you" (Acts 2:37b-38). That does not sound very evangelical to some who insist on the "only believe" of the gospel. But gospel believing is the most radical, the most revolutionary, thing in the soul of man. It demands action. There can be no true believing without repentance, a complete turning of the heart from sin, to be set in the new direction of Christ and holiness. There can be no saving faith without a readiness to be known as belonging to Christ; and baptism, among other things, is a public confession of union with Him.

Actually the question of the Jews, "What shall we do?" was itself indicative that they believed Peter's testimony concerning Jesus of Nazareth, that He is Lord and Christ. Peter answered their question by calling for the proof of their faith in a turning from sin and a symbolic, open identification of themselves with the Lord Jesus. This application concerns *you*. What will *you do with Jesus,* who is called Christ?

Note to Chapter 4

Baptism is a much abused ordinance, and has become a problem and a bone of contention because of the changes that have been made in both the doctrine and the practice of it. There was no such difficulty in apostolic times. Those who came to the knowledge and faith of the Lord Jesus were instructed to be baptized in public acknowledgment of their union with Christ, and they obeyed without question, not in order to be saved, but with respect to the salvation which they had received.

The words of Peter here have been frequently used in bestowing saving powers upon the ordinance. "Then Peter said unto them, Repent, and be baptized every one of you in the name of Jesus Christ for the remission of sins" (Acts 2:38). So reads the King James Version. On the last phrase Dr. A. T. Robertson in his *Word Pictures in the New Testament,* says:

> This phrase is the subject of endless controversy as men look at it from the standpoint of sacramental or of evangelical theology. In themselves the words can express aim or purpose for that use of *eis* does exist as in I Cor. 2:7 *eis doxan hemon* (for our glory). But then another usage exists which is just as good Greek as the use of *eis* for aim or purpose. It is seen in Matt. 10:41 in three examples *eis onoma prophētou, dikaiou, mathētou* where it cannot be purpose or aim, but rather the basis or ground, on the basis of the name of prophet, righteous man, disciple, because one is, etc. It is seen again in Matt. 12:41 about the preaching of Jonah *(eis to kērugma Iona)*. They repented because of (or at) the preaching of Jonah. The illustrations of both usages are numerous in the N.T. and the *Koiné* generally (Robertson, *Grammar,* p. 592). One will decide the use here according as he believes that baptism is essential to the remission of sins or not. My view is decidedly against the idea that Peter, Paul, or anyone in the New Testament taught baptism as essentia to the remission of sins or the means of securing such remission So I understand Peter to be urging baptism on each of them wht had

already turned (repented) and for it to be done in the name of Jesus Christ on the basis of the forgiveness of sins which they had already received.[1]

1. A. T. Robertson, *Word Pictures in the New Testament* (Nashville: Broadman, 1930), 3:35-36. Used by permission.

5

THE SPIRITUAL AND SOCIAL ORDER OF PENTECOST

Acts 2:41-47

In this chapter we have a glimpse of:

1. The spiritual life of the early Christians, expressed in close adherence to the means of grace
2. The social life of the early Christians, expressed in a magnificent application of the communal principle

Our Lord speaks of one who "heareth the word, and anon with joy receiveth it" (Matt 13:20), but He goes on to tell the sad story of that one's speedy defection under trial. His reception of the Word was in the surface soil of shallow emotion. John Bunyan has erected a monument to his tribe in his Pliable, Christian's first eager companion, whose endurance failed at the first hurdle, the Slough of Despond. The Pentecost harvest was a different strain. Another word than our Lord's is used to describe their acceptance of the gospel, an emphatic word suggesting the opening of their whole being to the entrance and operation of the blessed truth. The sharp arrows had pierced their hearts till they cried out, "What shall we do?" Then were they of the same mind as Christian, who, when warned by Mr. Worldly Wiseman of the "wearisomeness, painfulness, hunger, perils, nakedness, sword, lions, dragons, darkness, and death" likely to be met on the pilgrim way, replied, "Why, sir, this burden upon my back is more terrible to me than all these things which you have mentioned; nay, methinks I care not what I meet with in the way, if so be I can also meet with deliverance from my burden." Oh that the King would ride forth with His sharp arrows! Then would there be less of the partial receiving of the Word, the shallow emotional or the cold intellectual acceptance of it, and more of the deep, complete, decisive yielding to its penetrating power.

"Then they that gladly received his word were baptized" (Acts 2:41a). And they were given baptism without a year's probation, too, for the work of the Spirit was so evident that day that no such delay was needed. "Who can forbid water, that these should not be baptized who have received the Holy Ghost as well as we?" (10:47, author's trans.), asked the same preacher in the house of Cornelius.

What a baptismal service! Not at all impossible! There were plenty of pools in Jerusalem, and plenty of well-practiced apostolic hands for the task. Doctor J. E. Clough is reported to have baptized, with his own hands, in one day, 2,222 Telugu converts during the great movement in India. I am thinking how wonderful it must have been to receive and administer baptism in those Pentecostal days when there was no contention as to the proper mode, the rightful subjects, and "whether or not" one should be baptized at all. The innovations of man, both in the doctrine and in the practice, have wrought much confusion. "Reversion to type," a law in the natural realm, needs to be studied and practiced in the church.

"And the same day there were added . . . about three thousand souls" (Acts 2:41b). I am glad the record says "souls." Too often there are only "names" added, nothing having happened to the "souls" except to confirm them in their hypocrisy. When I was pastor in a Cleveland, Ohio, church, I received a letter from an evangelist inviting himself to hold meetings in my church, with a "guarantee" of a hundred additions to our membership! I'd rather have one the Pentecostal way of conviction and conversion than ten thousand that way.

There was no quick evaporation of the Pentecostal work. "They continued stedfastly" (2:42a). They were determined to go through with their newfound faith, and showed dogged persistence in what we sometimes call the "means of grace," those things whose neglect or whose merely formal practice is responsible for so much spiritual feebleness and backsliding. Here are the four building exercises: the teaching, the fellowship, the communion, and the prayers. The teaching was apostolic, whose content, both doctrinal and practical, we have in the volume of the New Testament, so that the sum of the teaching given to the instruction classes after Pentecost is available to us still. The New Testament, of course, is not apart from the Old, from whose pages the apostles drew their doctrine as the Holy Spirit taught them of its grand fulfillment in the new covenant. "All scripture is given by inspiration of God, and is profitable for doctrine, for reproof, for correction, for instruction in righteousness: that the man of God may be perfect, throughly furnished unto all good works" (2 Tim 3:16-17). So we, too, are exhorted, "Desire the sincere milk of the word, that ye may grow thereby" (1 Pet 2:2).

"The fellowship" was the exercise and realization of the new relationship into which the believers had entered with each other as "the body of Christ, and members in particular" (1 Cor 12:27). There was no need as yet to say to that group of Christians, "Forsake not the assembling of yourselves together" (Heb 10:25, author's trans.), for they were kin to those of whom Malachi spoke: "Then they that feared the LORD spake often one to another: and the LORD hearkened, and heard it, and a book of remembrance was written before him for them that feared the LORD, and that thought upon his name" (Mal 3:16). There can be no healthy Christian life in isolation. One who is providentially deprived of assembly privileges will doubtless receive special grace, but deliberate neglect of Christian fellowship will bring its inevitable harvest of spiritual atrophy. It is "with all saints," not in grand aloofness, that we comprehend "what is the breadth, and length, and depth, and height" (Eph 3:18) of the love of Christ.

"The breaking of the bread" (Acts 2:42b, author's trans.) no doubt refers here to the ordinance of bread and wine our Lord established for the church in connection with His last Passover. The two definite articles in the Greek, coupled with the context of church order, make the meaning clear enough. How often this "breaking of the bread" was observed in the first days of the church cannot be well determined. It may have been every day, as the climax of the common meal, as the institution of the new feast was the climax of the Passover supper. The feast and the Lord's Supper seem to have been regularly so related for some time, till the abuses of gluttony and drunkenness necessitated a separation of the two, and the love feast gradually fell out of use. Apart from all that, these first Christians engaged in the simple feast of bread and wine as a loving memorial of the Lord, as a proclamation of His death in its vicarious and redemptive value, and as a seal of their communion in this holy faith.

"And in the prayers" (Acts 2:42c, author's trans.). Yes, the article is in the Greek here, too, the reference being clearly to the public prayers in the assembly of believers. Various words are used for prayer in the New Testament. Archbishop Trench has dealt with seven of them in his "New Testament synonyms." Of all the words for prayer, that used here is at once the most exclusive and the most inclusive: the most exclusive in that it represents prayer offered only to God, being a sacred word; and the most inclusive in that it embraces all the exercises of the soul which can be denominated prayer. Adoration, confession, petition, and thanksgiving: all were included in "the prayers."

Now "the prayers" have fallen upon hard days. In liturgical churches they are given the place of prominence that they demand, but too often they are mere recitations of pious sentiments without heart or feeling. In nonconformist churches, apart from the sentence invocation, the offertory, and the benediction, "the prayers" have been reduced to "the pastoral prayer," which must not be too long, being part of that necessary nuisance baggage which we glorify with the title "preliminaries." As to the form of the prayers, nothing is indicated here, but I would not be at all surprised if, in addition to what we call free prayers, those first Christians, accustomed as they were to the stated prayers of the Temple and the synagogue, repeated in concert old prayers that took on new meaning in Christ, and perhaps new prayers taught them by the apostles. At any rate, the prayers were a carefully guarded exercise of the assembly, when they thoughtfully and earnestly worshiped God, adoring His glorious being, confessing their sins, petitioning His grace, and giving hearty thanks for the multitude of His mercies; and I only wish we could be more unhurried and worshipful in that part of our modern services.

Here, then, are the four aspects of church life to which the Pentecostal believers gave persistent attention: the preaching, the fellowship, the communion, and the prayers. Closer adherence to these would make stronger Christians today.

A brief word about the social order of the first church is not out of place, for spiritual order ought to have appropriate social expression. They had all things common, we are told. Here was a magnificent experiment in communism, the social scientist will say. Was it an experiment or was it an expedient or a bit of both? Dr. A. T. Robertson suggests that many of the new converts, who would normally have turned homeward right after the Feast of Pentecost, lingered in Jerusalem to learn more about their newfound faith, thus creating an economic situation that was met by this application of the communal principle, being a temporary expansion of the simple economy practiced in the apostolic band while the Lord was with them in the flesh. After the sad case of Ananias and Sapphira, we have no further mention of the plan being followed. Its necessity was probably short-lived.

Whatever interesting features of the phenomenon may be in doubt, some things are clear enough. It was quite a voluntary movement, not a matter of command, as Peter reminded Ananias. Again, it was an expression of a new sense of oneness in Christ. They were members one of another, and since they had Christ in common, it seemed only logical that the lesser things should be held in common also. It was a magnificent vision, but all too soon it became evident that too much common clay still persisted in the church to make it practical as a permanent measure, even if it had been so intended. An advanced degree of sanctification is required to deliver us wholly from covetousness, that rock upon which ideals are so often wrecked. But for all the failures of all the experiments, we must hold and practice the Christian principle which has inspired them all. We dare not regard our possessions as our own. They belong to our common Lord and Master and are committed to us in sacred trust, not for the gratifying of our own lust, but for distribution to the needs of His household.

I have just been reading about an early Archbishop of Canterbury, Hubert Walter, who died in 1205, and from whose tomb was taken, near the end of last century, a beautiful silver-gilt chalice which the ancient cleric used in Palestine on one of the crusades. This man ruled for King Richard, Coeur de Lion, during his absence from England, and so dominated King John that the latter said on the churchman's death, "Now for the first time I am king of England." But the chief fame of this strong ecclesiastic and statesman was his benevolence. It is recorded of him that "he was so bountiful in providing for the poor and the wayfarer that his income seemed common property." He carried out the spirit of the communal principle which is inherent in the Christian relation.

In view of the asceticism and the monasticism which later developed in the church, it is interesting to read this description of the combined spirituality and sociability of those early Christians in the first flush of the Holy Spirit's baptism: "And they, . . . [persevering] daily with one accord in the temple, and breaking bread from house to house, did eat their meat with gladness and singleness of heart, praising God" (Acts 2:46-47a). The social instinct was neither crushed nor perverted, but directed and guarded. A Christian man is likely to feel very much out of place in environments that are foreign and inimical to his renewed spirit, but he does have a social life that abounds in joy and ministers to the glory of God.

Christians at once so devoted and so radiant will be in favor, even when the tide of persecution rises; and their testimony will be the Lord's instrument in adding to the church daily such as are being saved.

6

PENTECOST IN DEMONSTRATION

ACTS 3:1-11

In this chapter we see:

1. A beggar in abject poverty
2. A preacher with ample provision
3. A Saviour with adequate power

I AM PUZZLED to know how this man remained a cripple for all the times that Jesus must have passed through that very gate where he sat daily begging. Perhaps he was a newcomer to Jerusalem, brought by his relatives to this center of their religion in the hope that he would secure a more bountiful living from the piety of Jews visiting the holy city from all over the world. Perhaps he was quite contented with his lot, and until this time cared not for a healing that would have robbed him of his easy living. For we have heard of beggars making fortunes. A sufficiently appealing exterior will play on the pity of the populace.

At any rate, here he was, doubly lame: lame in his feet by a congenital disease that had no cure, and lame in his soul with an apathy toward life that made him content to receive alms all his days. His forty years had aroused in him no fire of independence. So long as he was sustained in his disability, he did not attempt to rise above it. In all this he well pictures the sinner in his inability to serve God, to walk in the way of holiness, or to understand the things of the Kingdom of God; and particularly does he represent the sinner who is quite insensible to his lost condition, content so long as the world will provide such things as satisfy his natural appetites.

42

As this lame beggar sat at the gate Beautiful, which led into Solomon's porch, Peter and John came in midafternoon, for not yet were the Christians cut off from the Temple. The beggar recognized them as leaders in the events that had stirred the whole city but a few days before, for beggars know all that transpires in a community. They are a sort of listening post for all gossip. So our man was sure his luck was in when he saw Peter and John. They would be sure to give a substantial sum, and do it openly, so as to uphold their prestige as leaders of the new movement.

So right from the beginning the church has been regarded as a charitable institution, called into being for the sole purpose of distributing handouts to all and sundry. Of course, charity has kept pace with advancing civilization, and has been promoted to the rank of social service, so the church, while doing a little old-fashioned charity on the side, is called upon to lead the new charity, preach a social gospel, and promote the whole scheme of social betterment.

Now I have no objection to the church being a charitable institution; the church surely ought to have a prophetic voice against abuses and evils of all kinds, and Christians should not be so aloof from the world that they lose interest in the alleviation of distresses, injustices, and oppressions. Only the church must remember that she has a bigger job that she dare not neglect in zeal for betterment programs. The philosophy of the world says, "New conditions will make new men." We answer, "New men will make new conditions." And our job is the making of new men.

The evangelistic movement introduced by the Wesleys did more for social uplift in England than all other factors combined. It was the spiritual impetus of a whole age of reform.

See how Peter and John operated on this parabolic occasion. They did not help to sustain the man in his inability; they set about removing the inability. "Silver and gold have I none" (Acts 3:6a), began Peter. Now that was strange! For all the lands that had been sold and all the money that had been laid down at his feet, Peter did not have so much as a silver dime. Apparently he had not collected the apostolic revenue as his "successors" have done. "You see," said Pope Innocent IV to St. Thomas Aquinas as he sat before piles of money. "You see, Thomas, that the Church cannot now say as the Primitive Church

did, 'Silver and gold have I none.' " "Yes, holy father," replied
Thomas, "but neither can she say, as did St. Peter to a crippled man,
'Arise and walk.' "

"Money is power," we are told. And in this world money can do
and obtain almost anything. But when money becomes power in the
church, then the church has lost her power and picked up a poor
substitute.

Peter was making no apology for his poverty. He was rather introducing a boast. He had something far greater, far more precious,
than silver and gold. He had Christ! But is Christ really more precious than silver and gold? Do not some choose illicit gain before Him?
Do not even some who profess His name deny Him at times for profit?
And do not many evince far more zeal in driving for financial prosperity than in seeking after Him? Oh, to realize the preciousness of
Jesus! How many of your tears will money wipe away in the hour of
your sorrow? How much new courage will money inspire in the day
of affliction? How much rest of heart, how much peace of mind, how
much ease of conscience, will money buy? What will money do for
you in the day of death? It will secure for you an elaborate funeral
and a striking tombstone. Indeed, the moneyed man is poor without
Christ, and he can lend little help who has only money to give; but
rich beyond calculation is the man who has Christ, and whoso brings
us Christ is our greatest benefactor.

Ring out your boast, Peter! "Silver and gold have I none," which
would but support the man in his beggary and impotency. You have
that which will save him from both.

"But what I have, that give I thee" (Acts 3:6b, ASV). Now Peter
was not one whit the poorer for giving what he had. And that is a law
of the spiritual realm. The richest things are increased by distribution, and sharing Christ and His gifts multiplies our possession.
George Appia, a European Evangelical of last century, used to say,
"The Gospel is a strange merchandise. The more you export, the
more remains."

"In the name of Jesus Christ of Nazareth, walk" (3:6c, ASV).
Daring words these, by which Peter committed to the proof of demonstration that Jesus Christ was alive and present in power. The apostle
was not acting the part of a conjurer who has learned the trick from

another. He was representing a living, present, divine Saviour, whose power he invoked to meet this need and to establish the testimony.

As he spoke the word of command, Peter took the man by the right hand and began to pull him up. The confused thinking of the man was helped to take shape by that handclasp and that upward tug, until it dawned on him that Jesus Christ, of whose miracles he had heard much, was present in this simple but radiant man before him, offering him release from his life of mendicancy and helplessness. His soul awoke from its dead slumber, a surge of hope and faith rose within him, and, as he responded to the pull of Peter's strong hand, he felt a sudden firmness in his heretofore useless heels and ankles, and shot up with a snap that startled even himself. The miracle was complete. No gradual finding of his balance, no unsteady practice in locomotion; he immediately started to walk, and even went leaping like a delighted child, while his tongue, too, was unloosed, until the Temple courts rang again with the voice of his thanksgiving to God.

The word Luke uses in this passage for "feet" is interesting and suggestive. It is used for that upon which a thing rests, and anatomically it means that part of the foot upon which the leg rests. The word is *basis,* from which, of course, we have our own English "basis." The thought suggested by this little bit of etymology is that Peter, in the name of the Lord, did a basic work for this man, instead of a superficial work of just feeding his impotence. God wants us to stand and walk like men. Those who are brought up in a Christian environment are somewhat sheltered from certain forms of temptation, surrounded by wholesome and helpful influences. Be careful that you are not just being carried and fed in these good surroundings. Someday you may, you will, be in a very different atmosphere, and you must be able to stand and walk and leap in all weathers. See, then, that there is a basic work done in your heart, that your spiritual base is sound.

When Andrew Bonar died in Glasgow, one of his converts and admirers despaired of being able to continue as a Christian, deprived of the help of his good minister. He began walking through Kelvingrove Park, where many nursemaids bring the babies under their care for a daily walk. Now in those days many Christian parents named children after the godly and beloved minister. Just as the despairing Christian passed a baby buggy carrying twins, the nursemaid in charge said peremptorily to one of the little tots, "Don't lean on Andrew Bonar!" It proved God's message to him. Don't lean on human influences. Look to the Lord to do a basic work in you, to put His strength into your feet and anklebones, so that you can stand anywhere. And if you have fallen, let Him take you by the hand. He will lift you up and make you stand and walk and leap and sing!

7

PETER EXPLAINS

Acts 3:11-26

In this chapter we have:

1. An explanation of the miracle
2. An exhortation to the multitude
3. An expectation of the Messiah

FOR THE SECOND, and not the last, time Peter is under necessity to explain. This was one sort of situation which he was always able to turn to good account. We have already seen him turn the gaping wonderment of the crowds on the day of Pentecost to the uses of the gospel, making a statement well worthy to be called the manifesto of a new age. Here again the amazement of the people at the miraculous healing of the lame man calls for explanation, and becomes the occasion of another magnificent testimony.

"You may mention my name!" There is power in a name. Where we do not rate highly enough to secure what we desire for ourselves, the mention of a name may just tip the scales in our favor, whether the object be a position, a reservation on a plane, or other consideration. The most influential human name, however, is limited in the range of its power. The best of them cannot reach beyond the human sphere. What care the birds, the beasts, the trees, the rocks, for the name of a pauper or a king? The sun will scorch prince and peasant alike, the rain will soak them both, and death will stay for neither. Speaking of names to conjure with, Shakespeare makes Cassius declare that " 'Brutus' will start a spirit as soon as 'Caesar.' " But it will take a long time for either name to do it! As for God, He accepts the person of no man, nor will the name of any creature move Him.

47

Is there a name that can reach into every realm, supernal and infernal, celestial and terrestrial, and command obedience and obeisance? Yes, there is such a name. "God also highly exalted Him, and bestowed freely on Him the name above every name, so that in the name of Jesus every knee might bow, of things in heaven and of things on earth and of things below the earth, and that every tongue might acknowledge that Jesus Christ is Lord, for the glory of God the Father" (Phil 2:9-11, author's trans.). God "set him at his own right hand in the heavenly places, far above all principality, and power, and might, and dominion, and every name that is named, not only in this world, but also in that which is to come" (Eph 1:20-21). There is no creature beyond the power of that name. Animate and inanimate, mortal and immortal, material and immaterial, visible and invisible, all must bow at its very mention.

But may men use that all-prevailing name? Has this august Person said to mortals, "You may mention My name?" Yes; that is our hope of salvation: "for there is none other name under heaven given among men, whereby we must be saved" (Acts 4:12). That is our power in prayer: "If ye shall ask any thing in my name, I will do it" (John 14:14). And that is the answer to our problems: "In the name of Jesus Christ of Nazareth rise up and walk" (Acts 4:6c).

The exercise of the very simple principle of faith brings the power of the all-prevailing name into action. We come to God in all the vileness of our sin, seeking pardon, cleansing, deliverance. We offer only one plea—"Jesus told me to mention His name." Immediately, by the sacrifice that was made, by the blood that was shed, by the covenant that was sealed, God grants the plea, and the sinner is "accepted in the beloved" (Eph 1:6). We come with our need, our burden, our longing. We tremble at our daring, but we stammer, "Jesus told me to mention His name." At once there is made over to us, in the divine will, "exceeding abundantly above all that we ask or think" (Eph 3:20). Is it as simple as that? Yes, and that is what makes it so difficult. We have stumbled at the simplicity of it. We have lacked faith because we have lacked simplicity. We are so looking for mysteries that we let the wonder of simple prayer in the name of Jesus go by. "Mention My name!" "And his name through faith in his name hath made this man strong" (Acts 3:16).

Jesus! Jesus! Jesus! Sing aloud the Name;
Till it softly, slowly, sets all hearts aflame.

Jesus! Name of cleansing, washing all our stains;
Jesus! Name of healing, balm for all our pains.

Jesus! Name of boldness, making cowards brave;
Name that in the battle certainly must save.

If Peter's explanation of the miracle was correct, an act of repentance was certainly due on the part of the Jews, for their treatment of Jesus was found to be direct and bitter antagonism to God. This Jesus was none other than the Servant of Jehovah, of whom Isaiah the prophet had spoken so much; He was the Holy and Just One; He was the Prince, the Author, the Leader of life. Yet they had preferred a man who was a murderer before Him; they had betrayed Him, denied Him, killed Him. See how Peter aggravates their guilt by a series of contrasts! Their denial of the Servant of the Lord is contrasted with the Roman Pilate's futile attempt to acquit Him. Again, they denied the Holy and Just One and asked for a murderer. Again, they petitioned for a murderer and slew the Prince of life. Through all these runs the still more telling contrast between their betrayal, denial, and murder of Jesus, and God's answer, raising Him up, and glorifying Him.

So fearful was their crime, so deep their guilt, that repentance would have been useless, their turning of no avail, had not two factors entered into their action. First, it was done in ignorance, and had not the Lord Himself prayed, "Father, forgive them, for they know not what they do" (Luke 23:34)? Even the old Mosaic economy made provision for sins of ignorance in the trespass offering.

Still more important, their very crime had been made God's method of implementing His redemptive purposes. The prophecies concerning the sufferings of the Christ had thus been fulfilled, the sacrifice for sin had been offered, and the very murderers of the Holy One might now partake of the pardon, enter into reconciliation, and become sons of God.

Great God of wonders, all Thy ways
Are matchless, godlike and divine;

> But the fair glories of Thy grace
> More godlike and unrivalled shine:
> Who is a pardoning God like Thee?
> Or who has grace so rich and free?

Peter encourages the act of repentance to which he calls the Jewish people by holding before them the hope of Israel. Have not the prophets consistently taught them to look for the times of refreshing, which should be ushered in with the coming of Messiah? Messiah has visited them, but has been cast out. So the Scriptures have been fulfilled which spoke of His sufferings, and now the heavens have received Him, raised from the dead and glorified. He will not again visit the earth in humiliation, but must abide in glory until He brings the day of restoration and regeneration to a groaning, travailing creation. But, says Peter to the Jewish nation, that day waits for you. "Repent ye, and turn again, for the blotting out of your sins, that so times of refreshing may come from the face of the Lord, and that so He may send Messiah Jesus, who was foreordained for you" (Acts 3:19-20, author's trans.).

Here two important truths are indicated. First, God has not cast away the people of His ancient choice. The "times of [the] restoration of all things" (3:21, ASV) are "times of refreshing" (3:19) for Israel. Jesus, rejected, crucified, risen, glorified, is Israel's Messiah, foreordained for them, and in His coming again will fulfill His Messiahship toward them. The Messianic expectation has not been canceled.

This passage declares the relation of Israel's repentance to the return of the Lord. "Repent . . . that so He may send Messiah Jesus" is the undisputed reading of the grammar. That would seem to make it clear that the Lord's coming as Messiah to Israel is contingent upon a national repentance and conversion. If other Scriptures seem to suggest that the return of Messiah is the cause of Israel's national conversion rather than the divine response to it, those passages should be carefully examined in the light of this clear statement, and such comparing of more obscure passages with definite statements, instead of the contrary, will bring about more harmony of interpretation. The mourning of Israel on seeing "him whom they pierced" (John 19:37), and the opening of the fountain "for sin and for uncleanness" (Zech 13:1), spoken of by the prophet Zechariah, do not necessarily contradict the order of Peter—repentance and the coming of Messiah Jesus. I can well picture the godly sorrow of the repentant nation being intensified at the sight of the wounds which their unbelief inflicted, and their comfort in the realization that those very wounds are the fountain of cleansing.

Some indeed spiritualize this passage to avoid the teaching of a literal return of Christ to the earth, but the positiveness of the statement, coupled with the whole tenor of Scripture, surely demands that we regard this as referring to "that blessed hope, even the appearing of the glory of our great God and Saviour Jesus Christ" (Titus 2:13, author's trans.).

If it be so that this greatest of all events of the future waits for the repentance of Israel, we have here one of the strongest reasons for the evangelization of the Jews; yet it has been strangely omitted from the lists of reasons generally presented to Christian people.

Having tried to give the passage its dispensational setting, I wish to add this application: every soul that repents and turns to the Saviour for the blotting out of his sins brings nearer the times of refreshing and regeneration in the coming again of our Lord Jesus Christ.

> Let all that look for, hasten
>   The coming joyful day,
> By earnest consecration,
>   To walk the narrow way;
> By gath'ring in the lost ones
>   For whom our Lord did die,
> For the crowning day that's coming by and by.

8

A TILT WITH THE HIERARCHY

ACTS 4:1-22

In this chapter we see the leaders of Israel confounded by:

1. The unauthorized preaching of the apostles
2. The unquestionable power of the apostles
3. The unconscionable persistence of the apostles

JOHN BUNYAN was arrested three times, and spent in all nearly thirteen years in prison, all for the crime of "unauthorized" preaching. His first indictment was for "devilishly and perniciously abstaining from coming to church to hear divine service, and for being a common upholder of several unlawful meetings and conventicles, to the great disturbance and distraction of the good subjects of this kingdom, contrary to the laws of our sovereign lord the King." The warrant for his third arrest, resulting in his imprisonment in the "clink" of Bedford, where he wrote his great allegory, *Pilgrim's Progress,* read as follows:

> Whereas information and complaint is made unto us that (notwithstanding the Kings Majties late Act of most gracious general and free pardon to all his subjects for past misdemeanours, that by his said clemencie and indulgent grace and favour they might bee mooved and induced for the time to come more carefully to observe his Highenes lawes and statutes, and to continue in theire loyall and due obedience to his Majtie), yett one John Bunnyon of your said towne, Tynker, hath divers times within one month last past in contempt of his Majties good laws preached or teached at a Conventicle meeteing or assembly under colour or pretence of exercise of Religion in other manner then according to the Liturgie or Practise of the Church of England. These are therefore in his Majties name to com-

52

mand you forthwith to apprehend and bring the Body of the said John Bunnion beefore us or any of us or other his Majties Justice of Peace within the said county to answer the premises and further to doe and receave as to Law and Justice shall appertaine, and hereof you are not to faile. Given hour handes and seales the ffowerth day of March in the seaven and twentieth yeare of the Raigne of our most gracious Soveraigne Lord King Charles the Second.

The Jerusalem hierarchy of A.D. 30 was no more kindly disposed toward "unauthorized" preaching than was the English hierarchy of the seventeenth century. The first preachers of the gospel had their authorization from the Lord Himself, but since they had no diploma from the school of Gamaliel, nor letters from the high priest, nor license from the Sanhedrin, they were irregular, so "the priests and the captain of the temple and the Sadducees came upon them, being sore troubled because they taught the people" (Acts 4:1-2, ASV).

It may be that our democratic ways have carried us too far in the other direction, until there is apt to be a complete disregard of church order. Still we must recognize God's prerogative to raise up His testimony within or without the establishment of any place or time. The fact is that established orders have a tendency to drift from purity of message and practice. Important truths become neglected or perverted, false emphases are introduced, and abuses creep in. Then it is that God raises up a witness outside the regular channels, as in the Reformation of the sixteenth century, the nonconformist movement of the seventeenth century, and the evangelical revival of the eighteenth century. So long as the ranks of "unauthorized" preachers can list an apostle Peter, a John Bunyan, and a Dwight L. Moody, we shall do well to credit a man's message rather than his title.

If the established churches wish to prevent irregular, unauthorized preaching, they will do it not by means of persecution and suppression, but by the living message of the gospel. I have in my library a large folio volume published in the year 1641. It carries the ponderous title: *XCVI Sermons by the Right Honorable and Reverend Father in God, Lancelot Andrewes, Late Lord Bishop of Winchester. Published, by His Majesties Speciall Command, Whereunto is added a Sermon Preached before two Kings, on the Fifth of August, 1606.* For all the erudition of the noted cleric, and for all the heart-searching

qualities of his *Private Devotions,* which are a classic in more ways
than one, it must be admitted that there is more meat for the soul in
one page of John Bunyan's *Grace Abounding* than in the entire volume of Andrewes' ninety-seven sermons; so that if these represent the
established preaching of the seventeenth century, some unauthorized
preaching was fully due.

The hierarchy was not only disturbed by the unauthorized preaching of the apostles, but disconcerted by the unquestionable power
they displayed. Their message was accompanied and confirmed by
deeds of a miraculous order. The healing of the lame beggar was
evidence to all that these men were endued with power from above.
The marvel of it was all the greater that "the man was more than forty
years old, on whom this miracle of healing was wrought" (Acts 4:22,
ASV). The members of the council frankly admitted their dilemma
in face of the incident. "What shall we do to these men? For that
indeed a notable miracle hath been wrought through them, is manifest to all that dwell in Jerusalem; *and we cannot deny it"* (4:16, ASV,
italics added).

Can Christianity today produce something that the world cannot
deny? We have many excellent books dealing with the evidence for
Christianity, and we shall not discount their value for a moment.
Only, argument can always be met with argument. Dialectic is never
coercive, never indisputable. "The greatest evidence for Christianity
is a Christian."

When John the Baptist sent to our Lord his inquiry, "Art thou he
that cometh, or look we for another?" (Luke 7:20*b*, ASV), the Saviour
sent the messengers back, not with an elaborate apologetic, but with
an eyewitness account: "Go and tell John the things which ye have
seen and heard; the blind receive their sight, the lame walk, the lepers
are cleansed, and the deaf hear, the dead are raised up, the poor have
good tidings preached to them" (7:22, ASV). Healed lives are
Christ's great apologetic. "Seeing the man that was healed standing
with them, they could say nothing against it" (Acts 4:14, ASV). So
long as the gospel is demonstrably "the power of God unto salvation
to every one that believeth" (Rom 1:16*b*), we can afford to say with
Paul, "I am not ashamed" (1:16*a*). And the evidence is so abundant
that we can safely challenge the world with it. Harold Begbie's *Twice*

Born Men is the frank acknowledgment of a man of the world that the gospel of Christ brings superhuman power into the lives of men, for healing and recovery. "To convert the worst of men into a saint is a miracle in psychology," he says in his preface, and then devotes his book to the record of such miracles, from personal observation, every one being wrought through the message of Christ. Such power is both unquestionable and unanswerable.

A third element in the embarrassment of the Jewish leaders was the unconscionable persistence of the apostles. They were accustomed to see culprits quail in their august presence. They had learned even how to bend the Roman will to theirs. The unabashed boldness of these heralds of the crucified Jesus of Nazareth was, therefore, an unwelcome novelty. It was clear enough that they had received a strange power from this Jesus in their contacts with Him, for never had unlearned and ignorant men stood up to the masters of Israel with such assurance of statement, boldness of accusation, and reasonableness of appeal.

The astute Sanhedrinists were not up to their usual astuteness on this occasion. They really asked a leading question that called for the very testimony that Peter and John were waiting opportunity to give. "By what power, or in what name, have ye done this?" (Acts 4:7). The very question emboldened the apostles, and on the carnal side they must have been highly amused and pleased by this unconscious invitation to proclaim their message.

The masters of Israel thought of themselves as God's special favorites and representatives. It was no sweet morsel, then, to hear themselves listed in the category of God's opponents, and their actions declared to be the exact opposite of God's. "Jesus Christ of Nazareth, whom ye crucified, whom God raised from the dead" (Acts 4:10). And again, "You rejected this Stone as worthless, but God made Him the head of the corner" (Acts 4:11, author's trans.). And yet again, what an affirmation is this concerning the One they had cast out and thought to be rid of: "Neither is there salvation in any other: for there is none other name under heaven given among men, whereby we must be saved" (4:12). That is too dogmatic for our liberal-minded people who think that any man can build his own road to heaven, but how must it have sounded to those men, whose hands were still red with the blood of His crucifixion, to be told in such undisguised terms that the One whose death they had compassed was the sole way to God, the sole Giver of salvation!

What you do with Jesus of Nazareth determines your relation to God, decides your eternal destiny. Are you with those who crucified Him, or with God who raised Him from the dead? Are you with the builders who leave Him out, or with God, who gives Him preeminence? Your salvation rests on your answer.

A few weeks ago a charge from the Sanhedrin would have struck awe in the hearts of these Galilean fishermen, but they had seen the glory of God in the face of Jesus Christ; the voice of the Highest had sounded in their souls, and there could be for them no question as to prior obedience. The prohibitions of men could carry no weight with them in face of what they had seen and heard and known and felt.

There is little such persistence today. We are willing to obey God's injunctions provided they do not clash with the ordinances of men. The apostles indeed taught submission to the ordinances of man, but not where these interfered with their divine commission. I remember hearing the late Dr. R. V. Bingham speak of the governmental regulations that limited the work of the Sudan Interior Mission in Muslim territory. The conviction seemed to be forming in his mind that finally the missionaries might have to ignore those regulations for the sake of their prior obedience to the Lord's command, "Go ye into all the world, and preach the gospel to every creature" (Mark 16:15). It is only right and proper that every effort be made to bring governmental regulations into line with the divine mission, but the day may come when the church will have to stand with the apostles in their "We must obey God rather than men" (Acts 5:29, ASV), or be found unfaithful. We must in that case be willing to pay for our right to obey God first, even with our lives. "Sir," said Bunyan to Cobb, who came to him in Bedford jail to persuade him to submit at the next quarter session, "the law hath provided two ways of obeying: the one to do that which I in my conscience do believe that I am bound to do actively; and where I cannot obey actively then I am willing to lie down and suffer what they shall do unto me."

9

THE GHOST OF ACHAN

ACTS 5:1-21

In this chapter we examine:

1. The sin that threatened the church
2. The severity that saved the church
3. The sanctity that glorified the church

GHOST OF ACHAN!" I wonder, did Peter make that exclamation under his breath when he saw Ananias come into church that day? For Ananias and Sapphira had set their envious, covetous eyes on a Babylonish garment and a wedge of gold just as Achan had done, and were imperiling the early triumphs of the infant church just as their spiritual father jeopardized the conquests of young Israel.

Barnabas had just consummated a real estate deal that had occupied him for some time. The rich Cyprus estate was at last profitably sold, and the money was—no, not in the First National Bank of Jerusalem!—in the treasury of the church for common distribution. This shining example of Christian fellowship had clothed Barnabas with honor in the eyes of all the saints. The praise of his deed was in every mouth.

At last Ananias and Sapphira were stirred; not, however, with the shame of their tardiness in expressing the same fellowship with the saints, but with envy of Barnabas's halo. They, too, had real estate, and they would convert it into a robe of honor and glory for themselves. Simulated sainthood was their Babylonish garment.

But they wanted it cheap, at bargain price. Like Achan, they would have their wedge of gold, too; they would have their robes of honor fur-lined. So they "kept back part of the price" (Acts 5:2). They

57

talked it over in their perfect self-justification. This church communism was being carried too far, they said to each other, and unless a curb were put on this wild enthusiasm, many would find themselves in a state of dependency and beggary for their improvidence. They would be practical in their Christianity. Perhaps Barnabas himself would be glad someday for a little help out of their wise savings. Little Simon's education, too, would soon be making demands on the family exchequer, and a little caution now would enable them to give a well-trained minister to the church someday—a better gift than money! So the family of Ananias went out for the Babylonish garment with the wedge of gold to boot.

Now, it was not the mere keeping back part of the price that constituted the sin of these two. Peter made it quite clear that they were under no obligation to sell, and after selling they still were not required to give all or any of the proceeds to the apostles. The envy that prompted the sale and the offering, and the covetousness which urged the withholding, these were the sins—deep, dark sins of the heart—out of which sprang the further sin which Peter specifically named: the sin of lying.

Ordinarily it was nobody's business whether the offering of Ananias was the whole or part of the proceeds of his real estate deal, or whether it was a legacy from a deceased rich uncle. The fact was, however, that both of them intended the church to think that they were doing the same as Barnabas, never expecting the question to be raised. The lie was in their hearts, but poor Sapphira never dreamed it would spring to her lips. The only safeguard against lying lips is a clean, true heart. "Keep thy *heart* with all diligence; for out of it are the issues of life" (Prov 4:23, italics added).

> The heart aye is the part aye
> That mak's us richt or wrang.

Thus envy and covetousness produced a pair of liars, hypocrites, Pharisees in the church, and their seed, it is to be feared, is a numerous race. Every piece of religious pretense, every show of unreal consecration, is a repetition of the Ananias and Sapphira act. If God were to visit today as He did that first church in Jerusalem, I wonder how many ministers would have multiple funerals, and how many remnants of congregations would be burying their ministers! God have mercy on us!

The first breach of discipline in the ranks of conquering Israel, and the first outburst of sin in the equally conquering church, were alike punished with swift and complete retribution. Later in Israel's history and later in the church's history, multiplied sins of equal and perhaps greater enormity were not so immediately visited. Surely the swift stroke of judgment in each case was intended to manifest the holiness of God, His utter recoil from sin, and the surety of judgment, that, with these examples before them, His people might turn from sin with horror. But a continuance of the same swift retribution would create an abnormal situation, wherein men would lose the moral sense, and flee sin to avoid the penalty rather than for holiness' sake. The training of a dog is on the principle of immediate association. Associate in his mind certain actions with the pain of the whip, and he will learn to avoid them; again, link certain other actions with the pleasure of a bone, and he will perform. There is nothing moral in that. Man is higher than the dog, and must learn on a higher plane. Therefore, after the solemn lessons of the first exemplary visitations, God reverts to the slower processes of judgment, mingling long-suffering and patience with His allowance of the normal harvests of sin. Fools mistake the delays in judgment for immunity. "Because sentence against an evil work is not executed speedily, therefore the heart of the sons of men is fully set in them to do evil" (Eccles 8:11). Thus, they "forsake their own mercy" (Jonah 2:8). "Be sure your sin will find you out" (Num 32:23) is equally true when we seem to "get by" as if the ax fell the very moment of the transgression.

> Though the mills of God grind slowly,
>   Yet they grind exceeding small;
> Though with patience He stands waiting,
>   With exactness grinds He all.

The penalty was severe, but dare we say it was too severe? These two broke the fellowship of the saints; they introduced into the body of the church the very thing which in Adam brought universal woe and death, and which in Achan wrought humiliation and defeat for Israel. They made mock of those high acts of devotion of which

Barnabas was an outstanding example; they set their hearts on filthy lucre, while seeking to purchase a name for piety; they lied to the Holy Ghost, the blessed Paraclete of the church. For that, death was the solemn, but surely not too severe, retribution. *Poena duorum doctrina multorum,* exclaims an ancient writer; the penalty of two is the lesson of many. May it be sanctified to our learning, till we "abhor that which is evil . . . [and] cleave to that which is good" (Rom 12:9).

Let us not be too sure that God has altogether abandoned disciplinary measures, although the connection may not always be so close and evident. Paul distinctly attributed a wave of sickness and some untimely deaths in the Corinthian church to abuses of the Lord's Supper. In the story of Pastor Hsi of China it is related how one who foully turned against the godly pastor and sought to hurt both him and his work both lost a son and died himself in such circumstances as to make it evident to all that it was the hand of God. More than one death has come under my own observation which I could not but connect immediately with sin, especially sin which damaged the church's fellowship and testimony.

For all its severity, the death of Ananias and Sapphira was a great mercy, not only for the church, but for themselves, for it saved them from a growth in iniquity that would have been a far deeper tragedy than their death. The apostle Paul speaks of a certain Corinthian believer being delivered to Satan "for the destruction of the flesh, that the spirit may be saved in the day of the Lord Jesus" (1 Cor 5:5). Yes, the death of some saints is a double mercy, for themselves and for the church. A sanctifying exercise would be to pray, "Lord, take me home rather than let me live an unholy life!" But be careful! He might take you at your word.

It is the salvation of the church's life and testimony to have sin judged. Had Achan's sin been discovered and dealt with before the expedition to Ai, Israel would not have turned their backs on the enemy or suffered that humiliating defeat when their progress of victory was scarce begun. Well was it for the infant church that Peter obeyed the voice of the Holy Spirit and checked that sin which, if tolerated, would have corrupted the body, grieved the Spirit, and killed the testimony. A wholesome fear was engendered, both within and without the church: within, a fear of God, a dread of sin, a carefulness not to offend; without, a fear to join such a church except on the grounds of true repentance and regeneration. "Great fear came upon all the church . . . and of the rest durst no man join himself to them" (Acts 5:11-13). So the purity of the church was doubly guarded.

Human reasoning would suggest that with such standards, so rigidly enforced, there would be little growth for that church. The opposite was the case, for, runs the record, "believers were the more added to the Lord, multitudes both of men and women" (5:14). Where Christian standards are discarded in favor of conformity to the world, where sin goes unchallenged, where membership is offered to the unregenerate, even pressed upon them in the annual "drive," and where the only fear known is the minister's fear of losing his job if he speaks out, the masses lose interest in "organized religion." It is one of the paradoxes of the Kingdom of God that the church men are most afraid to join is the church that knows the biggest increase.

The testimony of this judged and purified church was with power, carrying every evidence of the presence of God. What a record is this! "And by the hands of the apostles were many signs and wonders wrought among the people. . . . Insomuch that they brought forth the sick into the streets, and laid them on beds and couches, that at the least the shadow of Peter passing by might overshadow some of them. There came also a multitude out of the cities round about into Jerusalem, bringing sick folks, and them which were vexed with unclean spirits: and they were healed every one" (Acts 5:12-16). We are reminded of our Lord's strong action in cleansing the Temple in Jerusalem, with this significant statement following, "And the blind and the lame came to him in the temple; and he healed them" (Matt 21:14). Purity and power: that is the order.

Such a testimony is not only fruitful and powerful, but it is irrepressible. See how the Sanhedrin tried to silence the apostles by imprisoning them, but the angel of the Lord released them, so that next morning they were found in their "pulpit" instead of in the prison cell. Persecution does not silence testimony! Madagascar and Ethiopia are classic illustrations of that. The return of missionaries to these fields after years of suppression of the gospel only found the native churches larger and stronger and more numerous than before.

Only one thing can silence the testimony of the church: *sin!* And that is as true of the individual as of the church. Nineteen centuries of Christian history bear witness to this challenging fact. Is your testimony silenced? Let "the spirit of judgment, and . . . of burning" (Isa 4:4) search out all the sin, and you will again have a vocal, fruitful, irrepressible witness.

I am glad this story is in the New Testament, to teach us that grace is no more tolerant of sin than is the Law. It ought to correct our one-sided conception of God and restore a sense of His awful holiness; it ought to give pause to our irreverence, establish in us a dread of sin, and magnify the love and grace by which we are saved. If such a God is saving us, there will be high morality and deep ethics in His salvation, the "everlasting burnings" (Isa 33:14) will be in the hearts of His saints, and the cry will be often on our lips: "Purge me with hyssop, and I shall be clean: wash me, and I shall be whiter than snow" (Psalm 51:7).

10

APOSTOLIC CERTAINTIES

Acts 5:29-32

In this chapter we see the secret of apostolic strength in:

1. A certainty of God
2. A certainty of Christ
3. A certainty of calling

AT THEIR PREVIOUS HEARING, the apostles, in reply to the charge of the council, had submitted a proposition: "Whether it is right in the sight of God to hearken unto you rather than unto God, judge ye" (Acts 4:19, ASV). That proposition has now crystallized into a life principle for them. It has become, to use Kant's phrase, a "categorical imperative": "We must obey God rather than men" (5:29, ASV).

Such a sense of "ought" demands a great certainty of God. No one will consistently give prior obedience to a hypothetical God. If "he that cometh to God must believe that he is" (Heb 11:6b), how much more he who risks standing alone against all men for His sake!

> Whoso has felt the Spirit of the Highest
> Cannot confound nor doubt Him nor deny:
> Yea with one voice, O world, tho' thou deniest,
> Stand thou on that side, for on this am I.

Such was the apostolic assurance, and it left no alternative to giving God first place in their obedience. For this obedience to God, and for such disobedience to men as it might demand, they were willing to pay the price of suffering, even unto death.

They did not assume that they were exempt from all obedience to man because of the higher loyalty. They gladly submitted themselves to the ordinances of man for the Lord's sake and for conscience' sake, but where the word of the Lord and the ordinance of man clashed, they had no doubt where their duty lay. "We must obey God rather than men." In such case, not only did these early heralds of the gospel refuse to bow before the Jewish Sanhedrin, but they defied all the might of Rome, till at last Rome bowed.

We are so accustomed to our freedom of worship that we easily forget the many in the world today who cannot serve God with good conscience without defying their governments. The Nazi regime of Germany has fallen, but not before many have had to pay for their allegiance to God with dire and awful suffering. The name of Martin Niemoeller will stand high in the annals of true martyrs, for he "endured, as seeing him who is invisible" (Heb 11:27*b*). Refusing to make his church a tool of the Nazi party, he obeyed God rather than Hitler, and accepted without complaint the brutalities of the Nazi concentration camps. Japan's insistence on universal acquiescence in Shinto worship made it impossible for a Christian there to be true without resisting the law of the land. The time is at hand, and even now is, when as followers of the Lord Jesus we must emblazon on our banners what we have inscribed in the archives of church history. "We must obey God rather than men."

This splendid allegiance of the apostles was reinforced by a threefold certainty with respect to Christ—the certainty of His resurrection triumph, His exalted rank, and His saving activity. Their obedience to God was in regard to this testimony of His Son, and indeed there could be no mightier incentive and support to a life of uncompromising obedience than such a realization.

"Consider him . . . lest ye be wearied and faint in your minds" (Heb 12:3), says the writer of Hebrews, for there is little hope of our standing up in face of our adversaries and our temptations unless we have our eyes and our thoughts and our heart set on Him. The vision of an enthroned Lord is the antidote for discouragement and despair. "What is man, that thou art mindful of him? Or the son of man, that thou visitest him? Thou hast put all things . . . under his feet" (Heb 2:6, 8*a*). So sings the psalmist in his ecstasy of vision. "But," replies our apostolic commentator in his Hebrews letter, "now we see not yet all things put under him" (2:8*b*), after so long a time. Man is no more a king, and just as much a slave, as ever he was, and the prospects for his attainment to sovereignty would be depressing indeed were it not for this further word: "But we see Jesus . . . crowned with glory and honour" (2:9). Without that we must be pessimists, but with that we have only the most radiant optimism. We can "run with patience the race that is set before us, looking unto Jesus . . . who for the joy that was set before him endured the cross, despising the shame, and is set down at the right hand of . . . God" (Heb 12:1-2). If only we hold the vision of a living Lord, highly exalted at God's right hand as a Prince and a Saviour, and bringing to His saving activity the full resources of divine omnipotence, the demands of obedience will never frighten or appall:

> We would see Jesus—this is all we're needing;
>   Strength, joy and willingness come with the sight:
> We would see Jesus, dying, risen, pleading,
>   Then welcome, day! and farewell, mortal night!

This certainty of Christ was not only the powerful stimulus of apostolic obedience; it was also the throbbing heart of the apostolic message. The crucified Jesus of Nazareth they proclaimed the risen Christ; they envisioned Him on the seat of universal sway, "far above all principality, and power, and might, and dominion, and every name that is named" (Eph 1:21), they regarded Him as the sole Minister of salvation, bestowing repentance, forgiveness, and life upon sinners from the throne of grace. But this gracious distribution looked back to the cross, where He "suffered, . . . the just for the unjust, that he might bring us to God" (1 Pet 3:18). That was their gospel, which proved at their preaching, and still proves to be, "the power of God unto salvation to every one that believeth" (Rom 1:16).

The apostles did not propound theories; they proclaimed certainties. That is the test of the Christian preacher. A man who desires to do something else should be honest enough not to do it in the garb of a minister of Christ. The pulpit is the place to give an authoritative message—not an "I think," but a "Thus saith the Lord." Says Dr. G. Campbell Morgan, in his excellent little book on preaching, "The mass of men are waiting for preaching of the New Testament kind, with a great message of grace to meet human need, delivered by men who realize that they represent a Throne, and have the right to claim submission to it." To the vendor of doubts most men will return the answer of Goethe, "Give me the benefit of your convictions, if you have any. Keep your doubts to yourself; I have enough of my own."

Added to a certainty of God which inspired prior obedience, and a certainty of Christ which gave them a living message, the first apostles had a certainty of calling which sustained them through all difficulties. The statement, "We are witnesses of these things" (Acts 5:32, ASV), means much more than "We saw these things." They had been solemnly and specifically appointed to declare the things which they had seen and heard and learned beyond all question. A widely accepted reading of this verse gives, "We are *His* witnesses of these things," reminiscent of our Lord's own declaration to them before His ascension, "Ye shall be my witnesses" (1:8, ASV).

Such divine appointment lays upon one a sense of weighty obligation, coupled with holy confidence. It means that a task is imposed which must be done. "Necessity is laid upon me; yea, woe is unto me, if I preach not the gospel" (1 Cor 9:16), said Paul of his commission, even as Jeremiah had declared long before, "If I say, I will not make mention of him, nor speak any more in his name, then there is in my heart as it were a burning fire shut up in my bones, and I am weary with forbearing, and I cannot contain" (Jer 20:9, ASV). Do I hear the Jewish Sanhedrin charge the apostles to speak no more in this name? As well might Alfred command the tide no more to flow, or Congress forbid the rose to open! That divine necessity brooks no challenge.

God's call inspires confidence, for He never lays a charge upon His ministers without such assurance as He gave to Moses, "My presence shall go with thee, and I will give thee rest" (Exod 33:14). The tides of circumstance, the wrath of men, the opposition of devils we need not fear in the prosecution of God's appointment. True, we may suffer in the process, we may even die for it—in which case that is part of the appointment, and the issue is sure. The Jewish hierarchy may seek to stay the outgoings of the gospel, but the Jewish state will be dispersed and the gospel will go on. Rome may attempt to blot out the church, but Rome will fall while the church reaches out for wider triumphs. Everyone who lifts a finger against a God-called man will be found fighting against God: and "woe unto him that striveth with his Maker" (Isa 45:9). The man upon whom God's ordination rests is invincible.

God's messengers do not stand alone. "We are witnesses of these things; and so is the Holy Spirit" (Acts 5:32, ASV). This divine partnership lends certainty and confidence. How does it operate? "The Spirit himself beareth witness [along] with our spirit" (Rom 8:16, ASV), adding assurance to conviction respecting the truth to be proclaimed. Thus the spirit of the witness is strengthened. Then the Holy Spirit energizes the messenger for the act of witnessing. Again the Holy Spirit works conviction of the truth in those who receive the witness. At times the same Holy Spirit gives special outward tokens to reinforce the message. Thus the servant, while obligated to give his all in the fulfillment of his divine calling, and to improve and utilize all human equipment available, is not dependent on "natural resources," but rejoices in the divine activity of which he is but a channel. "Who goeth a-warring on his own charges?" Certainly not the man called of God.

Back in 1928, Dr. F. B. Meyer was addressing a youth rally in London. In the course of his message he related an incident told him in Denmark by Lord Radstock. This Christian nobleman had been in a fashionable hotel in Norway, where a little girl, just beginning piano lessons, insisted on inflicting her practice on the guests in the drawing room. The child was usually left in sole possession! One day a noted piano virtuoso arrived with his bride. The next time the child chased out the bored guests, the artist did not follow the crowd, but instead took his seat by the child at the piano, and began filling in a beautiful accompaniment to the hesitating and discordant notes of the beginner. The guests began flocking back to the drawing room and for twenty minutes enjoyed a real concert. Then the musician led the child around the room to receive the thanks of the audience. So the Holy Spirit "helpeth our infirmities" (Rom 8:26), and Dr. Meyer adds: "Again and again when I have been preaching to congregations and have felt that I was doing poor work, I said to Him, 'Great Partner,

things have gone to pieces at my end, put on extra pressure on
Thine.' " "We are . . . witnesses . . . and so is . . . the Holy Ghost"
(Acts 5:32) .

11

GROWING PAINS

ACTS 6:1-8

In this incident we find some practical hints on:

1. How to handle problems in the church
2. How to appoint officers in the church
3. How to assure prosperity in the church

GROWING PAINS," was the diagnosis given in former days when a lad in his teens complained of rheumatic twinges. We are more advanced now, but all the same many a growing boy has growing pains, not in his joints and muscles but in his mind. He feels too big and awkward and clumsy, is embarrassed over the most trivial happening, and wants to keep out of sight. There are other sorts and stages of growing pains, too, before he comes to the strength and poise and freedom and dignity and full manhood.

Growing churches are likely to have growing pains. One hears the groaning of the very building taxed beyond capacity. There is the delicate task of adjusting the organization to the growing needs, and the feeling that despite the best efforts some are being neglected in the increasing demands.

The first church in Jerusalem was experiencing growing pains, and they became an acute case. A minority group is apt to develop a complex and become very sensitive to the slightest indication of neglect on the part of the stronger group. The Hellenists, or Grecian Jews, and the Hebrews, or Palestinian Jews, were both represented in the church, and had not altogether forgotten the scorn on the one hand, and the resentment on the other, that existed between those two factions of Jews. Grace had not yet perfected its work in those young believers, so in the matter of the daily distribution to the poor—and there were many of them—it was easy for the dominant Hebrews to prefer their own, and it was easy for the Hellenists to exaggerate the neglect of theirs.

The apostles faced the problem frankly, and put their finger on the cause—lack of organization. The burden of the church was too much concentrated on the shoulders of the apostles, instead of being distributed on many shoulders. The result was that the chief work of the apostles was in danger of suffering, while the other tasks for which they were responsible were not being done satisfactorily. In the meantime, good material was spoiling for lack of use in the church. Division of labor was, therefore, the proposed solution, and it is a principle of church operation from which we dare not depart.

The very fact that for some time the apostles themselves bore the burden of the service of tables is evidence that they did not regard it as a mean task, nor might mean men be appointed to take it over. It was not that the diaconate of tables was incompatible with the diaconate of the Word, but that the one interfered with the efficient fulfillment of the other. The new deacons of tables, therefore, as deacons of any order within the church, must be men answering to certain standards. Four qualifications were required.

1. "Look ye out, therefore, brethren, *from among you* seven men" (Acts 6:3, ASV, italics added). The deacons must be of the company of believers. It is a thing inconceivable in the New Testament that "men of the world" should be invited to take part in the operation of a church.

2. "Look ye out, therefore, brethren . . . seven men of *good report.*" Whatever a man's profession, if his neighbors and townfolk have no high regard for the reality of his profession, he is not eligible for church office.

3. "Look ye out, therefore, brethren . . . seven men . . . *full of the Spirit.*" Bezaleel was to work in gold and silver and stone and wood and linen, and for that he received the enduement of the Holy Spirit, even as Moses did for his administrative and legislative work, and Aaron for his priestly duties. Even so the man who handles the church's money must be filled with the Spirit, even as the man who occupies the pulpit.

4. "Look ye out, therefore, brethren . . . seven men . . . *full of . . . wisdom.*" A man who handles the affairs of the world is expected to be keen, shrewd, discerning. Will the ministers of God's house be less so? Nay, the business of the Lord will make demands on wisdom beyond the stock market and the trading house. It will require the "wisdom that is from above," which "is first pure, then peaceable, gentle, easy to be entreated, full of mercy and good fruits, without variance, without hypocrisy" (James 3:17, ASV).

High standards these! Blessed is the church that can call upon such men for its service! Woe to the church that disregards these standards and elects men to office with an eye to their bank account, their influence in the community, or any such consideration!

The democratic ideal was practiced in the apostolic church, and it is significant that the democratic procedure was not demanded by the congregation, but proposed by the apostles. "Look ye out . . . men . . . whom we may appoint" (Acts 6:3). "And the saying pleased the whole multitude: and they chose . . . whom they set before the apostles" (6:5-6). Thus proper representation was secured, and proper recognition given. This also becomes a basic principle of church polity.

The election of these seven to the diaconate of tables was indeed a triumph of grace. The Hellenists had complained about the neglect of their widows, and, if we may draw a conclusion from the seven Greek names, that so strongly Hebraistic church in Jerusalem entrusted the whole matter of distribution to Hellenistic hands. The Hebrews controlled the vote, and they gave it to their brethren who felt they had been wronged. Such a gracious gesture was calculated to kill the old feud, and effect a new realization of their oneness in Christ. I suggest that that kind of "politics" would end many a church faction.

That was a notable board of deacons. What church would not consider itself honored in having Stephen and Philip numbered among its officers! But, then, the local church could not contain these men. They and their gifts belonged to the whole church, and they became the gift of the church at Jerusalem to the wider field. But the local church, with the serving of tables, was their training ground. Where did Stephen come by that irresistible wisdom and spirit of his if not in the delicate situations that arose in the daily ministrations of the church? And where did Philip learn his ease or approach and sympathy of understanding if not in those many contacts with needy, perplexed people who came for spiritual refreshing as well as for material bounty? A good church will expect to lose the best of its younger officers to wider fields, and will accept it as a blessed ministry to train them for the larger call.

"And the word of God increased; and the number of the disciples multiplied in Jerusalem greatly; and a great company of the priests were obedient to the faith" (Acts 6:7). What was the secret of this new wave of prosperity? First, because the apostles were freed to give themselves to prayer and the ministry of the Word. You would expect the Word of God to increase in those conditions. And the Word of God will increase in all our churches and all our communities when our churches learn to free their ministers from the thousand tasks others can do, and when our ministers accept that freedom in order to give themselves to prayer and the study of the Word.

Second, the resources of the church were harnessed for service. A church can never be fully prosperous while skills and abilities are allowed to rot from lack of use. Discontent is bound to arise, for men of ability chafe when they see work lagging and opportunities passing for want of organization and leadership.

Third, the breach was repaired, until such a spirit of fellowship breathed throughout that church that people came flocking to feel the warmth of it. Even priests of the Temple discerned that the followers of Jesus had a fire such as never was kindled upon their sacred altars, and they bowed to the faith they had despised.

It was in such an atmosphere of emancipated ministry, cooperative service, and glad fellowship that Stephen, "full of grace and power, was doing wonders and great signs among the people" (Acts 6:8, author's trans.). Nothing is impossible in such a church.

12

FAITHFUL UNTO DEATH

Acts 6:8—7:60

In this chapter we consider:

1. The ministry of the deacon
2. The mastery of the apologist
3. The martyrdom of the witness

THAT PASSAGE of arms between the Grecian and the Palestinian Jews might readily have proved to be a rock of destruction for the infant church. Instead, it was a stone in the channel which gave direction to the stream of the church's life and operation. That is what God always makes of our difficulties when we seek His face. See what developed from that tense situation. First, the general principle of the division of labor was enunciated and established as a policy in the church, opening the door for the several offices that later took definite shape. Second, the church's right to a voice in the personnel of its leadership was recognized, while their selection was held subject to the approval of the apostles, with whom the final responsibility of appointment lay. In particular, the office of deacon of tables, that is, of temporal things, was defined as distinct from the ministry of the Word and the spiritual direction of the church. The qualifications for church office were laid down, adherence to which would have made church history a happier tale.

The whole incident, however, is full of interest in another sphere than ecclesiastical polity. It introduces us to personalities of rare quality, deacons of apostolic caliber. Two of them specially command attention—Stephen and Philip. In these men we see that appointment to the office of deacon did not deter a man from the exercise of

73

his gifts in distinctly spiritual ministry. The one becomes a foremost
defender of the faith and the first to seal his Christian testimony with
his blood; the other does the work of an evangelist and begins the
evangelization of Africa. It is Stephen who commands our attention
first.

"And Stephen, full of faith and power, did great wonders and
miracles among the people" (Acts 6:8), as if God purposed so to
attest and confirm and seal the spiritual witness of this first deacon
that none would ever dare to say to one of that rank and office in the
church, You mind your tables, look after your temporal affairs, and
do not intermeddle with things too high for you; leave the work of
teaching and preaching to those ordained for it! And from the days
of Stephen till now, the church has been blessed with many a deacon
who has excelled in the ministry of the Word. I know a large, thriv-
ing Kentucky church whose minister not only goes away for many
revival meetings, but also has to leave for the North every year for
nearly two months because of hay fever. It is taken for granted in that
church that in the absence of the pastor a certain deacon, who has been
a judge for several terms, will preach. The same judge and deacon
writes the Sunday school lesson for the church paper.

Stephen apparently carried his testimony to the synagogues of the
Grecian Jews, being himself one of them. Now in many respects the
Grecian Jews were more liberal in their attitude than the Hebrews,
but for that very reason they were held in suspicion by their stricter
brethren. It was only natural, then, that when opportunity was
afforded them, they would seek approval by showing themselves very
zealous for the Jewish faith. The rise of "the sect of the Nazarene"
gave them their opportunity, till all Jerusalem rang with the disputa-
tions between Stephen the deacon and the leading spokesmen of the
Hellenist synagogues. But "they were not able to resist the wisdom
and the spirit by which he spake" (Acts 6:10). If we would contend
for the faith we must have respect to both—the wisdom and the spirit
in which we speak. If many a well-meant argument has failed for lack
of logic and reason, many more closely knit and finely reasoned contentions have been lost by displays of bad spirit. Let the wisdom of
the Spirit and the Spirit of wisdom combine, and the result will be an
unanswerable testimony. By all means study the evidences and mass

them into unassailable argument, but give heed to the spirit, that it be not one of pride and self-assurance and bitterness.

No matter how wise and true and faithful and gracious our testimony may be, we shall not win all. Our adversaries may not be able to resist, but they will not therefore desist. Stephen's antagonists were silenced in argument and confused by the strong and noble spirit of the man, but they were not convinced. They turned from argument to accusation, stooping to bribery and perjury in order to destroy the man who had so thoroughly routed them in open debate. If wisdom and spirit were all that the faith needed to win, the decision should never be in doubt. But men's hearts are more perverse than their minds, and where there is a determination not to believe, the more convincing the testimony, the more obdurate becomes the antagonism. The depths of infamy to which men will stoop in their enmity to the truth of God is appalling, and these "liberal" Jews showed their kinship with the more strict of their race by employing the very tactics that had brought Christ to judgment and death.

Hailed before the Sanhedrin on trumped-up charges which were, like those brought against his Lord, perversions of the truth, Stephen ignored the accusations as such, and assumed the role of apologist rather than defendant. The word "apology," as we frequently use it, signifies a confession of wrongdoing with expressions of regret, and perhaps some little claim to exonerating circumstances. A true apology, however, is a statement in vindication of one's position; it does not say, I was wrong and I am sorry; but rather, I am right and here are my reasons in substantiation. Barclay's "Apology" and Newman's "Apologia" are classic examples. Now Stephen made his great apology, not so much to vindicate himself as to present the Christian position in the light of the history of Israel. His thesis was that the Christians stood in the place of the true Israel, accepting and obeying God's revelation, while unbelieving Jewry were the true children of their fathers who, generation after generation, had resisted God in His servants. History was called to the witness stand for an accumulation of evidence against them. The enmity against Joseph, the refusal of Moses, the rebellion in the wilderness, the persecution of the prophets: these the indomitable apologist presented in his gallery of the boasted ancestry of his people. And as Jesus, God's Just One and Anointed One, stood as the last and ultimate of God's messengers to Israel, so those who rejected Him were making up the full measure of their fathers' rebellion. It was such an aspect of their national history as was calculated to hurt their pride and jerk them up to a realization of their false position, somewhat as Christ Himself did in His address at Nazareth. The climax was an anomaly. The accused had not touched on the charges laid against him, except that at the end of his historical sketch he reminded them that God could not be localized, and therefore the Temple of which they boasted was no ultimate institution. Then, rising to the full strength of his argument, he became the judge arraigning his judges, laying to their charge high crimes against God the Holy Ghost, God the Son, and God the Father. Had they complained that he had spoken against the Law? What had they done with the Law but to make it of no account? They professed honor for the prophets who "shewed before the coming of the Just One" (Acts 7:52). Their fathers had slain these prophets, but they had played the Judas to the Just One Himself, compassing His death. So bound were they in their prison house of tradition that every attempt of the Holy Spirit to break in and free them was met by stolid resistance. Rebellion, treason, murder, lawbreaking! Think of the Sanhedrin sitting and listening to charges of that nature leveled against their respectable, religious selves! Do you wonder that they "gnashed on him with their teeth" (7:54)?

The outlook was bad for Stephen. Every face before him was a thundercloud. Every eye flashed deadly lightning. Every throat thirsted for his blood. But Stephen had another prospect. The uplook was glorious. "He, being full of the Holy Ghost, looked up stedfastly into heaven, and saw the glory of God, and Jesus standing on the right hand of God" (7:55). In face of a vision like that the gnashing teeth and lowering countenances of the council had no terror for him. Sometimes it requires a dark outlook to make us interested in the uplook. It was in the year that King Uzziah died that Isaiah saw the Lord high and lifted up, and the seraphim around the throne chanting their majestic Sanctus. When did you see the Lord? Captain Eddie Rickenbacker saw Him when horrible death stared at him out of every restless wave of the ocean around. But a dark outlook is no guarantee that the uplook will open for you. There may be no pack of wolves baring their fangs at you right now, no dread storm cloud wrapping its cold shrouds around you now, no tide of destruction galloping up your sands to engulf you now. Nevertheless, now is the time to establish the uplook, to save you from despair and darkness when the gloom settles. Stephen had his vision focused on the throne of God long before seventy sets of teeth began cringing out their murderous intent. And that is what gave him such easy superiority over his foes even in death. Get the upward vision right now, and be ready.

It was too much for good Stephen to keep to himself. To see the crucified Christ so exalted enraptured his soul till he could not hold it even from his enemies. He did not stop to calculate the reaction. These men must know that Jesus Christ was glorified at God's right hand, and he would tell them if it were the last thing he did. So, oblivious of the danger, this faithful martyr cried out, "Behold, I see the heavens opened, and the Son of man standing on the right hand of God" (Acts 7:56).

Exalting Christ is a crime that this world can never deal with in the calm course of justice. From the council that passed sentence on our Lord, a bloody trail of violence, perversion of justice, and base treachery has marked the course of opposition to the gospel. No formal charge was laid against Stephen, no evidence weighed, no finding of guilt announced, no sentence passed. The council of law and order became a mob of unrestrained violence, as, with dignity thrown to the winds, these rulers of Israel hustled this blessed witness to the stoning ground and wreaked their vengeful ire upon him.

But Stephen won. "Fear not them that kill the body, and then have no more that they can do" (Luke 12:4, author's trans.). The spirit of Stephen was in hands that once knew the nails but had conquered. "Lord Jesus, receive my spirit" (Acts 7:59). It was an echo from the cross. It was the triumph of faith. And then another: "Lord, lay not this sin to their charge" (7:60). It was the triumph of grace. So in death as in life he walked in the steps of the Master. In him the prayer had been answered:

> Lord, speak to me, that I may speak
> In living echoes of Thy tone.
> FRANCES RIDLEY HAVERGAL

He went out, bearing the marks of the Lord Jesus. The promise of his name was fulfilled. "Be thou faithful unto death, and I will give thee a crown [*stephanos*] of life" (Rev 2:10*b*).

> A noble army, men and boys,
>   The matron and the maid,
> Around the Saviour's throne rejoice,
>   In robes of light arrayed;
> They climbed the steep ascent of heaven,
>   'Mid peril, toil, and pain;
> O God, to us may grace be given
>   To follow in their train!
>   REGINALD HEBER

PART TWO

The Expansion Begins

13

PRESSURE EXPANSION

Acts 8:1-24

In this passage we learn:

1. How the Good News was brought to Samaria
2. How the Good News was received in Samaria
3. How the Good News was confirmed in Samaria

THE LORD HAD MADE His program of evangelism clear enough. "Ye shall be witnesses unto me both in Jerusalem, and in all Judea, and in Samaria, and unto the uttermost part of the earth" (Acts 1:8). The apostles set to with a will after Pentecost, till Jerusalem resounded with their message of a risen Christ. Indeed, this phase of the undertaking was progressing so satisfactorily that the witnesses seem to have forgotten all about Judea and Samaria and the uttermost part. Despite the opposition of the rulers, converts were being counted in the holy city itself by the thousands, even great numbers of the priests becoming obedient to the faith. There is no suggestion that in the midst of this prosperity the apostles assembled in council to pray about and discuss any extension of their activities to the wider regions. Success carries with it the danger of complacency, blinding us to the needs just beyond.

But the Lord of the harvest does not forget His own orders, and He has wonderful ways of seeing that they are carried out. If the apostles will not organize evangelistic bands to carry the Good News farther afield, the Lord will thrust forth His messengers without apostolic organization. So "they stoned Stephen. . . . And there arose on that day a great persecution against the church which was in Jerusalem; and they were all scattered abroad throughout the regions of Judea and Samaria. . . . They therefore that were scattered abroad went about preaching the word" (Acts 7:59—8:4).

That was a fierce persecution, one that threatened the very existence of the infant church. I do not wonder at its intensity when I discover young Saul of Tarsus taking the lead in it. He had been so baffled and confused and humiliated in debate with Stephen that he would never be satisfied with anything short of the utter annihilation of this pestiferous sect of the Nazarene. If he could not defeat them in argument, he would avenge his hurt pride with a sterner weapon, and be doing God service to boot!

"As for you, ye thought evil against me; but God meant it unto good" (Gen 50:20). So said Joseph to his guilty, penitent, cringing brothers. That is one of the ways of God. "Surely the wrath of man shall praise thee: the remainder of wrath shalt thou restrain" (Psalm 76:10). So it came to pass that Saul's wrath, and the wrath of the Sanhedrin, became the unwilling instrument of the good purposes of God, and the affliction that was meant for destruction wrought expansion. The gospel is like metal; it expands with heat. "They therefore that were scattered abroad went about preaching" (Acts 8:4, ASV). Who can tell how long Samaria might have been without the Word had not that persecution driven the messengers forth?

Other dispersions have had like effect. For many years the evangelization of inland China was small and slow. We shall not minimize the heroic efforts that were made to reach those vast stretches with their teaming millions. But "what were these among so many?" (see John 6:9). It seemed as if the cry of the unreached multitudes must continue indefinitely. Then the Japanese entered China, not for evangelization but for conquest, not for benevolence but for oppression. Then did God take up that bitter thing as His instrument of good. The great, tragic trek inland began and continued, but it carried with it a host of witnesses. Once again, "they that were scattered abroad went every where preaching the word" (Acts 8:4), till it came to pass that there was more spreading of the gospel in five years than there had been in half a century.

> God moves in a mysterious way
>   His wonders to perform;
> He plants His footsteps in the sea,
>   And rides upon the storm.
>
> Deep in unfathomable mines
>   Of never-failing skill,
> He treasures up His bright designs,
>   And works His sovereign will.
>
> Ye fearful saints, fresh courage take;
>   The clouds ye so much dread
> Are big with mercy, and shall break
>   In blessings on your head.
>
> WILLIAM COWPER

Philip, the deacon, then, was thrust out into the career of an evangelist by the pressure in Jerusalem, and came, during his journeys, to "the city of Samaria" (Acts 8:5), that ancient center of Israelitish apostasy and new center of the imperial cult, which Herod had rebuilt with great magnificence and renamed Sebaste in honor of the emperor. Philip was not one of the apostolic band, but his preaching was apostolic in both content and power. He preached "with the Holy Ghost sent down from heaven" (1 Pet 1:12). That the Holy Spirit wrought with the evangelist was evidenced by the signs following, "for from many of those that had unclean spirits, they came out, crying with a loud voice: and many that were palsied, and many that were lame, were healed" (Acts 8:7).

The manner, therefore, in which the Samaritans received the Good News, is expressed in a significant phrase, "hearing and seeing" (8:6b). Psychologists insist that we retain much more of what we see than of what we hear. Certainly demonstration will carry further than mere statement. The simplest high school science course does not consist of a catalog of statements made by a lecturer to be learned by rote. We were not given definitions of the principles of Archimedes until we had carried through experiments under the direction of our instructor, as a basis in demonstration for them. So men want to see exhibits of the gospel as well as to hear expositions of it. We are not asked to produce the same kind of miracles as were wrought in those days of the first confirmation of the message, but we are required to give evidence of the miracle of grace. If we preach righteousness, we must exemplify it. If we teach holiness, we must display it. If we proclaim Christ, we must reveal Him. What men see in us will determine the measure of their heed to our message.

What they heard and what they saw were in such agreement, that "the people with one accord gave heed unto those things which Philip spake" (Acts 8:6a). Surely a response to gladden the heart of any evangelist! Without an advertising manager or press agent, without a city-wide organization, without inducements of gifts, recognition, or musical parties, this evangelist had a whole city hang on his words, while great numbers came to a saving knowledge of the Lord Jesus Christ. If all our modern innovations will catch more ears for a hearing of the gospel, and be thus the means of salvation to some, more power to them! Yet it is still true that more living exhibits, and more preaching "with the Holy Ghost sent down from heaven," are God's basic method.

The gospel is the gladdest thing in the world. The news of the end of the war in Europe sent the cities of liberated lands into a veritable panic of delight. London, freed from the long terror of air raids, buzz bombs, and blackout, went wild with excitement. Now the joy of salvation, when it comes to a city, does not require extra police to hold it in control, extra ambulances to care for the casualties, extra rations of beer to help on the fun. The joy of sins forgiven, the joy of the new life in Christ, the joy of the new relationship with God, does not disrupt life, but lifts it from the drab to the glorious, and keeps it there. The Scots convert expressed it quaintly when he said, "I'm gladder noo when I'm no' glad, than I used to be when I wis gladdest."

The gospel was confirmed in Samaria by the visit of an apostolic delegation, a delegation, be it noted, not appointed by Peter as pope, but appointed and sent by the group of apostles, Peter being a member of it, and taking orders, just like John. What a strengthening of the hands of Philip was the arrival of the two apostles! And what confirmation services, as they gathered the converts, exhorted and assured them, and blessed them with prayer and the laying on of hands!

But why did not these believers receive the Holy Spirit till the apostles came down and laid their hands on them? They had heard the Word, they had believed, they had been baptized. Why, then, the delay in this further experience? A little later pure Gentiles received the Holy Spirit with Pentecostal signs in the middle of the saving sermon, before they were even baptized. Is there, then, a reason?

There was nothing lacking in the preaching. Philip's preaching is described by two words, one meaning *to herald,* the other *to tell good news.* He heralded Christ, announcing His rank, title, rights, and demands. He told the Good News of remission of sins through the name of Jesus. There was nothing lacking in Philip's message.

Neither was there a lack in their baptism. It was true Christian baptism, not defective like that of the twelve men of Ephesus, converts of Apollos, who knew only the baptism of John.

Pentecost was the birthday of the church, and *in its phenomena* cannot be taken as typical of universal experience. The spiritual baptism of the Samaritans, that of the household of Cornelius, and that of the Ephesian disciples, seem all to be special cases, marking certain crises in the history of the gospel, and all related to apostolic ministry. The Samaritans were a mixed race with a corrupt Judaism as their religion, Cornelius and his household were the first pure Gentiles to be given official recognition in the church, while the case of the Ephesians marked the passing of the preparatory baptism of John in favor of the full Christian message and its ordinance. We cannot, therefore, build a doctrine on any one of these incidents. In view of their variety, and the manifest sovereignty of the Spirit in them all, we remember the words of our Lord to Nicodemus, "The wind bloweth where it listeth, and thou hearest the sound thereof, but canst not tell whence it cometh, and whither it goeth" (John 3:8). Yet the sovereignty is not arbitrary nor meaningless, for there is a beautiful fitness in the order of each of these events.

The gospel is well confirmed in a community which has a church of Spirit-filled people.

The confirmation of the gospel has its negative aspect also. In this case it is seen in the rebuke of the pretender.

The baptism of Simon must have been hailed as a great triumph for the new faith, and no doubt contributed to the general turning to Christ in Samaria. Yet it was not a complete heart submission which the former magician and demigod gave to the Lord Jesus, and he soon began to chafe at the loss of his power over the people he had held in thrall so long. When, therefore, he saw that by the laying on of the hands of the apostles the believers received the Holy Spirit, Simon thought he saw a way back to power and prominence even greater than he had enjoyed before. Philip had not exercised this function, and the apostles were only visiting. If, then, he could secure the secret, he would have a monopoly of it on the departure of the apostles, and wield a unique influence in the Christian community, as he had in the pagan city. So he came with his offer of money to Peter and John, thus giving his name to a practice which is regarded as one of the meanest and most despicable of all church sins—simony, the purchase of preferment.

Peter, filled with the Holy Spirit, not only spurned the offer, but read the guilty heart behind it. What a scathing rebuke, yet mingled with a tender appeal to repent, and hope of pardon! "Your silver go to perdition with you! Because you thought to obtain the free gift of God with money. You have no share or inheritance in this matter, for your heart is not right before God. Repent, then, of this iniquity of yours, and beseech the Lord if perchance the purpose of your heart may be forgiven; for I perceive that you are in the gall of bitterness and in the bondage of unrighteousness" (Acts 8:20-23, author's trans.). I wonder did Peter think of Judas's thirty pieces of silver that day? Judas sold the Lord for money, and Simon tried to buy the Holy Spirit with money.

Simon's answer seemed humble enough, but contained no confession of sin, no thought of repentance—only a plea to be spared the judgments spoken. If tradition speaks truly, he never did repent, but sought to retrieve his lost powers by forming a sect of his own to whom he gave his name. He drew many after him, and introduced teachings which blossomed into the Gnosticism of the second century. Better to have a rival and heretic without than a pretender within. The church is safer thus.

14

RURAL EVANGELISM

ACTS 8:26-40

In this chapter we consider:

1. Philip, the bearer of the evangel
2. The eunuch, the receiver of the evangel
3. Jesus, the theme of the evangel

THIS MAN PHILIP was appointed to serve tables, but when he reappears in the story twenty years after the incident before us, he is referred to as Philip the evangelist. An ecclesiastical appointment is one thing; a divine ordination is another. Yet it is often through the lesser assignment that the larger call emerges. It was so with Stephen, and it was so with Philip. But Philip was more hesitant than his fellow deacon to undertake a public ministry of the Word in the presence of the apostles. When, however, he found himself thrust out by persecution from Jerusalem, and in the semipagan city of Samaria, the fire of the gospel burned in his soul till he could not forbear. He found his lips in the presence of an imperious need, with no apostolic preference to consider nor apostolic authority to command. "Necessity is laid upon me; yea, woe is unto me, if I preach not the gospel" (1 Cor 9:16b). That is how a deacon became an evangelist—and I know of no better way. Philip had discovered his life's work. He will always be identified as "one of the seven," but he will be designated the evangelist.

The divine leading in this man's life, particularly at this point, is so marked as to command our attention. It would surely require unmistakable leading from God to induce a man to leave such a work as occupied Philip in Samaria. Yet we may read the wisdom of the great

Head of the church in the removal of His honored servant from the scene of his first successes. Few can endure the pitch of such experiences for very long. The intensity of Carmel nearly broke Elijah, and God sent an angel to nurse him in the sanitarium of the wilderness. To leave Philip longer in Samaria might have spoiled him for the more than two decades of obscure but faithful labor which lay before him.

God knew his man. Philip was susceptible to divine leading, able to discern between the impulses of nature and the voice of the Spirit. That is a faculty which calls for development, and requires both study and practice. Our airmen have to learn the principles which govern "blind flying," and they have to exercise themselves according to those principles. The better they understand the principles, and the more frequently they employ them, the surer they become in their flying. The more we study the principles of the will of God and His methods of leading men, and the more faithfully we obey His known will, the surer do we become in walking the path of guidance. Disobedience to the known will of God is bound to dull our sensibility and cloud our discernment. It certainly looked like strange leading to be called from the revival in Samaria to a desert road. But,

> His not to make reply,
> His not to reason why,
> His but to do!

for it was not as in The Charge of the Light Brigade, where "the soldier knew Someone had blundered."

During World War II a newspaper article suggested that the early stages of the North African campaign were slowed down because the enlisted men were not always sure that their officers were masters of the situation. This produced hesitancy at times in obeying commands. Philip knew that his Lord was Master of the situation, and he went, as under sealed orders.

We must look now at this Ethiopian eunuch to whom Philip was sent. A question immediately emerges as to his race. Was he a Jew or was he a Gentile, a true son of Africa? Joseph in Egypt, Daniel in Babylon, and Disraeli in England are outstanding examples of sons of Abraham rising to places of leadership in the great nations of the world, so it is not beyond possibility that the chancellor of the Ethiopian exchequer might have been a Jew. On the other hand, it would be no unique thing to see a prominent Gentile among the proselytes to Judaism, whose high conception of God and whose robust morality appealed to many, dissatisfied with the gross superstitions of paganism. It is generally received that Philip's convert that day was a true African, and it is not necessary to regard him even as an official proselyte.

If we accept that this Ethiopian was an Ethiopian indeed, that opens a most interesting question. It means that not Paul, the apostle to the Gentiles, not Peter, the holder of the keys, but Philip, the deacon-evangelist, first brought the gospel to the Gentiles and sent it hastening on its glad way to dark Africa. Later, when Philip was actually resident in Caesarea, Cornelius was directed to send to Joppa for Peter; but Peter had no hand in *this* affair. We generally speak of Peter as opening the door of the Kingdom, first to the Jews on the day of Pentecost, and then to the Gentiles in the house of Cornelius. If Philip forestalled him, by divine command, in bringing in the Gentiles, we may have to modify our interpretation of the keys.

Whatever the race of this Ethiopian treasurer, three conclusions may be drawn from the incident:

1. God has a care for individuals, and does not consider a preacher engaged in a city-wide campaign too busy to deal with one soul. The fact is, salvation is a most individual matter, and there is danger that one handling crowds all the time become too mass-conscious and lose the sense of the value of the individual. He needs the discipline and the corrective of person-to-person work, such as comes in the pastoral office. One queried recently whether weddings, since I perform them so frequently, did not become a matter of routine. I answered, "No! For weddings are the most distinctive and individualistic of events. We are dealing with personalities of divers tastes and outlooks, so that, although there may be a general sameness in the service, each wedding calls for its own individual touches, its differences of emphasis, its own measure of formality or informality. We do not run weddings off an assembly line." Woe to the minister who loses the individual in the crowd! Our Lord was always careful of the individual, and preached some of His greatest sermons to one person, as

Nicodemus and the Samaritan woman. Even in the jostling crowds He would stop to give particular attention to a Zacchaeus and a Bartimaeus.

2. God had His heart on the ever expanding program of the gospel. There was a divine impatience to hasten the glad tidings to "the uttermost part." None of the apostolic group seemed ready yet to carry the message to Africa, nor had the vision of such a mission, so the Lord brought an African to Jerusalem to receive it and carry it back with him. And although this stranger, this seeker after God, left Jerusalem unenlightened, untouched by even the apostolic band, God saw to it that he was met on the homeward journey. For this purpose He chose Philip, who had already broken through the Jewish-Samaritan prejudice, to send the gospel on its winged way to the regions beyond.

3. "Ye shall seek me, and find me, when ye shall search for me with all your heart" (Jer 29:13). The seeking heart God will not despise, but will summon resources of heaven and earth, commission men and angels, to meet the soul that cries out for him. Here is a man to whom the knowledge of God is paramount. His search has brought him into touch with the fullest revelation of God yet given, but the stewards of that revelation have so overlaid it with traditions and forms that it is but a far glimpse that a seeker can obtain. He knows he is in the vicinity of a gold strike, but he has not yet unbared the precious metal. He is returning, somewhat disappointed with the results of his pilgrimage, but still searching, poring over the sacred volume which he believes must contain what will enlighten his eyes and satisfy his heart. God *must* meet that man.

Let us give a little attention to the sermon of this great occasion. We might consider that Philip's approach was rather impudent. What if I came across the secretary of the treasury of the United States reading on a train, and broke in on him with, "Do you know what you are reading?" But unusual circumstances demand unusual methods. I heard once of a painter who was working on an interior quite close to an artist engaged on an elaborate mural. The artist was absorbed in his task, and, forgetting that he was on a scaffold, began stepping backward to gain the perspective of what he had done. Another step would have hurtled him from the height to almost certain death. The common painter saw the situation, and, with marvelous inspiration, threw a brush loaded with paint on the beautiful mural. The artist stepped forward in an instinctive move to save his work, and was saved himself.

Instead of being angry at the intrusion and the impudence of Philip, the great man recognized in his unexpected visitor a teacher who might help him, and soon the two were engrossed in the chapter which the seeker had been reading aloud. The quotation indicates that he was reading the prophet Isaiah in the Greek, and of all sections of that so evangelical prophet he was reading that most evangelical chapter, the fifty-third. Concerning this leading passage he asked a leading question: "Of whom speaketh the prophet?" (Acts 8:34). Everything depends on that question and its answer.

The eunuch's question reveals that he was not deeply learned in the Jewish faith. For not yet had the meaning of this great passage been clouded by diverse interpretations invented to cover unbelief. It was fully recognized as a Messianic passage, and not till the eleventh century of our era was this seriously questioned among the Jews. Then its application to Israel as a nation began to take hold, and has continued to this day. Isaiah himself, Jeremiah, Hezekiah, Josiah, and Job have variously been made the subject of this chapter. These are all unsupported inventions. Philip introduced no novel interpretation in referring it to Messiah, only he showed from this Scripture that *Jesus* was Messiah. That was the Christian innovation. "Beginning from the same Scripture, he preached unto him *Jesus*" (Acts 8:35, author's trans.). Now I declare that Philip had it very easy that day. It is surely not difficult to preach Jesus from Isaiah 53, where every line and word and syllable is instinct with His wonderful person and His redemptive work. The only trouble is that there is so much of Jesus in the chapter, that in half an hour one would be just well begun. But Philip did not have to watch the clock. Out on that desert road he could be as leisurely as if he had a whole eternity to expound his text; and, indeed, if his one-man audience had not interrupted him with a proposal for baptism, he might have preached all the way to Africa. Yes, the least among us could begin from Isaiah 53 and preach Jesus. We have a broader task than that, however, in which the Lord Himself is our model. "Beginning from Moses and from all the prophets, he interpreted to them in all the scriptures the things concerning himself" (Luke 24:27). That is a task for a lifetime. Oh, to be so full of Jesus that every Scripture would become for us pregnant with Him! That is a goal for every preacher, as it is the real meaning of Paul's exhortation to Timothy, "Study to shew thyself approved unto God, a workman that needeth not to be ashamed, rightly dividing the word of truth" (2 Tim 2:15).

Jesus is the answer to Isaiah 53, Jesus is the answer to all the Law and the prophets, and, also, Jesus is the answer to the cry of the human heart. No man in all sacred story echoed the questions of the soul as did Job, and Jesus is the answer to them all. "How should man be just with God?" (Job 9:2); "He was made sin for us, that we might be made the righteousness of God in Him" (2 Cor 5:21, author's trans.); "If a man die, shall he live?" (Job 14:14); "I am he that liveth, and was dead; and, behold, I am alive for evermore" (Rev 1:18); "Oh that I knew where I might find him [God]!" (John 23:3); "He that hath seen me hath seen the Father" (John 14:19*b*). Whatever form the human question takes, Jesus is the answer, the ultimate answer. Oh that we could adequately state Him, till questing men, believing, would go on their way rejoicing!

15

THE ARRESTER ARRESTED

Acts 9:1-16

In this chapter we light on:

1. Two little words that tell a big story
2. Two blessed truths that emerge from a conversation
3. Two distinguishing features that mark the new man

THE "AND" that opens the ninth chapter of Acts in the King James Version should be a "but." The eighth chapter tells of the splendid work of a man fired with zeal to push the gospel farther and farther afield. But here is another man possessed of a consuming passion to block the progress of the Christian message. So we ought to read, "Saul, on the other hand, still breathing out threatenings and slaughter . . . went unto the high priest." Let us not miss the contrast here.

That other little word "yet," or "still," is also full of interest, reminding us that we have already met Saul in the way of persecution. Going back, we trace progression in this young man's destructive zeal. At the end of chapter seven we find him standing as guardian over the clothes of those who were carrying out the stoning of Stephen, and the Spirit of inspiration adds this significant statement, "And Saul was consenting unto his death" (Acts 8:1). Many years later the apostle, in one of his defenses, recalled the scene, and his guilty part of consent to the deed. Whether he had given his consent in a formal vote of the Sanhedrin is a matter of some doubt. It is not evident that that august body even took a formal vote, unless it was before the trial, which really ended in a mob riot. At any rate, the issue was well pleasing to this young Cilician Jew, who, for all his combined Greek learning and

93

Pharisaic indoctrination, had not been able to answer the wisdom of Stephen in debate in the Hellenist synagogues.

Tigers, we are told, naturally avoid man, but if once a tiger tastes human flesh, he becomes a dread menace to the community. The taste develops the appetite. Saul of Tarsus was intense by nature, but in the first scene of persecution against the saints he is found playing a passive, though consenting role. That taste of Christian blood, however, was enough to turn him into a man-eating tiger, and he started on a course of relentless persecution, laying waste the church, disregarding the sanctity of the private home, caring not for any distinction of sex. Ruthless cruelty marked the second stage of his career as a persecutor of the church.

Finally he so sold himself to this baneful activity that it became his very breath. The ninth chapter begins, according to the King James Version, with Saul "breathing out threatenings and slaughter" (9:1). Actually the Greek verb is "breathing in." Such was the deadly atmosphere which he came to regard as his breath of life, till it was not enough that the movement was fairly broken up in Jerusalem; he raged with madness that the central persecution was the very means of its spread to other parts, and determined to pursue it wherever it might take root. It seems quite clear that Saul, not the high priest of Jewry, became the chief inquisitor.

There is one indication that the young persecutor had moments of pause and doubt. When the Lord appeared to him on that day of all days, a significant sentence fell from the divine lips: "It is hard for thee to kick against the . . . [goads]" (Acts 9:5b). Now goads are used on oxen only when they give signs of stalling, and it is far easier for the most stolid ox to keep going than to fight against that sharp-pointed weapon that urges him on. So when remembrance of Stephen's unanswerable reasoning, or of his angelic and triumphant countenance, or the invincible testimony of some of his victims, gave him pause in his desperate course, the goads of pride, prejudice, and fanaticism would urge him on; rather than face these with frank reasoning and open inquiry, he dashed forward yet more fiercely, raging with fresh hate.

Thus it stood with Saul the day he met Christ, and was conquered. Conversion, in the evangelical sense, is always a miracle. There can be no true conversion without supernatural action. Not always are supernatural accompaniments in evidence, but that even these should at times appear in such a distinctly divine operation should not be difficult to receive. That light which outshone the midday sun is the very light which shines in our hearts, and the voice which spoke audibly is the same that speaks to our inward sense. It is not ours to demand such outward signs, nor yet to dispute them. A conversion is no more miraculous with them, nor less miraculous without them; he is no better converted who is given them, nor worse converted who is not granted them. The enlightening of a little child is as truly a wonder of divine grace as the sensational, dramatic turning to God of a noted sinner.

Here is a remarkable example of the sovereignty of God in the work of salvation. I am all for the freeness of grace, all for a bona fide offer of salvation to the world, but I cannot read my Bible and observe the work of God without discerning a very distinct sovereignty. Others were journeying with Saul. They all saw the light and fell on their faces, but that light was focused on Saul, who was conscious of its beating upon him as the others were not. He only was blinded by it, and—more important—he only saw, though blinded, a presence in that light, which enabled him to say years later, in defense of his apostleship, "Have I not seen Jesus Christ our Lord?" (1 Cor 9:1). Again, they all heard the voice, but it was articulate only to Saul. He alone discerned the words and recognized the sound as the utterance of the God-man, Jesus. The vision in the light, the message in the voice, were both withheld from Saul's companions, and were sovereignly directed to him.

Now after fully granting the uniqueness and the dazzling superiority of the great apostle, I make bold to say that grace was no more sovereign toward him than toward me. A view of my experience tells the story of a life hemmed around and hemmed in with sovereign grace. Only that can account for the multiplied providences which shut me up to Christ, hedged up the ways of escape from Him, and made His call irresistibly imperative. All this I can say while still recognizing the responsibility of every man to seek the face of God, to turn from his sins, and obey the gospel.

How that proud spirit was subdued before Christ! Suddenly enveloped in heavenly light, prostrate on the ground, he beheld a glorious figure wrapped in supernal radiance and heard himself addressed, so kindly, so sorrowfully, so reprovingly, "Saul, Saul, why persecutest thou me?" (Acts 9:4). Now there was only one form of address for this glorious Being. "Who are thou, *Lord?*" (9:5*a*, italics added) ; "I am Jesus whom thou persecutest" (9:5*b*).

In that brief dialogue two tremendous truths emerged—both multiple truths, supertruths. First, Jesus is Lord. That there was one called Lord, Saul knew very well. From infancy he had repeated the basic statement of the Jewish creed, "The LORD our God is one LORD" (Deut 6:4), and like all other Jews he would not breathe the supreme, ineffable name of the Lord for very awe, but substitute the secondary title lest the utterance of the all-holy name with his lips should be blasphemy. He knew, too, that there was one Jesus, of Nazareth, who had been crucified for calling Himself the Son of God, so "making himself equal with God" (John 5:18). But to acknowledge that there was any relation between these Two, much less an identity, was unthinkable to the youthful Pharisee. It was to avert the possibility of such a link being established that he was turning from the peaceful pursuit of the rabbinic office to the fiery course of an inquisitor. Yet here, prostrate and overwhelmed, he finds himself addressing this very Jesus as Lord; nor does he retract the title after the glory-enswathed Man proclaims Himself Jesus. Instead, this will be the throbbing heart of his message all his apostolic days. Peter may proclaim to Jewry that Jesus is the Christ, and draw further conclusions from that as his basic tenet, but Paul will go to all the world with this watchword, that Jesus is Lord. It is not only a bit of doctrine—it is cosmic truth. To Paul it is the sum of all theology and philosophy and history, and he does not hesitate to define its universal and eternal scope: "for of him, and through him, and to him, are all things" (Rom 11:36). It is the focus of the movement of the ages: "that at the name of Jesus every knee should bow, of things in heaven, and things in earth, and things under the earth; and that every tongue should confess that Jesus Christ is Lord" (2:10-11).

If there was only one form of address for this glorious person, there was only one logical attitude to follow the confession that He was Lord. "Lord, what wilt thou have me to do?" (Acts 9:6). There is no value in owning His title if we do not submit to His sway. Peter was not always logical or consistent, but the most illogical and most inconsistent of his illogical and inconsistent sayings was this: "Not so, Lord!" (10:14). These words are an utter contradiction. We cannot say, "Not so," while calling Him Lord. We are verily guilty, are we not? Let us get back to the logic of Paul: "Lord, what wilt Thou?"

The other multiple truth which Saul learned that day, and which became exceedingly precious to him, was the oneness of Christ with His people. "Why persecutest thou me? . . . I am Jesus whom thou persecutest" (9:4b-5). So then, every stone that bruised the body of faithful Stephen had struck Jesus, the Lord! Every manacle, every chain that he had fastened on the wrists and ankles of the saints were laid on Jesus, the Lord! No wonder the crime of his persecutions haunted him all his days, till he challenged the world to produce a greater sinner than himself. How often have you injured the Lord in injuring one of His people? "In all their affliction he was afflicted" (Isa 63:9).

Now follow through the wonderful epistles of the apostle Paul and mark those majestic passages which treat of our union with Christ. See him developing the doctrine of the body. Underline this: "For we are members of his body, of his flesh, and of his bones" (Eph 5:30). Or this, with exclamation marks in the margin: "As the body is one, and hath many members, and all the members . . . being many, are one body: *so also is Christ*" (1 Cor 12:12, italics added). And this: "Ye are dead, and your life is hid with Christ in God. When Christ, who is our life, shall appear, then shall ye also appear with him in glory" (Col 3:3-4). Where does it all spring from? From that day and hour, when One spoke to him from the light of heaven, "I am Jesus whom thou persecutest" (Acts 9:5).

We shall from now on have many glimpses of Paul, the man in Christ. In closing the present study, note with me two marks of the renewed man emphasized in this chapter. First, he is a praying man. "Behold, he prayeth" (9:11b), said the Lord to Ananias. If it is a significant thing to the Lord that a man was praying, it ought to be significant to us. Men are not saved by praying, but when men begin to pray it is a sign that something has taken place or is taking place. Some unregenerate men can parrot the language of prayer very elo-

quently, but most men out of Christ stall at praying. I know many
who would be embarrassed beyond words to give thanks at their own
table. The news that such men were praying would be good news
indeed.

But was not Saul a praying man, brought up in a devout Jewish
home, taught in the prayers of the synagogue, trained in biblical lore
at the feet of Gamaliel? Certainly he went through the prescribed
prayers at every hour of prayer, and did it devoutly and earnestly. Yet
it all counted for nothing with God, since in all that he was going
about to establish his own righteousness. Not until he quitted the
place of the Pharisee and joined the breast-beating sinner, calling for
mercy; not until he lay broken and humbled and subdued in the
house of Judas on Straight Street, Damascus, did the Lord say, "Behold, he prayeth." And He gave that as the guarantee to Ananias that
Saul was a changed man of whom he need no longer be afraid or stand
in doubt. Prayer is human need reaching up to divine help. How
often can the Lord call to an attendant of His throne and, pointing to
us, say, "Behold, he prayeth!" The changed man is a praying man.

Then the changed man is "a chosen vessel" (Acts 9:15a). No man
is saved just to be saved. There is purpose in God's call. It is easy to
discern divine purpose in such men as Paul and Augustine and Luther
and Wesley and Moody and Hudson Taylor, but the humblest saint is
just as truly a chosen vessel as any of these. Some vessels are put to a
use which gives them great prominence, while others are used in the
secret place. The cup which the old Scottish peasant woman kept
under glass in the window of her cottage because Queen Victoria had
drunk out of it was no more "a chosen vessel" than the old "mug" out
of which she herself drank her tea in the kitchen. To fulfill God's
purpose for his redeemed life is the greatest glorification that can
come to any man, whether it be conspicuous or obscure.

The Lord defined the use of His chosen vessel to Ananias, "to bear
my name" (Acts 9:15b). That is exactly the purpose for which every
one of us is called. We may not all bear His name before kings as Paul
did, but we are asked to bear it before our own households, our neighbors, our workmates, our friends, and it is only our earthly habit of
regarding face and rank and title that makes that seem less honorable
and urgent than the witnessing before kings. Indeed, the one whose

witness brought Queen Victoria to the assurance of salvation was not one of her notable clergymen, but an obscure and humble servant of the Lord, John Townsend. The late Bishop Taylor Smith himself said that when he was chaplain to the royal household of England he directed his sermons to the servants in the back pews of the chapel.

Preaching is neither the only nor the main way of bearing the Lord's name. His name is laid upon every believer, to bear it in all his conversation, in all his conduct. Our manner of life can greatly honor and exalt the precious name, but it can also drag it down to dishonor and reproach.

Bearing His name involves suffering. "I will show him how many things he must suffer for my name's sake" (Acts 9:16, ASV), said the Lord of this conquered Pharisee. That was no exaggeration. Years later Paul put forward his sufferings as a token of his apostleship: "Are they ministers of Christ? . . . I more; in labors more abundantly, in prisons more abundantly, in stripes above measure, in deaths oft. Of the Jews five times received I forty stripes save one. Thrice was I beaten with rods, once was I stoned, thrice I suffered shipwreck, a night and a day have I been in the deep; in journeyings often, in perils of rivers, in perils of robbers, in perils from my countrymen, in perils from the Gentiles, in perils in the city, in perils in the wilderness, in perils in the sea, in perils among false brethren; in labor and travail, in watchings often, in hunger and thirst, in fastings often, in cold and nakedness" (2 Cor 11:23-27, ASV). This also is not uniquely the lot of the great apostle. The call to suffer comes upon all who bear the name of the Lord. "To you it hath been granted in the behalf of Christ, not only to believe on him, but also to suffer in his behalf" (Phil 1:29). "This honor have all his saints" (Psalm 149:9, ASV).

16

SAUL IN RETIREMENT

ACTS 9:8-30

GALATIANS 1:15-17

In this chapter, after some general considerations, we see:

1. Saul's retirement for confirmation (Acts 9:8-9)
2. Saul's retirement for instruction (Gal 1:15-17)
3. Saul's retirement for discipline (Acts 9:29-30)

THE STEPS of a good man are ordered by the LORD" (Psalm 37:23) . "And his stops too," throws in one of our quaint old commentators. One acquainted with the music of Handel knows with what rich effect he uses the pause. God is the master Artist, and well knows when the heavy pace needs to be broken. "Come ye yourselves apart . . . and rest a while" (Mark 6:31) , said our Lord to His followers when He saw tension gathering on their faces.

Saul was given three periods of retirement between the transforming vision on the Damascus road and his first official appointment as a minister. The first was three days' duration, in the house of Judas, on Straight Street, Damascus. The second was in Arabia, and lasted for some portion of three years that we cannot well determine. The third was of longer extent, covering a period variously reckoned from six to nine years, in his native city of Tarsus. There was, then, a space of from nine to twelve years between Saul's conversion and his entrance into regular ministry at Antioch. Not that he was idle during those years, or refrained from witnessing; but they were years of preparation, with such ministry intermingled as occasion offered.

Here is something for young men to ponder who wish to enter the ministry. It is no work for a novice. Moses, the great apostle of the old covenant, was given forty years' training in the wisdom and prudence of Egypt's law schools and military colleges and diplomatic services, and a graduate course of forty years with God in the wilderness of Horeb, before he was entrusted with his important commission. Paul, the great apostle of the new covenant, had his humanity courses in the Greek city of Tarsus, his seminary training in the strict Pharisaic school of Gamaliel, and then a decade of varied disciplines and instructions, before God sent him his first "call." Jesus, Moses' Lord and Paul's Lord and our Lord, allowed Himself thirty years of preparation in the flesh for but three years of public ministry.

Shortcuts into the ministry are dangerous, and costly, as I can testify from personal experience. I would not dispute God's leading in my own life, nor seek to block God's leading in another's life, but from the travail through which I had to learn what I ought to have known before starting, I would urge diligent, thorough training for every aspirant to this most taxing, most demanding, most glorious office. My contention is borne out by the increasing number of pastors who are returning to college and seminary, conscious of their need. Others, lacking the ambition of these, frequently drop out, like the young man who assured me he was called to preach without training, but soon was making his living bottling horseradish. In saying this I do not forget the men who have been thrust out to the work over their own cries, "I am a child," after the order of Jeremiah, and like him have submitted to strenuous disciplines, till they rose to places of distinction in the service of the Lord.

It is significant, too, that when Saul was finally given an official appointment, it was not the sole, nor even the chief, pastoral burden of the church at Antioch. He was there associated with Barnabas, who for all his willingness to take second place, was still regarded as first minister. Now this also would be a means of grace to a young minister, not to be taken directly from college to the pastorate of a leading city church, but to be given as assistant, or junior associate, to some experienced man of God under whose tutorage he would increase in wisdom and stature, and in favor with God and man. What a privilege it would have been to walk for a season in the shadow of

Alexander Whyte, that Gibraltar of a man, or of Spurgeon, mighty preacher of grace, or of the saintly Bishop Moule!

I am thinking, too, that periodic retirements are quite as necessary for the minister who has entered upon his labors, for ministerial recuperation and enlargement. God gave Moses two sessions of retreat in the mount, of forty days each. He sent his tired servant, Elijah, on a forty days' walk, after feeding him with "bread from heaven" (see 1 Kings 17:6). Free St. George's Church, Edinburgh, soon learned that the wealth of ministry that it enjoyed under Alexander Whyte could not be sustained without such periods of retirement. A winter recess was granted him in addition to the summer vacation, which was increased from one month to three months. The ardent student took a young library with him to his highland retreat, and there gathered the wealth with which his people were enriched in the ensuing season. Not every church can relieve its minister for so long a time, but longer vacations, spent in quieter study and deeper devotion, would pay big dividends. The fishing and boating need not be eliminated! A Sabbatic year, too, for travel, or for refresher courses in college, would also repay a congregation richly. Perhaps the Millennium will have come when ministers and churches alike learn these things!

Saul's first retirement was for confirmation. His conversion took place out there on the highway, when he saw Jesus and called Him Lord. It was now necessary to learn what was involved in conversion. For this purpose he was shut out from normal contact with the world by his blindness, and given three days to reflect on the startling change which had come. Then it was that the Pharisee's pride was abased, till he joined the breast-beating publican, crying, "God be merciful to me a sinner!" (Luke 18:13). Then it was that he counted the cost of confessing and bearing the name of the Lord Jesus, and determined to suffer the loss of all things, that he might gain Christ. Then it was that he faced and accepted the demands of the new relationship, and gave himself up to be the bondslave of Jesus Christ.

Thus it was that conversion took on its larger, deeper meaning for this so thoroughly converted man, even before Ananias came with his brotherly exhortations to cleansing, confession, and consecration, and he was ready to submit to the rite of baptism in token of all three.

That was the crossing of Saul's Rubicon. The die was openly cast that day.

The Arabian retirement was for instruction. Saul began witnessing in Damascus immediately after his baptism. His theme was "Jesus is the Son of God" and "Jesus is the Christ." He made such strides in Christian polemic that he "confounded the Jews which dwelt at Damascus" (Acts 9:22), doubtless with the very arguments by which Stephen had confounded him in Jerusalem. The keen mind of the young convert soon realized, however, that there were implications to this basic truth which called for further study, avenues of thought inviting exploration, questions demanding answers. He was not content to ring the changes on the one great revelation that had come to him and refuse the challenge of the intellectual "regions beyond" (2 Cor 10:16). It was no easy step to pull away from the Christian circle and the opening ministry, but his duty was clear, and he went off to retirement in Arabia, in search of a systematic theology.

For those who boast of being satisfied with "the simple gospel," let me call to mind a striking passage in the epistle to the Hebrews:

"Of whom we have many things to say, and hard to be uttered, seeing ye are dull of hearing. For when for the time ye ought to be teachers, ye have need that one teach you again which be the first principles of the oracles of God; and are become such as have need of milk, and not of strong meat. For every one that useth milk is unskilful in the word of righteousness: for he is a babe. But strong meat belongeth to them that are of full age, even those who by reason of use have their senses exercised to discern both good and evil. Therefore leaving the principles of the doctrine of Christ, let us go on unto perfection; not laying again the foundation of repentance from dead works, and of faith toward God, of the doctrine of baptisms, and of laying on of hands, and of resurrection of the dead, and of eternal judgment. And this will we do, if God permit" (Heb 5:11—6:3).

If this was written for the ordinary "lay" believer, what will be required of the minister of the gospel? "Art thou the teacher of Israel, and . . . [knowest] not these things?" (John 3:10, ASV) is a question which may come not inappropriately to some of us.

As yet no theological seminary had been established in the Christian church. The foundations were just being laid. Years later, when the body of divinity was thoroughly established, the aged Paul would write to young Timothy, "The things which thou hast heard from me among many witnesses, the same commit thou to faithful men, who shall be able to teach others also" (2 Tim 2:2, ASV). That is the basis of our training schools, but it was not yet. Saul went into private tuition to the Holy Spirit, and received instruction by revelation, as he affirmed in his letter to the Galatians.

"But I certify you, brethren, that the gospel which was preached of me is not after man. For I neither received it of man, neither was I taught it, but by the revelation of Jesus Christ. For ye have heard of my conversation in time past in the Jews' religion, how that beyond measure I persecuted the church of God, and wasted it: and profited in the Jews' religion above many my equals in mine own nation, being more exceedingly zealous of the traditions of my fathers. But when it pleased God, who separated me from my mother's womb, and called me by his grace, to reveal his Son in me, that I might preach him among the heathen; immediately I conferred not with flesh and blood: neither went I up to Jerusalem to them which were apostles before me; but I went into Arabia, and returned again unto Damascus" (Gal 1:11-17). Can we accept the tradition that Saul's retreat was on Mount Sinai? It would be a dramatic thought that the same hill witnessed the giving of the Law and the enlightening of the great apostle of grace, but it is an unconfirmed report.

Revelation does not preclude work. Saul carried his Old Testament with him into Arabia, and as he pored over it, the Holy Spirit did for him what the Lord Himself had done for the disciples after His resurrection: "Beginning at Moses and all the prophets, he expounded . . . the things concerning" (Luke 24:27) Jesus, till Saul could not read of Adam or Abraham or Sarah or Hagar or Moses or Mount Sinai or the seed of David without seeing Jesus.

"Never did any other lord receive his own again with such usury as when Paul went into Arabia with Moses and the Prophets and the Psalms in his knapsack, and returned to Damascus with the Romans and the Ephesians and the Colossians in his mouth and in his heart."

Thus does revelation not only give us the body of Christian truth, but teach us how to read the Word of God with fullest profit.

I read Thy Word, O Lord, each passing day,
And in the sacred page find glad employ:
But this I pray—
Save from the killing letter. Teach my heart,
Set free from human forms, the holy art
Of *reading Thee in every line,*
In precept, prophecy, and sign,
Till, all my vision filled with Thee,
Thy likeness shall reflect in me.
Not knowledge, but Thyself my joy!—
For this I pray.

Saul's witness in Jerusalem did not have the desired effect. Instead of carrying weight, it stirred up a hornets' nest. The plot of the Jews against him convinced the brethren that he ought to leave for other parts, but he doubtless would have held out at Jerusalem and followed Stephen to death, had not the Lord met him in a vision and distinctly told him that the Jews would not accept the message from him, that he was appointed to the Gentiles, and that he must leave Jerusalem immediately. Thus frequently does God with a push and a pull lead His dear children along.

So he came to Tarsus, and entered the period of disciplinary retirement. He was not indeed idle those years. The biographical section of the Galatian letter suggests not a little preaching, but it was obscure labor, far from the main current of testimony. There was, however, no loss of apostolic vision accompanying the lack of apostolic appointment. He was gaining experience and understanding and being prepared for the tasks that lay just ahead.

This was a time of further enlightenment, and further testing. The remarkable visions in which he heard words unlawful to utter belong to this period, as also the coming of that bodily affliction which he ever after called his thorn in the flesh. For even this so sanctified man needed the humiliation of such a "messenger of Satan" (2 Cor 12:7b) to keep him in the place of useableness. Whether this thorn in the flesh were an eye ailment, or epilepsy, is of secondary importance. Of more value to us is that it became an occasion of grace, as your thorn and mine will be, instead of a handicap, if we carry it as from the Lord.

All this retirement, all this obscurity, all this instructing, all this restraining, all this buffeting and bruising went into the training of an apostle. It is stern discipline, but saints are not made without it. "We must through much tribulation enter into the kingdom of God" (Acts 14:22*b*). But the Kingdom of God is worth it!

17

AN EPISCOPAL ITINERARY

Acts 9:32-43

In this chapter we see:

1. Peter in the wake of the evangelist
2. Peter in the steps of the Master
3. Peter in the control of the Spirit

WE LAST SAW Peter as he was returning to Jerusalem from Samaria, whither he had gone with John to examine and confirm the gracious work being done at the hands of Philip, the deacon-evangelist. We now find him on an episcopal tour of the centers touched by the gospel in Judea and Samaria, and remarkably enough, he is still trailing Philip. Philip had been called from the scene of the Samaritan awakening to the meeting with the Ethiopian in the desert of Gaza, after which he "was found at Azotus: and passing through he preached in all the cities, till he came to Caesarea" (Acts 8:40), his hometown. Lydda and Joppa were two of those cities. A look at a Bible map of Palestine will show Gaza, Azotus, Lydda, Joppa, and Caesarea roughly on a curved line on or near the Mediterranean Sea.

"And it came to pass, as Peter passed through all quarters, he came down also to the saints which dwelt at Lydda" (9:32), and thence north to Joppa and Caesarea. Lydda and Joppa were not the only points touched by Peter between his departure from Jerusalem and his arrival at Caesarea. These have special mention because of the unusual events which took place there. There can be little doubt that the "all quarters" included Azotus, where Philip began his preaching itinerary after bidding farewell to the Ethiopian. So we see the apostle in the wake of the evangelist.

107

If Lydda and Joppa are picked out as examples of what Peter wrought on that memorable journey, they may also be taken as a sample of what Peter found in the tracks of Philip. We already know the good work which the apostles found in Samaria. Now, coming after Philip, Peter discovered some grand saints in both Lydda and Joppa. And who can say whether the preparedness of Cornelius of Caesarea may not be somewhat traced to the influence of Philip's godly household? At any rate, there are enough statement and suggestion in Scripture to indicate that Philip's goings were marked by a trail of blessing.

As surely as a ship leaves a wake in the deep, so surely does every man leave a trail of blessing or cursing behind him. There are those "who passing through the valley of Baca make it a well" (Psalm 84:6), while others poison the wells they touch and leave behind them vales of weeping. We touch lives, and leave them lifted or fallen, stronger or weaker, more courageous or more craven, nobler or baser.

In July 1927, Commander Byrd visited the Invalides, the Paris hospital which housed the "Broken Wings" of the First World War. There he met Captain LeGendre, who nine years before had crashed, and broken, it was said, nearly every bone in his body. He had never walked since, but was wheeled about in an invalid's chair. After the visit at the hospital Byrd started out for the tomb of Napoleon, a short distance off. LeGendre went too, in his chair, the commander walking beside him. Suddenly the wounded man called for a halt, and, saying to the great explorer, "You give me courage," he got out of his chair and walked.

If a man may so inspire and bless others through psychological impact, what should not our touch on others do in the spiritual realm! Does our passage through leave lives richer or poorer, elevated or sunken, nearer heaven or closer to hell? D. L. Moody passed through the cities of Great Britain and Ireland and left behind him a trail of Bible institutes, evangelistic associations, missions, revived churches, and redeemed lives. I wonder would the effects of a lecture tour of Bob Ingersoll, the noted infidel, bear comparison with the results of an evangelistic itinerary of Moody! How many broken hearts comforted, broken lives mended, broken homes rebuilt, would one have found in his trail? You may be neither a Moody nor an Ingersoll, but in whose company are you?

Philip needed Peter's follow-up. Peter had something that Philip had not. In Samaria the presence of the apostles was required to bestow the Holy Spirit on the believers. In Lydda, Peter's ministry was needed for the recovery of Aeneas and the consequent city-wide turning to the Lord. In Joppa the death of Dorcas called for the miraculous gifts of the apostle, while in Caesarea the new work of the Spirit necessitated apostolic testimony. This by no means discounts the work of Philip. It just illustrates the distribution of the gifts, and the interdependence of the ministry. "And he gave some to be apostles; and some, prophets; and some, evangelists; and some, pastors and teachers; for the perfecting of the saints, unto the work of ministering, unto the building up of the body of Christ" (Eph 4:11-12, ASV). All are required. The apostles and the prophets and the evangelists and the pastor-teachers need each other; they supplement each other, and all together, with the blessing of God, bring about the perfecting and the building up. So let not Peter despise the partial work of Philip, nor let Philip resent the coming of Peter.

This Petrine interlude reads very much like a page out of the gospels. The scene at Lydda cannot but recall our Lord's healing of the paralytic "borne of four" (Mark 2:3), while Peter's "Arise, and make thy bed" (Acts 9:34), recalls the words of Jesus, "Arise, and take up thy couch, and go unto thy house" (Luke 5:24, ASV). There is striking similarity, too, between the raising of Dorcas and the raising of the daughter of Jairus, even to the expelling of the crowd. Peter, then, while geographically in the wake of Philip, was spiritually in the steps of the Master, who "went about doing good" (Acts 10:38*b*).

"The former treatise have I made, O Theophilus, of all that Jesus began both to do and [to] teach" (Acts 1:1). Now He is continuing, in His apostle, what He began in the days of His flesh. "Jesus Christ maketh thee whole" (9:34), said Peter. It is still Jesus Christ, not now the Man of Galilee, but the Man in glory, doing His mighty works through chosen men filled with the Holy Spirit.

The signs which accompanied the beginnings of the gospel—miraculous healings, prophecies, the raising of the dead—may not show

forth in us. These are in the hands of the sovereign Spirit. The fact
of special note is that the works in which our exalted Lord engages,
as a continuance of what He began in the days of His flesh, He ac-
complishes through the ministrations of His servants; and these are
greater works than were wrought before the cross, as He Himself said,
"I have a baptism to be baptized with; and how am I straitened till it
be accomplished!" (Luke 12:50). "Greater works than these shall
. . . ye [do]; because I go unto my Father" (John 14:12). If the redemptive blessings of the cross are being realized and manifested, we
need not be anxious about spectacular works in the physical realm. If,
for purposes of evidence or as a matter of grace, the Lord grants these,
they are the lesser accompaniments of the greater works. That such
accompaniments are granted, especially where the gospel is making
a new beginning, is a matter of record. Mr. Mickelsen, a missionary
from Borneo, in the course of an address related this incident. He
was far in the interior, in uncharted territory, virgin soil for the
gospel, a native came to him, coughing violently and complaining of
terrible pain in head and chest. The missionary was without medical
supplies, and the case seemed critical, so he quietly and simply prayed
for the man, who was healed immediately, and listened earnestly to
the gospel. Leaving the missionary, the healed man returned to his
own people and told them what had happened to him. One of the
company who sat listening began to scoff and jeer. Suddenly he was
seized with a paroxysm of pain in his head and chest. The ailment
which had been lifted in answer to prayer fell on the reviler. He
quickly changed his attitude, and came to the missionary, coughing as
if his body would be rent to pieces, and crying for mercy. The missionary prayed again, and the erstwhile scoffer was delivered also. Yes,
these things do happen, but our concern is with the "greater works."

Peter was walking in the control of the Holy Spirit, as various
operations of the Spirit in his life testify. First, there are distinct
evidences here of the Spirit's leading. Now the Spirit leads in divers
manners. He led Peter to Samaria by the appointment of his brethren.
He led him to Lydda in the course of a prepared plan, to Joppa by the
request of the saints there, and to Caesarea by vision and direct command. Yet, despite the diverseness of the leadings, there is a remarkable orderliness, a steady progression as toward a fixed goal. The

leading of the Spirit is not a multiplication of unrelated "hunches," producing a jitterbug sort of life, but is reasonable, significant, whole, progressive, purposeful. It is vexing at times to hear young people speak so flippantly of God telling them to do this and that, when their lives are manifestly a bundle of contradictions. David was still praying, "Teach me to do thy will" (Psalm 143:10), after long experience with God. The basic secret of the leading of the Spirit is in yieldedness to His control.

The empowering of the Spirit accompanied the leading. Control and power go together. A giant of the air has power to stay aloft and to sustain its flight so long as it is held in control, but let it get out of control, and it soon lies a helpless wreck on the earth. An uncontrolled man is a powerless man. A self-controlled man is a forceful man. A Spirit-controlled man is one through whom the divine power flows in the accomplishment of works beyond the scope of merely human endeavor.

In Samaria the power of transmission of the Holy Spirit rested upon this controlled vessel. In Lydda the power of the Spirit enabled him to invoke the name of the Lord Jesus for the healing of the paralytic. In Joppa the power of prevailing prayer was granted him to raise Dorcas from the dead. In Caesarea the power of the Holy Spirit was in his words to convince, enlighten, and convert Cornelius and all his house. So the power of the Spirit is as varied in its operations as are His leadings. When we submit to the control of the Spirit, we learn His leading and realize His empowering.

The preparations of the Spirit work in those appointed for His services. This refers not only to general fitness for the ministry at large, but equally to special preparedness for particular requirements. Sometimes the accomplishing of one task is a preparation for the next. The miracle at Lydda fitted Peter for the greater demand in Joppa. Then in Joppa the Holy Spirit put the apostle through a course of instruction to condition him for the new departure in Caesarea.

Without the preparations of the Holy Spirit no man is fit for the ministry, even if he have the most thorough training which our best institutions of learning can give. The best mind and the highest learning are none too good for the holy calling of the gospel, but academic honors in college and seminary are no guarantee of true success. The

Holy Spirit has courses of training far more taxing, far more difficult, far more effective than the stoutest curriculum ever followed by the schools. When a man has come through the liftings up and the castings down of the school of the Spirit, the bruisings and the healings, the humiliations and the exaltations, the tears and the laughters, the chastisements and the caressings, the instructions and the applications, he is fit, and he fits. And what is true of the Christian minister is equally true of the Christian mother and the Christian businessman and the Christian teacher.

A case of special aptitude for a specific task in a Spirit-controlled life has just come to my notice. James Fraser was a born musician. From childhood it was his passion, and he gave himself to the mastery of its difficulties until he himself was a master of the classics. Although he prepared himself for the engineering profession, graduating from the London University with the B.Sc. degree, he was urged to make music his career, and was greatly inclined toward it. Then came his call to China, and he followed His Lord "behind the ranges" to the wild, forgotten China-Burma border to labor among the unknown tribes. Surely it seemed like burying his talents, recklessly throwing away a useful career for the sake of a work which less talented men could do! But God had been preparing his man. These highly developed skills, especially his music, were part of the equipment required for a definite, unique ministry. The Spirit-prepared man fit the job. The Lisu language turned out to be one of the most tonic in all that part of the world, having no less than twenty tones. None but a musician with a trained ear could have discerned these and mastered them. Fraser did, and not only reduced the strange tongue to writing, but applied to the phonetic script a system of tone symbols which gave accuracy to learning and reading, for both native and foreigner, where otherwise there would have been confusion. The Holy Spirit makes no mistakes.

What a man is the Spirit-controlled man! For he is Spirit-led and Spirit-empowered and Spirit-prepared. I should not wish to be found opposing that man! I should like to walk in that man's company! I want to be that man!

18

TACKLING A PROBLEM AT BOTH ENDS

ACTS 10:1-45

In this study three great truths emerge:

1. God will not allow a seeking soul to perish
2. Almsdeeds and prayers are no substitutes for the gospel
3. "At the Cross of Christ the Ground is Level"

CORNELIUS is not the only devout soldier on record. Many who have borne arms for their country have been "good soldiers of Jesus Christ." F. W. Robertson, whose title of fame is simply "Robertson of Brighton," was son, grandson, and brother of notable soldiers. It was his own early ambition to follow the family tradition, and to be "the Cornelius of his regiment." I write this during the Second World War, when nearly a hundred and fifty of my own young people are under arms. Most of them might justly bear the title, "the Cornelius of his regiment," for they "serve the Lord Christ" (Col 3:24). Not a few of them are doing chaplaincy work on the invitation of their commanding officers, where no regular chaplains are assigned. "Onward, Christian soldiers!"

Where and when Cornelius came under the influence of Jewish teaching we are not told, but his assignment to Palestine would bring him into closer contact with Jewish life and thought than ever before. The lofty conception of God and the high standards of righteousness were the characteristics of Judaism which attracted him, so that while he did not become a Jew, it is likely enough that he had taken some steps toward being a "proselyte of the gate." "A devout man, and one that feared God with all his house, which gave much alms to the people, and prayed to God alway" (Acts 10:2), is certainly the description of a man who had turned his back on all pagan practices and had set himself to seek the Lord with all his heart, accompanying his search with such deeds of righteousness and kindness as he judged to be consistent with the fear of God. That "all his house" followed him in his godly practices is evidence of his strength of character, and of the respect and veneration in which he was held by those closest to him.

Cornelius was definitely not a self-righteous man. He must not be classed with the Pharisee who went up into the Temple and prayed with himself, saying, "God, I thank thee, that I am not as the rest of men. . . . I fast twice in the week; I give tithes of all that I get" (Luke 18:11-12, ASV). Cornelius was sincerely seeking to fulfill the requirements of God as announced by the prophet Micah, "to do justly, and to love mercy, and to walk humbly with thy God" (Mic 6:8b). He acknowledged himself "a sinner of the Gentiles," and making the Lord God his God, he ordered his life according to the light he had, while eagerly seeking more light.

"Ye shall seek me, and find me, when ye shall search for me with all your heart" (Jer 29:13), saith the Lord. To the devout soldier, God sent an angel, instructing him to send to Joppa for Simon Peter. Now Caesarea was the home of Philip the evangelist, so the centurion might have been directed to send for him. God's purpose, however, required the light to come from thirty miles away, for this was not simply a matter of salvation for one man and his household; this involved the whole question of the salvation of the Gentiles. This thing must not be incidental to an evangelist's ministry; it must be climactic in an apostle's career.

What was the further light that Peter brought? It was "good tidings of peace by Jesus Christ" (Acts 10:36b, ASV). This Jesus "is Lord of all . . ." (10:36c, ASV), said Peter, then went on to relate the chief facts of the incarnation—the anointing, the ministry, the death, and the resurrection. Then followed the solemn announcement of the universal judgeship of Jesus, and the glad proclamation of remission of sins through His name. It is evident that Peter would have launched into an enlargement of all these points, had not the Holy Spirit interrupted with the miraculous evidence that the regenerating work was even now accomplished. A skeleton outline of the gospel was all that this so prepared company required, till their quickened tongues began to sing:

> 'Tis done, the great transaction's done!
> I am my Lord's and He is mine.

God will not leave a seeking soul to perish. A dear friend of ours, Francis Dickie, who labored many years in China, once told us this incident. He was preaching to a little congregation in a city of inland China. Thinking that all present were Christians, he was minded to give a word of kindly exhortation to them, but by a strong impulsion proceeded to a simple exposition of the way of salvation. Suddenly a wizened man at the rear of the hall leaped to his feet, shouting, "I have it! I have it!" The meeting broke up, and Mr. Dickie, engaging the man in conversation, learned that for years he had been going from shrine to shrine, undergoing many self-disciplines, measuring his length over many hundreds of miles, in an effort to find peace of heart. At every point he had failed, and was ready to give up in despair, when he was pulled by an invisible power from street to street and impelled to enter this little hall, not knowing the reason. Here he heard the story of Jesus and His love, and peace flooded his heart. The records of heaven hold multitudes of such incidents, and not until they are opened for our reading shall we know the wonderful ways of God in bringing to the knowledge of the truth those whose hearts were stirred up to seek Him.

Almsdeeds and prayers do not suffice. When Peter exclaimed, "Of a truth I perceive that God is no respecter of persons: but in every nation he that feareth him, and worketh righteousness, is acceptable to him" (Acts 10:34-35, ASV), he did not imply that the gospel, or faith in Christ, was not necessary, or that such devoutness as Cornelius exhibited, lacking Christ, was sufficient. As Dr. Vaughan says at this point, "If Cornelius was safe in his prayers and his almsgivings, why was Peter sent to tell him words whereby he and all his house might be saved?" What God does for true seekers is not to accept their seeking as sufficient, but to send them the light. It remains true that "there is none other name under heaven given among men, whereby we must be saved" (Acts 4:12*b*).

God had a problem thirty miles long: that is, if God has problems, and if you can measure a problem geographically. For Cornelius was in Caesarea, and Peter in Joppa, thirty miles away—thirty miles, not only of walking distance, but of inborn, inbred, inwrought prejudice which must be broken, crucified, trampled down every step of the stubborn way.

Peter was still Peter, even in his trances and his visions. He interrupted and contradicted and snubbed his Lord more than all the other apostles together. If the Master spoke of His own coming death, Peter was ready with his "Not so, Lord." If the condescending Saviour stooped to wash the disciples' feet, only Peter would answer with a "Not so, Lord." Or if it were a solemn warning of danger ahead, Peter's "Not so, Lord," was sure to be heard. So here, even in a transport of vision, the Lord's direct command is countered with a most emphatic "Not so, Lord."

What a contradiction in terms! What a denial of the Lord's truthfulness, wisdom, knowledge, and right! We attribute no lordship, no sovereignty, no right of command, to whom we say, "Not so!" We had better change our nay into yea, or else honestly leave out the "Lord." Our Lord Himself had a different answer for Him to whom He yielded allegiance. "Even so, Father" (Matt 11:26), was the Son's constant reply to the Father's will.

It was indeed a hard thing that the Lord asked of Peter that day. It would not have been hard for you and me who have not been bound all our days by the law of ceremonial clean and unclean, but to an Hebrew of Hebrews like Simon Peter the very thought of killing and eating indiscriminately of those four-footed beasts and reptiles was abhorrent. "I have never eaten anything that is common and unclean" (Acts 10:14, ASV).

Did the Lord's reply, "What God hath cleansed, make not thou common" (10:15, ASV), signify the abrogation of the ancient ceremonial law of clean and unclean beasts? Or was it simply a parable concerning the equality of all men before God? We can hardly ignore the primary, literal, though lesser meaning. The cosmic embrace of the blood of Christ demands such a release from the category of the unclean for the animal world. Because of the blood of Christ we can no longer discriminate between beast and beast on religious, ceremonial grounds. Whatever in the old discriminations has hygienic value we may preserve, and ought to, but as guided by wisdom, not as bound by Law.

The vision only left Peter puzzled, until he saw a first glimmering of its larger sense in the coming of the messengers from Cornelius and the encouragement of the Holy Spirit to go with them, "making no discrimination" (Acts 11:12, author's trans.). It was the vision plus the voice that prepared him to say to Cornelius, "Unto me hath God showed that I should not call any man common or unclean" (10:28, ASV).

The story of Cornelius carried Peter still further along the road of emancipation from the old prejudices. That God would send an angel to a Gentile seeker and bid him summon an apostle, and that God would "turn the works" on that same apostle to prepare him for the mission, was such a confirmation and demonstration of the character of God that Peter felt he was just learning for the first time what his Bible consistently taught. "I perceive that God is no respecter of persons: but in every nation he that feareth him, and worketh righteousness, is acceptable to him" (Acts 10:34, ASV). That "I perceive" means "I lay hold for myself." How many a truth of God we know, but only some crisis experience brings it home till we say, "I perceive," "I lay hold for myself!"

But it was that "little Pentecost" which bore Peter all the way, and fully convinced him that God had broken down every barrier, that "in Christ" there is neither Jew nor Gentile, neither bond nor free, that we are "all one in Christ Jesus" (Gal 3:28). The token of full membership in the church could not be denied to those who had manifestly received the deeper baptism of the Spirit.

Despite all these divine dealings, it was hard for Peter to break away finally and completely from the old exclusiveness. It remained for Paul to champion the full freedom of Gentile believers and to establish, under God, the "no difference" (Acts 15:9) of Jewish and Gentile sinners in condemnation, and the "no difference" of Jewish and Gentile believers in salvation.

Have we learned the lesson? Are we really like our heavenly Father in being no respecters of persons? A missionary family came home to America from three years in a Japanese concentration camp in the Philippines. They came to our Sunday school their first Sunday home.

The older boy was taken to the intermediate department and found
that his teacher was—a Japanese! Would the Christian grace have
been as strong in you as in that boy, who accepted his teacher as a
Christian, not as one of an alien race?

In the city of Madras, India, is a chapel, on the wall of which there
is a strange cross. At the end of one arm of the crossbeam is a pierced
hand, brown in color. At the end of the other arm there is another
pierced hand, a white one. Christ died for white, brown, black, and
yellow, and in Him the distinctions are forgotten.

> In Christ there is no East or West,
>   In Him no South or North;
> But one great fellowship of love
>   Throughout the whole wide earth.
>   JOHN OXENHAM

19

AS FAR AS ANTIOCH

Acts 11:19-30; 12:25

In this chapter we see:

1. The origin of a Gentile church (vv.19-21)
2. The ordering of a Gentile church (vv. 22-26)
3. The offering of a Gentile church (vv. 27-30)

THAT YOUNG MAN Saul did worse than he knew and better than he knew. Not till years of apostleship had ripened his spiritual senses did he gauge the enormity of his crimes, and then he wrote it down against himself, "I am the least of the apostles, that am not meet to be called an apostle, because I persecuted the church of God" (1 Cor 15:9). At the same time, not till he saw the flourishing Gentile church in Antioch which sprang from his persecuting zeal, and its daughter churches scattered over Galatia and Asia and Macedonia and Achaia, did he realize how God had turned his evil into boundless good.

The refugees from Saul's rage became a great army of evangelists. Uncommissioned by any church body, but fired with the love of Christ, they turned their flights into preaching tours, till they left behind them a trail of witness reaching Phoenicia, with its famous towns of Tyre and Sidon, the rich island of Cyprus, and Syrian Antioch, that strategic center of culture and business. Antioch was three hundred miles north of Jerusalem, situated in a deep pass between the Taurus and Lebanon ranges, sixteen miles from the sea, and on the main travel and trade route to Mesopotamia.

The dispersed Christians were Jews, and for the most part confined their witness to fellow Jews. They were not yet emancipated from the old bondage. Some of the Hellenistic Jews, however, found their

119

broader sympathies getting the better of them as they journeyed farther from Jerusalem and its rigid prejudices. By the time they reached Antioch, with its vast need and its strategic opportunity, they could not forbear, and they launched the noble experiment of telling their wonderful story to Greeks, with what hesitancy and questioning of the outcome we can only guess as we put ourselves in their place. They knew nothing about what had happened in Caesarea, in the house of Cornelius. They had no precedent for their action, no authority save the inward urge which they believed and hoped was from the Lord.

What was their surprise and delight to find their courage and faith rewarded beyond all expectation! "The hand of the Lord was with them" (Acts 11:21), says the King James Version, but there is an air of excitement in Luke's statement, produced by the order of the words and the omission of the articles, which our more stolid English fails to convey. How the trembling of these gospel experimenters gave place to boldness as evidences of the Lord's pleasure multiplied! When "a great number believed, and turned unto the Lord" (11:21), inexperienced churchmen as they were, they found themselves with a church on their hands, a Gentile church at that, the unforeseen outcome of their daring venture.

This also is one of the ways of the Lord. The Kingdom of God finds itself straitened in the encasements of tradition, custom, and established order, till the entrance is well-nigh blockaded. Then God raises up a man who is bold enough to break through the established order, and a host of violent men rush for the breach and take the Kingdom of God by force. So it was in the days of the Reformers So it was in the days of the Wesleys. So it was in the modern missionary movement. So it was in the establishment of the Sunday school. So we trust it is in our contemporary youth movements. Pioneers are needed for such projects—men of passion, of sympathy, of imagination, immune to criticism and the denunciations of the traditionalists. Their reward is to perceive the hand of the Lord working with them, and to find a development before them that they scarcely know what to do with.

By this time the broken up church in Jerusalem had grown again to good proportions, what with the return of some of the fugitives and the new fruitage of apostolic labors. So, while it was an act of the apostles to send a delegation of inquiry and help to Samaria, it was now the church which, upon hearing rumors of the mighty awakening and the new departure in Antioch, voted to send a representative to examine the amazing situation. They chose Barnabas, commissioning him to follow the trail of the refugee preachers as far as Antioch, taking note of their labors at the several points touched.

A better than Barnabas could not have been appointed to this delicate task. "Son of Consolation" as the apostles had named him, he seemed to have a special aptitude for relieving situations. His only quarrel was over his determination to give a man who had failed another chance. His must have been a happy journey from Jerusalem to Antioch, as he saw at every stopping place new and varied evidences of the work of the Holy Spirit through the witnessing of the dispersed believers. But the climax of that happy journey was at the end of it. When he came to Antioch and observed all that had been developing there, he had only one word to describe it. "This," he exclaimed, "is the grace of God!" (see Acts 11:23). And he was glad.

Very different would have been the reaction of some at Jerusalem. The Judaizers, "those of the circumcision" (11:2, author's trans.), would have tried to kill the whole movement. They would have said, "this is all out of order. First of all, the preachers had no commission from the apostles and elders. Second, they had no right to offer salvation to Gentiles save through the Law. Now, to bring everything into proper order, we shall establish courses in the Law of Moses for these Gentiles, and when they have embraced the Jewish faith and submitted to circumcision, then shall we grant them Christian baptism and give them the hand of fellowship into the church." So would the church have perished in its infancy, had not the great Head of the church ordered that Barnabas, the 'Son of Consolation,' should go forth on this mission of encouragement and confirmation.

Now Barnabas was a great man in the church at Jerusalem, but he had never done anything as big or as notable as this that he saw accomplished in Antioch at the hands of obscure believers who were scarcely regarded in the mother church. Yet not a shadow of jealousy creeps over his lovely spirit. This is not the last time that Barnabas will be eclipsed, but now and always he will champion and support and encourage those who eclipse him. Surely the grace of God over which Barnabas rejoiced was outdone by the grace of God in the man himself. Where meaner souls would have criticized, "he exhorted them all, that with purpose of heart they would cleave unto the Lord: for he was a good man, and full of the Holy Spirit and of faith: and much people was added unto the Lord" (Acts 11:23b-24, ASV).

Such grace is for us, too, and we who are ministers of Christ need it above all others. At the World's Fifth Sunday School Convention, held in Rome in May 1907, Dr. F. B. Meyer said in the course of a message: "I find in my own ministry that supposing I pray for my own little flock, God bless me, God fill my pews, God send me a revival, I miss the blessing, but as I pray for my big brother, Mr. Spurgeon, on the right-hand side of my church, God bless him; or my other big brother, Campbell Morgan, on the other side of my church, God bless him, I am sure to get a blessing without praying for it, for the overflow of their cups fills my little bucket." That is the spirit of Barnabas. If we can encourage what we did not originate, if we can rejoice in the successes of those who surpass us, we are becoming sons of consolation.

What an opportunity Barnabas had to mount the saddle and assume the leadership in Antioch! He had come with the authority of the church in Jerusalem, and might well have claimed apostolic rights in this irregular church founded by unauthorized preachers. But Barnabas was made of different stuff. For all the help he was able to give by his own ministry, he determined that this Gentile church should have nothing short of the best. His thoughts flew to Tarsus, where young, ardent Saul had now spent some years in obscurity, waiting the leading of the Lord. A conviction was borne in upon the soul of Barnabas that this was the right man for Antioch, and Antioch was the right place for Saul. His Hellenistic background, his call to the Gentiles, his expulsion from Jerusalem, his years of disciplinary retirement, all clamored for his entrance into just such ministry as waited him here. Now Barnabas did not know Saul's address in Tarsus, but he determined to find him, so, crossing the Gulf of Issus, he searched the city for his man, and brought him to Antioch. This is now the second time that Saul has been beholden to Barnabas: the first time for breaking down the reserve of the believers in Jerusalem and securing for the newly converted persecutor the hand of fellowship; and now for introducing him to this sphere of active ministry in the church.

Some boast that the dust of their shoes is on no man's shoulders. I am not as independent as that. I thank God for every Barnabas who has helped me on my ministerial way, and shall want to acknowledge my debt to them in that great day when we stand together before the throne. Not a few of them are in my own present congregation. They have ministered to me more than I have ministered to them.

What a year was that, rich in fellowship and ministry! It was during this year, too, that the community of believers grew in number and influence till it commanded the attention of the populace. Whether in scorn or banter or for mere convenience of designation, the people of Antioch dubbed them "Christians," a name which they gladly accepted, and bore with pride.

This Gentile church soon proved itself. The reports which Barnabas sent back to Jerusalem stirred the hearts of the generous saints there, so that some of the more gifted among them desired to visit Antioch, not now as a delegation of inquiry, but for their own enrichment—just as warmhearted ministers visit scenes of revival in the hope that they may carry the blessing back to their own churches.

In the group was Agabus, who appears once and again at strategic moments with a prophetic message. On this occasion he announced the approaching famine. Barnabas, who had had experience of difficult times in Jerusalem, knew how hard hit the poor saints there would be. It required only his statement of their peculiar hardships to stir the Gentile church to action. They would immediately start a fund for the purchase of food, and have a great supply ready to ship in to the church in Jerusalem when the famine struck.

Sir William Ramsey believes that Agabus made his prophecy in the year 44, and that the famine came in 46. If this is so, the church at Antioch had two years to raise their fund. The same scholar further believes that the contribution was sent in the form of food supplies, not money, which seems sensible. America did not ship gold to Europe to feed the hungry nations there after disastrous and destructive years of war!

Barnabas and Saul were entrusted with the ministry of this bounty. If it were simply a matter of carrying money to Jerusalem and depositing it with the elders there, little time would have been required, but the insertion of other events between their commission and their return suggests that "their ministration" was not accomplished in a day. They may indeed have acted as "relief officers," supervising the daily distribution during the months of crisis.

All these are points of interest, but we are more concerned with the principles involved. Later, in another connection, Paul wrote to the Corinthians: "If we sowed unto you spiritual things, is it a great mattter if we shall reap your carnal things?" (1 Cor 9:11, ASV). From the persecuted in Jerusalem had come to Antioch the "things that pertain unto life and godliness" (2 Pet 1:3). It was only meet that now a return of carnal necessities should flow from Antioch to Jerusalem. Again, more generally, Paul laid it down as a principle of Christian conduct to the Romans, "distributing to the necessity of saints" (Rom 12:13). Such are some of the good works which believers are required to maintain. So the saints in Antioch showed their faith by their works, and, having been justified by faith, were now also justified by works.

20

PRAYER CHANGES THINGS

ACTS 12:1-24

In this sequence of events we discern:

1. The call to prayer (vv. 1-5)
2. The answer to prayer (vv. 6-17)
3. The sequel to prayer (vv. 18-24)

GOD'S PEOPLE must be kept praying.

Prayer is the channel of communion. Without it the heart becomes estranged from the love of Christ, the life loses the luster of His likeness, the mind grows carnal and worldly, the witness of our lips becomes burned out ashes instead of coals of living fire.

Prayer is a condition of the divine operation. In sovereign grace and infinite condescension, God has imposed this necessity upon Himself, that not without the prayers of His people will His purposes be realized and His decrees fulfilled. Read the eighth chapter of Revelation, and see how the thunders and the voices and the lightnings and the earthquakes of God's goings in the earth wait for the prayers of the saints. Why did God lay a strange anguish of prayer on that mother the very night her son's submarine was sent to the bottom, and hold her in prayer till that hour of the morning when it surfaced by a means which neither the commander nor any of the crew could explain, except the boy who had a praying mother? Or, why does the Lord teach His church to pray, "Thy kingdom come!" (Luke 11:2), and, "Even so, come, Lord Jesus!" (Rev 22:20)?

For our own souls' sake, and for the Kingdom of God's sake, we must be kept praying.

But it is not easy to keep us praying. Praying, for all its glory and its eternal reward, is the most demanding, the most exacting, and the most crucifying exercise that we know. There is more blood and sweat and tears, more crushing and wounding, more groaning and travailing in half an hour's real praying than in a whole year of preaching. So it comes to pass that if we could "get by" without praying, we would. Too much ease, therefore, and smooth sailing and prosperity are exceedingly perilous for us, for they tempt us to slack praying. In such times "saying prayers" is likely to take the place of "praying," till we endanger our own souls and the Kingdom of God.

"He knoweth our frame; he remembereth that we are dust" (Psalm 103:14). Therefore He stirs up our nest and brings upon us stark necessities. Then we cry out, "Why is all this come upon me and the work committed to my hands?" And He answers, "Let me see thy countenance, let me hear thy voice!" (Song of Sol 2:14).

"Now about that time Herod the king put forth his hands to afflict certain of the church. And he killed James the brother of John with the sword. And when he saw that it pleased the Jews, he proceeded to seize Peter also . . . intending after the Passover to bring him forth to the people. Peter therefore was kept in prison" (Acts 12:1-5). It was God's call to prayer. Since the departure of Saul to Tarsus, the church in Jerusalem had enjoyed a season of great peace and enlargement, till there was danger of the saints being "at ease in Zion." It was for the salvation of His church that God sent this discipline, to avoid slackening in prayer and the softening influence of prosperity. When Sir Bernard Montgomery was general officer commanding southeastern command in England, between December 1940 and August 1942, he laid out a six-mile course over which he commanded all ranks up to brigadier to run once a week, frequently covering it himself. This was part of his "keep fit" program. Such strenuous discipline made the Eighth Army the keen instrument that it became for the 1,400-mile rout of Rommel and his Nazis. God's "keep fit" program for His people includes hurdles that hold them to prayer. That is how God's victories are won.

Herod Agrippa I, nephew of that Herod Antipas who had John the Baptist beheaded and who collaborated with Pilate in the death of our Lord, was elevated from disgrace by the Emperor Caligula in A.D. 37, being given two tetrarchies and the royal title. In the year 41, Claudius further advanced him, adding Samaria and Judea to his domains. Despite the profligacy of his youth, he gave himself to the observance of Jewish practices, and sought the alleviation of his country's oppressed state. Apparently it was for political reasons, to secure his position in Jewry, that he undertook oppressive measures against the church in the year 44, little knowing that he was writing his own death warrant while acting as God's unconscious agent in saving the church.

"Peter therefore was kept in prison: but prayer was being made intently by the church unto God on his behalf" (Acts 12:5, author's trans.). A new eagerness, a new earnestness, entered into the prayers of the people. They had been shocked and confused by the sudden slaying of James, the first of the apostles to win the martyr's crown, but it required the arrest of Peter and the imminent peril of his death, to stir them to this sort of praying, this praying after a stretched-out fashion, as Luke's word has it. Do you see these two runners nearing the tape, neck to neck, each stretching himself to the utmost to gain only one inch on the other and touch the tape first by but a fraction of a second? That is how the church in Jerusalem prayed, as those who were racing to beat death. And the form of the verb tells us that it did not let up. This intent, insistent prayer kept on arising to God. The church had accepted the challenge—the threat of the powers of evil to destroy the church, which was God's instrument to save the church. "The gates of hell shall not prevail against it" (Matt 16:18).

"Peter . . . was kept in prison . . . *but* prayer" (Acts 12:5, italics added). Here the prayer of the church is put over against the bondage of Peter, as spiritual opposition to it. Strangely enough, the soldiers and the chains and the guards are not indicated in the same antagonism to the presence of the angel. "Peter was sleeping between two soldiers, bound with two chains: and guards before the door kept the prison. *And* behold, an angel of the Lord" (12:6-7a, italics added). As if the soldiers and the chains and the guards were a sort of added ornament to the whole picture of deliverance, just as the water which Elijah poured upon and around his altar on Mount Carmel contributed to the completeness of God's triumph in the answer of fire. May we not believe that the very circumstances which seem to aggravate our affliction are there to enhance the blessing?

God's resources are exhaustless. He does not require our drugs to put men into a sound sleep, nor our keys to open doors, nor our implements to unfasten chains. He has worlds at His command that we know not. The hosts of heaven wait upon His will.

> His state
> Is kingly; thousands at His bidding speed
> And post o'er land and ocean without rest.

We do not see the angels of God in their constant ministrations, but they are here nonetheless. "Are they not all ministering spirits, sent forth to do service for the sake of them that shall inherit salvation?" (Heb 1:14, ASV). "Open ... [the young man's] eyes," prayed Elisha, and "behold, the mountain was full of horses and chariots of fire round about Elisha" (2 Kings 6:17). Those were the warrior hosts, for it was a day of battle. They work invisibly, inaudibly, these servants of the saints, and the only footprints they leave behind them is a sweet sense in our hearts that God has wrought for us.

God does not commission His angels to do for us what we can very properly do for ourselves. The angel that night took care of the soldiers and the guards and the chains and the locked and bolted doors and gates, but Peter had to fasten his own belt, buckle on his own sandals, and throw his cloak around his own shoulders. Part of God's way in answering prayer is to show us what we can do for ourselves, while He takes care of the things beyond our power.

"Thou art mad! ... It is his spirit!" (Acts 12:15). So said the praying saints to Rhoda when she confidently affirmed that Peter stood at the door. What hopeless unbelievers they were! Let him among you that is without this sin of unbelief cast the first stone! Nay, these dear people—and it is just possible that Barnabas and Saul were of the company!—believed God enough to shake sleep from their eyes and stretch every spiritual sinew in unceasing prayer. Who would not have been amazed at the manner of this answer to their prayers? I suppose they were thinking of the deliverance of Peter through some turn of events at the trial on the morrow. To have the man walk in on them, when they knew he was guarded with all security in prison, was too much like an apparition. We had better learn not to be amazed at anything when we begin to pray. God has a way of doing what we ask, and by strange means, too.

Missionary friends of ours, Mr. and Mrs. Huber, related the following experience to us in our home a few days ago. They were expecting to leave their hill station in Africa in about two months, and found that they had hardly enough powdered milk to meet the needs of their five-year-old girl and their five-month-old baby. No more would be available, and great economy must be exercised. Just then a single lady missionary arrived at the home, took ill, and could take only— milk! About the same time there was brought to them a black baby whose mother could not take care of it and whose father they had earnestly sought to win to Christ. The black baby, of course, needed— milk! The meager supply of the missionaries could not begin to provide for four for two months! They gave themselves to prayer. That evening at prayer, Mrs. Huber's eyes fell upon a verse of Scripture to which she had never given heed in her reading, and of whose very existence she was unaware. Amazed, she brought it to her husband, and they read it together: "And thou shalt have goats' milk enough for thy food, for the food of thy household, and for the maintenance for thy maidens" (Prov 27:27). Now they did not know of any goats in the neighborhood, but this looked like a promise from God. Next day a most ungodly man at the government post, one who had never offered help to the missionaries, but always charged them top price for everything, asked them if they could use some goats' milk. He had just returned from a three thousand-mile round trip, bringing back with him in trucks a herd of goats from fifteen hundred miles away. He would have a gallon of milk going to waste every day. Could they use it? Well, could they! "Before they call, I will answer; and while they are yet speaking, I will hear" (Isa 65:24).

God goes beyond prayer's requests. The prayers of the saints operate in a certain direction, and the events begun carry on farther in that direction, setting forward the greater and more comprehensive purposes of God. The prayer of the church in Jerusalem was answered in the deliverance of Peter, but that started a whole sequence which brought the slumbering judgments of God into action, and still more increased the work of the gospel. Herod's pride was sorely hurt when his plans for a public trial and execution of Peter went awry, so he quit Jerusalem in a fit of temper and tried to recover face in the garrison center of Caesarea by organizing a great holiday festival in honor of the emperor, giving himself full measure of prominence. He set his throne toward the east, Josephus tells us, and sat on it in silvery garments that shone resplendently in the rising sun. From here he made his orations to the obsequious throngs, and here the climax of fulsome adulation was reached when the group from Tyre and Sidon raised the cry, "The voice of a god, and not of a man!" (Acts 12:22). Herod accepted the divine homage, and in the heat of his pride was suddenly smitten with a fell disease which rapidly increased in loathsomeness till he died, his rotting flesh consumed with worms.

How modest is the language of Holy Scripture! Here was an act of God calculated to give warning to His enemies and comfort to His people for all time, yet it is all told, including the reason for the judgment, in eighteen words in the Greek. The similar death of Antiochus Epiphanes, that raging beast against the Jews, is related in great detail and with much comment and manifest gratification, in the second book of the Maccabees. These two passages present an instructive contrast between human accounts and inspired records.

"But the word of God grew and multiplied" (Acts 12:24). Herod stretched forth his hand to stop the progress of that Word, "and he was eaten of worms, and gave up the ghost" (12:23), and one is reminded that our Lord has said something of a place "where their worm dieth not, and the fire is not quenched" (Mark 9:46). While the very Word that this royal fool opposed "grew and multiplied." Thus the prayers of the saints in Jerusalem secured Peter from death, but they did more—they brought the judgments of God upon the earth, and hastened the coming of the Kingdom of God. "This honour have all his saints" (Psalm 149:9).

Recent history has produced a remarkable parallel. Benito Mussolini turned his "civilized" might on Ethiopia, crushed that inoffensive nation, and expelled the Christian missionaries. What was the answer of the expelled missionaries? Such prayer as they had never put into their missionary labors, assisted by the prayers of aroused Christians everywhere. What was God's answer? The protection of the native believers? Yes! The reopening of the door of Ethiopia to the gospel? Yes! But God went beyond their prayers. These prayers opened the sluice gates of God's judgments and mercies. The military pride of Italy was laid in the dust, and Mussolini, Il Duce, was bound before a firing squad of his own countrymen to die as national enemy number one, his body being left unburied, exposed to spitting and ridicule, for many days. "But the word of God grew and multiplied" in Ethiopia, so that returning missionaries found a larger, stronger church than they left. One field, occupied by the United Presbyterian Mission, was left with sixty believers. The missionaries, on their return, found that the sixty believers had grown to thirty churches with a membership of sixteen hundred! "So mightily grew the word of God and prevailed" (Acts 19:20).

Thus does God save His church, by calling His people to prayer. Thus does His Kingdom come. "Lord, teach us to pray!" (Luke 11:1).

PART THREE

Into All the World

21

OFF TO A NEW START

Acts 13:1-4

In this chapter we look in on:

1. A significant prayer meeting
2. A notable ordination service

THERE HAVE BEEN some remarkable prayer meetings in the history of the church. I think of the Moravian prayer meeting which began with the spiritual awakening of August 13, 1727, in Hernhut, and lasted for one hundred years, the first quarter of which saw the sending forth of more than one hundred missionaries. I think of the noonday prayer meeting which Mr. Lamphier called in the lecture room of the old Dutch church on Fulton Street, New York City, for September 23, 1857, out of which grew the widespread revival of the following years and the established institution of the midday prayer hour. I think of the Haystack Prayer Meeting, where three young men prayed while sheltering from the storm, and started the streams of witness flowing from America to the uttermost parts of the earth.

None of these can rival in importance the prayer meeting held in the church at Antioch in the year A.D. 46 or 47, and recorded so briefly and simply in these opening verses of Acts 13. World missions, not in its conception, for that was in the mind of God from the beginning, but in its realization, began in that prayer meeting.

The largest prayer meetings are not necessarily the most significant. We should all like to see our prayer meetings grow immeasurably, but this is one institution of the church which cannot be "popularized." As soon as the attempt is made to popularize it, it ceases to be a prayer meeting, and becomes something else. Our Lord said, "Where two or three are gathered together in my name, there am I in the midst of them" (Matt 18:20), and again, "If two of you shall agree on earth as touching any thing that they shall ask, it shall be done for them of my Father which is in heaven" (Matt 18:19). This prayer meeting, which changed the current of history, had an attendance of five. We have heard of the Cambridge Seven, whose prayer and consecration meant so much to the evangelization of China, but here we have the Antioch Five, whose ministry of prayer launched the church on its world mission. So significant was that gathering that the Holy Spirit considered it profitable that the record should contain the names of those present. Barnabas we know, and Saul we know, but who are Simeon and Lucius and Manaen (Acts 13:1)? Apart from the statements made in this brief reference, we have no certain knowledge of any of them. Was Simeon Niger an African proselyte, or just a swarthy Jew? Is Lucius to be identified with Luke, the writer of the gospel and the Acts, or was he one of the Cyrenian Jews who dared the great experiment of preaching Christ to the Greeks of Antioch? Was Manaen foster-brother of the Herod Antipas who murdered John the Baptist, or his companion of early, profligate days? In either case, it was a far cry from that to this holy service in the church of Jesus Christ. There was no dearth of inspired ministry in that first Gentile church!

These were earnest men, to whom the work of the ministry was serious, responsible business. For all their gifts and graces, they did not dare go warring on their own charges. They were men of much prayer, and when burdened with some problem or sense of urgency, denied themselves sleep and food, that they might wait upon the Lord without distraction. I have no doubt that they kept the Jewish fasts, but these had become more than a custom or ritual with them. It may be that on this occasion they had a presage of some unusual work of the Spirit, or a special burden for the expansion of the gospel to the farther reaches. Had young Saul been stirring them with a recital of the need and the opportunity in Cilicia and beyond? I have seen churches and groups sent to prayer by such means.

"Draw nigh to God, and he will draw nigh to you" (James 4:8). But do not be surprised if He draws nigh in an unexpected manner. I should not wonder a bit if some of those good ministers were praying that day, "Lord, lay Thy hand and Thine ordination on some of the fine young men of this Gentile congregation, and send them out to preach the gospel to their fellow Gentiles in Cilicia and Asia and Bithynia and Macedonia and Achaia and Italy and Lybia and Spain and Gaul," when suddenly the Holy Spirit broke in upon them with this startling communication: "Set apart for Me Barnabas and Saul!" (Acts 13:2, author's trans.). Two of their own number! And the chief of them at that! Was not Barnabas sent from the mother church at Jerusalem to them, and did he not bring Saul from Tarsus as one specially suited to the work here? When extraordinary tasks were to be performed, when appointments of high trust were to be made, did anybody ever think of other choices than Barnabas and Saul? "Set apart for Me Barnabas and Saul!" The more unreasonable it seemed, the more imperative it became.

This also is one of the ways of God. "Pray ye therefore the Lord of the harvest that He will thrust forth laborers into His harvest" (Luke 10:2, author's trans.). So our Lord exhorted His first disciples; and scarcely had they begun to pray as they were taught when "He chose them, that . . . He might send them" (Mark 3:14, author's trans.). God has a way of having us do the things we pray should be done.

Some years ago the Telugu field of the Canadian Baptist Mission in India experienced a notable work of the Holy Spirit, and it came about, in part at least, this way. Three missionaries at different points were independently burdened with the spiritual ebb tide of the work, and each gave himself to prayer that God would deal with the hindering sins in the native Christians and raise up chosen vessels from among them for a work of revival. All three had the same answer from God: What about *your* sins? And why not *you* be My instrument? Then the Holy Spirit brought to light the hidden things of darkness in their hearts, and having these put away, used them in signal fashion throughout the Telugu field, and later in Canada, when their story stirred the churches at home.

Mother, do not pray the Lord of the harvest to send forth laborers into His harvest unless you are willing to have your boy or your girl chosen. Young men, do not dare to pray for the regions beyond unless you are prepared to answer, "Here am I; send me" (Isa 6:8).

That significant prayer meeting issued in a notable ordination service. The Holy Spirit had revealed His mind to the leaders, but the action concerned the whole church. A solemn assembly was therefore called to announce and recognize the call to the apostolate so sovereignly imposed upon these two beloved ministers.

Here the three elements present in every true ordination are clearly marked—the action of God, the action of the church, and the action of the called.

No man is truly ordained who has not been indicated by the Holy Spirit as a chosen vessel, though a thousand councils or ten thousand bishops should lay their hands on him. The manner in which the Spirit points out His chosen ones will vary, but it is still the obligation of the leaders of a local church to be seeking the face of the Lord in this regard, expecting that their church will be honored in such fashion. And when a young man begins to give evidence of special devotion and special aptitude, the elders ought to surround him with earnest prayer and loving encouragement, till they and he together know the mind of the Lord. In too many instances young men whose hearts incline to the work of the gospel are left to find the will of God for themselves, without the counsel and prayers of older, more experienced, and discerning men of God.

Not only the appointing was the work of the Spirit of God, but the sending forth also. The specific sphere of labor as well as the choice of the servant is in His sovereign hands. His leadings in this matter also are infinitely varied, but the man of God will learn to recognize the hallmark of divine operations as against spurious calls, offers, and openings. I do not wish to be critical or unsympathetic in these matters, but I hardly think that God's man will have to send out a host of applications accompanied by impressive stacks of letters of recommendation. This may be appropriate to the world of commerce, but the sending Spirit of God does not require it. He has wonderful ways of bringing His laborers and their tasks together.

While the Holy Spirit does the choosing and the sending, it is His manner to do so in cooperation with the church, not apart from it. "Separate [to] me Barnabas and Saul" (Acts 13:2), He commanded the church at Antioch through its prophets and teachers. An interesting word is that translated here "separate." It signifies marking off as with a boundary line, setting apart for special use. When you "rope" off—with ribbon, of course, not with rope—a block of pews in your church for some group that is to take special part or receive special recognition, you do to those pews what the Holy Spirit asked the church at Antioch to do to Barnabas and Saul. They were now "reserved" for the Holy Spirit, so that no other could claim them for any office or service.

A friend of mine who operates a restaurant told me of a visit he paid in wartime to the packer's warehouse. He saw an unusually fine section of meat, and was closing the deal for it when an army sergeant came up behind him, touched the carcase, and said, "Army." That constituted a federal order to the packer to reserve that meat for the forces. It could be put to no other use, disposed of in no other way. In regard to all the meat which the sergeant indicated, the packer became an agent of the government to reserve it for military disposition. So the Holy Spirit lays the church under obligation with respect to those whom He marks for His own use.

Such a demand on the part of God called for a responsive action by the church, namely, the releasing of those two men from the ministry which they exercised in Antioch. It looked like a big loss to the local church to surrender their most powerful leaders and foremost ministers. I do not know what persuasions and exhortations and reasonings were required to induce them to concede to the demand, but the issue is stated for us in the simple but striking phrase, "They loosed them" (Acts 13:3, author's trans.). They set them free from all responsibility for service in the local church, that they might attend to the business laid upon them by the Holy Spirit.

Early in my ministry I was led out to engage in evangelistic endeavors in Canada, after a brief period in my first pastoral charge. Both the church and I thought that I should retain my relation as pastor and return to duty there in six months. I soon discovered that a man cannot do the work to which the Holy Spirit calls him, with strings tied to him. He must be freed. I think the church learned that, too. I shall not deny that "leave of absence" for a stated time and for a special ministry may sometimes be successfully arranged, but it is sound principle that when the Lord marks a man for another task than that in which he is engaged, all previous ties should be severed. He should be released. The church at Antioch, not without a sense of irreparable loss, loosed Barnabas and Saul for the new call.

Realizing the solemnity and the profound import of this new step, the church at Antioch called for a season of fasting and prayer. They could not let those two valiants set out on their hazardous journey or launch their new, vast program, with just "a word of prayer." True, they did not foresee the universal results which are common knowledge to us, but they were conscious that something stupendous was happening, and they knew that their two brethren would be in jeopardy of their very lives as they carried their witness to Jew and Gentile in the "regions beyond." Therefore they linked their action of releasing them with a long period of undistracted and uninterrupted prayer. The missionaries would never forget that joint ordination and farewell, and when the hands of their brother ministers were laid upon their heads, they knew that they represented a host of holy hands that for hours had been lifted up to God on their behalf. We may refuse to call ordination a sacrament; we may disavow it as a "means of grace" in the sacramental sense; but no man can have such a service performed for him as Barnabas and Saul had for them that day, and fail to carry with him through all his earthly ministry and up to the throne itself a profound sense of the grandeur of his calling, a deep realization of his own unworthiness, and a strong assurance of divine enabling.

I want to ask Simeon and Lucius and Manaen one question when I see them in heaven: "Why did not your church at Antioch finish its obligation to Barnabas and Saul by supporting them financially?" For years later Saul, now known universally as Paul, wrote to a church not yet born when he started off from Antioch: "Now ye Philippians know also, that in the beginning of the gospel, when I departed from Macedonia, no church communicated with me as concerning giving and receiving, but ye only" (Phil 4:15). More than that, the apostle again and again supported himself and his party by plying the trade of tentmaking. "Yea, ye yourselves know," he affirmed to the Ephesian bishops, "that these hands have ministered unto my necessities, and to them that were with me" (Acts 20:34). I am going to hold that against the church at Antioch until Simeon and Lucius and Manaen give me a true reason. And I think the Lord will hold it against many a miserly church that it said to its called and consecrated missionaries, "Depart in peace, be ye warmed and filled" (James 2:16), and gave them not that bounty which would have supported them and their toil in fields afar.

Now the action of the called: they went. They went obediently, they went trustingly. True sons of Abraham, they "went out, not knowing whither . . . [they] went" (Heb 11:8). It was a heroic venture. It would have been a mad venture had not the Lord been with them. From now on we shall see Paul the restless, Paul the insatiable, Paul the vagabond for Christ, Paul whose only rest this side the heavenly rest was in prison cells and dungeons—and even they were transformed into gospel workshops. Who follows in his train?

> Ye Christian heralds, go proclaim
>   Salvation through Emmanuel's name;
> To distant climes the tidings bear,
>   And plant the Rose of Sharon there.

22

COMBAT FOR A SOUL

Acts 13:4-13

In this chapter we have:

1. A study in human personality
2. A study in demonic power
3. A study in divine passion

THERE IS SOMETHING fascinating about a beginning. The source of the Mississippi has little interest in itself, but just because we see in it that mighty stream which divides a continent we are held in awe by it. It was an unpretentious landing which those few pilgrims made on Plymouth beach, but because it enshrined the history of a great nation and of a great freedom we glorify the very spot.

These verses challenge our attention because they relate the beginnings of an universal movement, the initial steps in the program of world missions. Jerusalem was not the starting point of the movement because Jerusalem would not accept the vision, being blinded by traditions and prejudices which shut out the great world of Gentiles. Antioch of Syria, which received the gospel through the daring experiment of a few refugee believers, was chosen as the center of the wider-reaching activity of God. The Holy Spirit had indicated His choice of workmen for the task, laying His call upon their hearts, and demanding their release from the ministry of the local church. Now, loosed by the church, and sent forth by the Holy Spirit, Barnabas and Saul, with John Mark as an assistant, started the first journey of planned world evangelization. A small beginning for so great an undertaking! But "who hath despised the day of small things?" (Zech 4:10).

It is surely significant that the first step in the journey was to Cyprus, island home of Barnabas, where that estate was located which this son of consolation had sold in order to swell the treasury of the church in Jerusalem for the needs of the saints there. Saul had already had opportunity to give the testimony in his hometown, Tarsus, during the years of obscurity. The ministry at Salamis, the landing place, is mentioned without enlargement, as is the progress across the island to Paphos, for the recorder Luke is not giving a log of the apostolic journeys. However curious we are to know how these ministers of Christ fared in the first days of their great mission, we are given no incident till they reach the farther end of the island.

By the time we follow them to Paphos, an important change has taken place in the leadership of the party. Saul, from now on known only as Paul, has stepped to the forefront, till it is no longer "Barnabas and Saul" (Acts 13:2), but "Paul's company" (13:13, author's trans.). Doubtless Paul had both names previous to this time, Saul his Hebrew name, and Paul his Roman name, but it is surely significant that the Hebrew name is dropped and the Roman name assumed in connection with the opening of the world missions campaign. He is the apostle of the Gentiles, and he carried his Gentile name.

Barnabas had long realized Saul's worth. It was he who recognized the sincerity of the converted persecutor when others were afraid of him, and secured for him the hand of fellowship in the church at Jerusalem. It was he who recognized his ability as a minister, and set out for Tarsus to find him and bring him and his rich gifts of mind and heart to the service of the church in Antioch. Now, as they set out together in pioneer, apostolic labors, Barnabas quickly recognized the superiority of his junior, and, where others might have been resentful and tried to curb the younger man, graciously yielded place, not by any formal agreement, but by quiet encouragement of the other to take the initiative; till it became evident, by the time they had traversed the island of Cyprus, that Paul, not Barnabas, was the dominant personality in the company. Once again Barnabas grows by diminishing. The Holy Spirit knew well whom to send with Saul of Tarsus to turn him into Paul the apostle.

That this transfer of leadership was the work of the Holy Spirit is seen in the events which transpired at Paphos. Not the leadership of

Paul, but the spiritual combat, is the matter of supreme importance here, but it is significant that Paul was the one who received the special enduement to press the battle to its issue.

It was a battle for a soul. Sergius Paulus, the Roman official, was a thoughtful man. He was convinced that there were powers beyond the human, spiritual forces available for our help. He was therefore willing to give a hearing to any who promised some light on the spiritual realm. The best that his world knew was represented by the magi, who practiced the "black arts" and professed to bring help from the spirits. There was a varying amount of trickery indulged by these men, but they also had varying degrees of power in their occult practices. It was no uncommon thing to find a magus of this sort attached to a household of means and influence. Our Roman friend, then, had his court magus, who gave him the contact with the spirit world that he sought.

But Sergius was thoughtful enough not to be satisfied with a sorcerer and spirit medium, although that was the best he knew. He realized that this was not fellowship with God, and often enough he suspected chicanery. When, therefore, report was brought to him of two itinerants preaching the living God, and salvation, he determined to hear for himself. The missionaries were summoned to his presence, and might have had a most pleasant interview had not Elymas been there also. The combat was drawn.

The issue of the struggle was the soul of a man, a man desirous to know the truth and obey it. Here were the missionaries, the ministers of God, bearers of the glad tidings of salvation through a crucified and risen Redeemer. There was the opposition, Elymas the sorcerer, a prophet of falsehood, the apostate Jew who had sold himself to Satan for illicit powers. The men of God "reasoned of sin, and of righteousness, and of judgment to come" (see John 16:8), as was their wont. The man of Satan interrupted with scornful, blasphemous remarks calculated to distract the listener and turn the interview into a fiasco. Soon it became evident that no progress could be made with the inquirer while the antagonist was allowed to pursue his iniquitous course. Then it was that the Holy Spirit laid hold of Paul, filled him in an extraordinary way, and bore him along to a direct assault on the powers of darkness as represented by this hinderer of the gospel.

Paul turns his eyes upon Elymas, and Elymas returns the steadfast gaze. Their attention is no more directed to Sergius Paulus, the prize for which both are striving, but to each other. You are not looking at three men now—Sergius, Paul, and Elymas. You are looking at the powers of darkness and the forces of light ranged against each other for a high stake—a man's soul. Elymas is full of the spirit of evil, energized by Satan. Paul is filled with the Holy Spirit. The man of God takes the offensive. He fastens a searching, determined look on the opponent, takes his full measure, then looses a terrific barrage: "O full of guile and villainy, son of a devil, foe of all righteousness, wilt thou not cease perverting the way of the Lord, the true way? And now behold the hand of the Lord is upon thee, and thou shalt be blind, not seeing the sun for a time" (Acts 13:10, author's trans.). They were no empty words, for darkness fell immediately upon the startled man, and the powers of evil were put to confusion as their braggart representative begged for a guide to take his hand. There was no more interference after that. The seeker gave awed, rapt attention, and his amazement at the demonstration of stern judgment was surpassed only by his wonder at the glorious doctrine to which he now listened without distraction. The Spirit of God had won; the man's soul was saved.

That is the story, and we look for some practical lessons in it.

First, soul-winning is a great conflict. We are not dealing with human personalities alone. That would be difficult enough, for human personality is a twisted, perverse thing, fearfully deformed by sin, and far from responsive to such demands as accompany the offers of the gospel. There is that in the gospel which so humiliates and casts down before it exalts and lifts up that human nature spontaneously reacts against it. A man is asked to confess himself a sinner, admit the judgment against him as fully just, acknowledge his helplessness and the utter inadequacy of anything he might do to make atonement or secure merit. He is pointed to the cross, told that that is at once the measure of his sin, the token of God's love and the instrument of his salvation, and invited to rely wholly upon the work of substitution, satisfaction, and atonement wrought for him there by the man Christ Jesus, the Son of God. That is not palatable to the natural man, and it would require more than the impact of another human personality, however forceful and persuasive, to bring a man to an acceptance of that message.

In addition to the perverseness of the human personality and the unpalatableness of many implicates of the gospel, we have the operation of satanic powers to blind men to the truth, to center their attention on those aspects of the message which will stir their anger and rebellion. These spiritual forces of evil exert themselves to confirm men in their sin, their self-sufficiency, and their misconceptions. In incredibly varied ways they oppose and hinder a hearing of the truth, or an apprehension of it if it is heard. "We wrestle not against flesh and blood, but against principalities, against powers, against the rulers of the darkness of this world, against wicked spirits in heavenly places" (Eph 6:12, author's trans.) .

We are apt to think that conflict with evil spirits is confined to heathen territory. It is true that where the gospel has not been long established, and where heathenism has had full sway, the spirits of wickedness range more freely, more boldly, more openly. Missionaries in such parts feel at times as if they were breathing the foul air of the pit, and they know the awful reality of conflict with demons in the rescue of a soul, a household, a village. But we are asking for defeat if we fail to recognize the spiritual forces arrayed against us here at home. The antagonism may be more subtle for being more hidden, and therefore more dangerous. Every unsaved soul is in the grip of the "strong man armed," who must be disarmed and defeated if he is to be dispossessed and the soul delivered. Military experts have laid the repeated defeats of Germany to the tendency of its leaders to underestimate the enemy. That is fatal in spiritual warfare. We must take full measure of our foe.

There is another side to the story. Paul went out to do battle with spiritual forces, but he had more than the force of his own personality to throw into the combat. Paul himself would be a host against any array of men, but Paul himself, for all his strength of character, would be no match for Satan. "Paul, filled with the Holy Spirit" (Acts 13:9, ASV) , is something different again. That partnership is equal to everything the enemy can muster and more. Paul has much on the human plane, but in this alliance he is contributing only the vessel, the instrument, while the Holy Spirit supplies the inexhaustible and completely adequate power. "Not by might, nor by power, but by my spirit, saith the LORD of hosts" (Zech 4:6*b*). "We have this treasure in earthen vessels, that the excellency of the power may be of God, and not of us" (2 Cor 4:7). Having, then, taken the measure of the adversary, let us exult as we remember that "greater is he that is in you, than he that is in the world" (1 John 4:4*b*). A man "filled with the Holy Spirit" is more than a match for all hell.

One of my dearest friends, a missionary of long service in India, had the following experience. He attended a heathen festival in the district where he was pioneering with the gospel. Great feats of strength were to be displayed by those into whom the demons came, including the hauling of nine heavily loaded carts which would ordinarily require many oxen to move. While the natives were going through their ritual dances and working themselves up into a frenzy, my friend stood without the circle, quietly praying against this manifestation of demonic power. Somehow the dance lagged, the frenzy was slow to come. At last the chief medicine man of the district felt himself equal to the display, and the whole multitude yelled with devilish excitement as he strained to move the great load. But it would not budge. An old woman, noted for her superhuman feats when in the control of the spirit, rushed forward to take hold of the traces, but was likewise helpless. Such failure had never been known before. Suddenly the medicine man caught sight of my friend, and with a wild cry, "The Jesus-man is hindering! The Jesus-man is hindering!" he rushed like fury at him to render him to pieces, as a demonized man could easily do. The missionary stood his ground prayerfully and fearlessly. The frenzied man continued his mad rush till, but a few feet from the "Jesus-man" he suddenly stopped, groaned, and fell at the feet of the missionary, limp and helpless. That day the powers of darkness were rudely shaken, and the Word of God gained many eager hearers. We, too, may withstand all the power of the enemy, "filled with the Holy Spirit."

Did you note the sternness of Paul's words to Elymas? Yet they were words spoken in the fullness of the Holy Spirit. Is the Spirit of God therefore stern? We have spoken of Him as the Spirit of grace, the Spirit of love, and heaped epithets of meekness and mildness upon Him. But we have done Him the same injury that we have inflicted on the Father and the Son in not recognizing the sterner aspect of the character of God. There is a wrath of God which is but the reverse side of His great love. There are the judgments of God which are but the sterner expression of His mercy. A man, therefore, who is filled with the Holy Spirit, will not forever be speaking in soft numbers. His words will at times be coals of hot fire, words that sear and burn. But when a man filled with the Holy Spirit pours out indignation and rebuke, it will be in no vindictiveness and carnal anger, but in a holy jealousy for God and a holy zeal for the souls of men. Paul's anger, which was the anger of the Holy Spirit, burned on behalf of the soul of Regius the Roman, aye, and on behalf of the soul of Elymas the apostate Jew, if perchance through judgment he might seek mercy. The Holy Spirit is "the spirit of judgment, and . . . the spirit of burning" (Isa 4:4), and the more control the Spirit has in the life of a man or the life of a church, the sterner will be the rebukes against sin and the more glorious will be the work of salvation.

23

HISTORY AND THE GOSPEL

ACTS 13:14-41

This sermon of the apostle Paul teaches us:

1. The apostolic technique of preaching
2. The apostolic philosophy of history
3. The apostolic doctrine of Christ

MANY HAVE WRITTEN, and written well, on the technique of presenting the gospel to Jews. Paul's sermon in the synagogue of Pisidian
Antioch, the first of the great apostle's addresses to be preserved for us,
is a pattern upon which we have not improved, nor are likely to improve. See how he penetrates deep into Israel's history for his foundation; then erects his superstructure of Christological truth, fortified by
the well-tempered mortar of the prophets; then emblazons over the
portals of his gospel temple the blessed evangelic offer, underlined
with solemn admonition.

This simple, effective formula is good for Gentiles, too. For there
were in Paul's audience that day not only "children of the stock of
Abraham" (Acts 13:26a), but also men who feared God, that is,
Gentiles, mostly Greeks by culture and many Romans by citizenship,
who had been drawn to the synagogue by the teaching of the one living and true God, and who had abandoned their polytheism and their
idols to serve Him. The apostle's historically founded, prophetically
sustained, and solemnly enforced gospel made a tremendous appeal to
this group.

What we have in the text is only the outline of what must have
been a sermonic masterpiece, which I shall ask the angel in charge of
the heavenly recording machines to put on for me. Whether we

149

preach to Jews or Gentiles, we should preach sermons more worthy of preservation if we modeled them more on this and others left for us in this same book of Acts. John Fraser of Lisuland, when seeking to formulate his preaching practices in preparation for ministry to the Chinese and tribespeople of the China-Burma border region, made a special study of these apostolic declarations. The effectiveness of the resultant ministry is well told by Mrs. Howard Taylor in her story of Fraser, *Behind the Ranges*. Simplicity, directness, urgency—these are some of the principles he learned and practiced, to the salvation of thousands.

One can scarcely avoid a comparison of Peter's Pentecostal address, Stephen's apology, and Paul's Antiochean sermon. The purpose of Stephen, as over against that of Peter and Paul, accounts for the marked difference in his statement. He was bringing an indictment against the Jewish leaders, while the two apostles were presenting the offer of salvation to their nation. In another respect, however, Stephen and Paul are more alike, in that they both trace the history of their people as a basis for their message, while Peter begins with a current event, the coming of the Holy Spirit, and the accompanying phenomena, and from that leaps immediately into his Christological argument.

Stephen and Paul carry their historical surveys to different points, each as suits his special purpose, the former to Solomon and the Temple, the latter only to David. Stephen covered enough ground to give ample evidence of the resistance which their fathers constantly raised against the message of God, while Paul brought his hearers as far as the king to whom the Messianic seed was promised.

Now the history of no other nation is so closely related to the coming of Christ and the message of the gospel as is the history of Israel. Nevertheless, unless we read all history as His story, we shall be lost in confusion out of which no philosophy of history will help us. See how the apostle attributes every step in his people's history to an act of God. God chose, God exalted, God brought out, God destroyed, God divided, God gave, God removed, God raised up—so the story runs. And I am persuaded that we must so read all history, or else we have no starting point and no landing place.

I am writing this on V-J Day. The global war of 1939-45 has come to an end with the surrender of Japan. As we review these terrible years, can we fail to see the action of God? Was it an air umbrella that covered the 365,000 Allied troops who evacuated from Dunkerque, or was it the hand of God? Was it fear of British resistance that hindered the thoroughly planned invasion of Britain, or was it God? Did God have anything to do with turning the hand of Hitler against Russia? Did God have any part in the defense of practically defenseless but vitally strategic Malta? The defender, General Dobbie, says, Yes! Was it only Montgomery and his Eighth Army that turned Rommel within sight of Alexandria and chased him fourteen hundred miles across North Africa? Montgomery says, No! Did God have a part in the fearful debacle of the German armies and the spectacular ending of the war in Europe? Was Douglas MacArthur right when he said on his return to Manila, "By the grace of God I have returned"? Was God's hand in the withholding of the secret of the atomic bomb from Germany and the revealing of it to American and British scientists? Was God in the picture when three successive days brought the news of the first use of the atomic bomb, Russia's declaration of war on Japan, and Japan's offer to surrender? In the larger view, too, one does not require to be a "crank" on prophecy to see that this fearful conflict, like its predecessor of 1914-18, has contributed to the "one increasing purpose" of God. The great prophecies of the Scriptures assume new proportions, and passages which once seemed fantastic carry a sense of awesome reality and imminence.

H. G. Wells has given us a history of the world from the naturalistic and evolutionary point of view. Would that some great Christian scholar might give us a textbook on history as the work of God, eliminating the distinction between "sacred" and "secular." Some there are who grant God a degree of overrulership in order to the final preservation of His ultimate purposes, which seem to be in constant jeopardy! We believe God has wider and completer dominion than that. For all the rebellion of angels and the sin of man, God rules in the armies of heaven and among the children of men. "He maketh the wrath of man to praise Him, and the remainder of wrath Thou wilt restrain" (Psalm 76:10, author's trans.) .

> Truth forever on the scaffold,
>   Wrong forever on the throne!
> Yet that scaffold sways the future,
>   And behind the dim unknown
> Standeth God amid the shadows,
>   Keeping watch above His own.

History is built on redemptive lines. Paul's purpose in this sermon is to show that God's dealings with Israel from the beginning were all toward the one end of bringing the Messiah Saviour into the world. Now these preparations of God for the coming of His Son were certainly not confined to Israel. Few lives of Christ are written without dealing with the place of the Greek culture and the Roman power in preparing the way of the Lord; and if only we had eyes to see and minds to discern, we should read our history books and our newspapers as records of God's redemptive works and redemptive preparations. The "one far-off, divine event to which the whole creation moves" is not so far off as the poet dreamed.

> Mine eyes have seen the glory of the coming of the Lord,
> He is trampling out the vintage where the grapes of wrath are stored,
> He hath loosed the fateful lightning of His terrible swift sword,
>   Our God is marching on!

> I have seen Him in the watch-fires of a thousand circling camps;
> They have builded Him an altar in the ev'ning dews and damps;
> I can read His righteous sentence by the dim and flaring lamps:
>   Our God is marching on!

Notice the redemptive facts concerning Christ, the facts which Paul denominates "the word of this salvation" (Acts 13:26*b*). They are three: that Christ came of the seed of David, "according to . . . promise" (13:23) ; that Christ was slain at the behest of the leaders of Israel, in fulfillment of the word of the prophets; that Christ was raised from the dead, as the Scriptures foretell, and as many eyewitnesses avouch. The incarnation, the crucifixion, the resurrection: these are the sine qua non of the gospel. It is Christ come in the flesh, Christ crucified, Christ risen, that is our Saviour. Leave any one of these out, and we have no Saviour. Our Redeemer is none other than the Son of God made Son of Man by the miracle of the incarnation;

our Redeemer has paid no less a ransom than His own precious blood; our Redeemer is "able . . . to save them to the uttermost that come unto God by him, seeing he ever liveth to make intercession for them" (Heb 7:25).

Only such a Saviour could bear the weight of such an offer as is made in His name: "Be it known unto you therefore, men and brethren, that through this man is preached unto you the forgiveness of sins: and by him all that believe are justified from all things, from which ye could not be justified by the law of Moses" (Acts 13:38-39). But such a Saviour as we have is fully able to bear such a burden. Are you under the guilt and condemnation of sin? Then forgiveness and justification, pardon and release, are yours for the coming, for the believing, for the receiving.

> Lo! the incarnate God, ascended,
> Pleads the merit of His blood;
> Venture on Him, venture wholly,
> Let no other trust intrude;
> None but Jesus
> Can do helpless sinners good.

Such good news is solemn business. It lays a burden of responsibility on every man. The prophets spoke out not only of the coming of the Just One, of His incarnation and His crucifixion and His resurrection and the great salvation which He should thus bring nigh to men; they spoke also of men who should refuse to believe the report, who should despise the proffered mercy, and who should perish in their sins. Be not you one of them! Let others, if they will, justify the prophets in their prediction of the despisers who perish; but as for you, accept the witness, and enter into life!

24

TRIUMPHS AND TRIALS

ACTS 13:42–14:23

In this chapter we observe:
1. The apostles' prosperous preaching
2. The apostles' severe suffering
3. The apostles' courageous comeback

IN THIS PASSAGE we have the same story told three times over. That is, the general pattern is the same, the essentials are identical, while the details, the incidentals which give color to the picture, differ. Triumph and trial, prosperity and persecution, acceptance and rejection, that is the story of Antioch, Iconium, and Lystra.

First let us look at the progress of triumph.

Should a preacher repeat his sermons? A sermon that is worth preaching once is worth preaching many times. Paul's first sermon in the synagogue of Antioch was worth repetition. So stirring and arousing was it that he was pressed on all sides to give it again the following Sabbath. There were many who wanted an opportunity to go over that ground again, for it seemed so unanswerable, yet they were cautious and did not wish to commit themselves prematurely.

That was all very encouraging. More satisfying to the heart of the apostles, however, were the many Jews and proselytes who required no more convincing, but became followers of Paul and Barnabas in the truth of the gospel, and spent the succeeding days in becoming established in the grace of God.

Never was a service better advertised than that of the following Sabbath. There were no newspaper announcements, no handbills, no placards, no window cards. I have seen in some business houses this

154

motto: "Our best advertisement is a satisfied customer." "Satisfied" in this instance means "wanting more"! That was the kind of advertising Paul and Barnabas had that week, till never a Barnum and Bailey circus nor a World Series nor an election so completely commanded the interest of a city. "The next sabbath almost the whole city gathered . . . to hear the word of God" (Acts 13:44, ASV). In Chicago we rejoice exceedingly if we can assemble sixty thousand, out of a population of about four million, for a great youth rally that has been advertised for months by radio, newspaper, mail, and every conceivable means—with super attractions, such as patriotic pageants, world championship running, and top-ranking music. I do not say this to criticize (for we are profoundly thankful to have such a witness in our big center of population), but only to indicate that we are a long way from this spontaneous gathering in Antioch of Pisidia, which had one attraction only—the hearing of the word of God! No place would hold that crowd but the public square. How John Wesley would have reveled at the sight!

Iconium also had a synagogue of spacious proportion, and here, too, God-fearing Greeks as well as Jews attended the services for the reading and hearing of the Law, and the worship of the God of Abraham and of Isaac and of Jacob. Paul's first sermon there had telling effects, for we are told that "a great multitude both of Jews and Greeks believed" (Acts 14:1*b*, ASV). Opposition only increased the boldness of the apostles, and their ministry was sustained there for a long time. Here the miraculous element was marked, the Lord confirming the witness at the hands of His servants by signs and wonders.

It is no small movement that has a city fairly split in two in a matter of weeks. The Lord Himself declared that He came not to send peace, but a sword. The gospel, He warned, would be a divider even of households. But the sword is being wielded with mighty force when it divides a city into two contending factions! I have seen such a division in a village during a season of revival, but to have a large city so affected indicates the power in which the apostles were witnessing, and the extent of their influence. In Iconium, as in Antioch, they were on the crest of the wave.

The prosperity in Lystra took a different, and a very dangerous, turn. In the course of still successful evangelizing, Paul came upon an impotent man, lame from birth. The Lord opened this needy man's heart until saving faith was wrought in him. Then Paul, conscious of the power of the Lord resting upon him, pitying this earnest fellow's plight, and seeking a confirmation of the testimony, cried out, "Stand upright on ... [your] feet" (Acts 14:10). The miracle was immediate and complete, and the man walked with all the steadiness and assurance of one who had been doing it from childhood.

To the heathen population of Lystra there could be but one explanation of such a notable demonstration of power. "The gods are come down to us in the ... [form] of men!" (14:11b). If the tradition about Paul's appearance is correct, it must have puzzled the Lycaonians that a god should appear in such unattractive guise! Greek reppresentations of the gods at least attribute to them wonderful grace and beauty of form. But perhaps this was part of the incognito! At any rate, the performance was the ultimate evidence.

Jupiter and Mercury are the Roman counterparts of the Greek Zeus and Hermes, Zeus being chief of all the gods, and Hermes his messenger, the fabled inventor of speech. According to the Latin poet Ovid, these gods had once before visited this region in human form, and the temple to Jupiter at the gates of the city was a memorial of that signal event. This inclined the inhabitants to look for a second visit, so it was the easier for them to believe that their expectation was now fulfilled. Would that we were as expectant for the return of our Lord! Only we must avoid the "Lo, here ... there" (Matt 24:23) error.

This was the greatest peril that ever beset Paul and Barnabas. Prosperity of any kind is dangerous, but praise is the most subtle and deceitful, and in measure as it approaches worship it increases in deadliness. Not that praise should never be given, if by that we mean the warm, sincere word of appreciation. That may save a soul, and lift a life from despair to hope and courage. It is praise become extravagant, become fulsome, become flattery, become adulation, that is deadly. Few men can resist it; and the more completely it merges into worship, the more difficult it is to refuse. Fandom is full of it, and the very language of idolatry is shamelessly used. Those who receive it live for it, knowing not that it is the asphyxiation of the soul. "Woe unto you, when all men shall speak well of you!" (Luke 6:26).

The apostles had grace to reject the proffered worship, and turned the occasion to good account for the gospel, using the error of the populace as a text on the folly of idolatry, which Paul treated much as he did later in Athens. But so convinced were the natives of the divinity of Paul and Barnabas, and so intent on their purpose, that "with these sayings scarce restrained they the people, that they had not done sacrifice unto them" (Acts 14:18). Let us who serve the Lord keep this prayer much in our hearts and on our lips, especially in times of prosperity: "Not unto us, O Lord, not unto us, but unto thy name give glory!" (Psalm 115:1).

Trial followed triumph, not to make the triumph less, but greater. All his life long, Paul looked back to those days as among the most bitter and the most blessed of his apostolic experience. On the eve of his departure he still held those scenes vividly in mind, and wrote in his farewell letter to Timothy: "But thou hast fully known my doctrine, manner of life, purpose, faith, longsuffering, charity, patience, persecutions, afflictions, which came unto me at Antioch, at Iconium, at Lystra; what persecutions I endured: but out of them all the Lord delivered me" (2 Tim 3:10-11).

One is saddened to see how the Jews were consistently and persistently the instigators in these persecutions against the apostles. Among the perils which Paul listed as falling to his lot were "perils from my own nation" (2 Cor 11:26, author's trans.). Specifically he declares, "Of the Jews five times received I forty minus one (stripes)" (11:24, author's trans.). Despite the multiplied wrongs that he suffered at their hands, Paul never wavered from that yearning love for his own people so ardently expressed in his letter to the Romans: "I have great heaviness and continual sorrow in my heart. For I could wish that myself were accursed from Christ for my brethren, my kinsmen according to the flesh" (Rom 9:2-3). Nevertheless, in face of their action against Christ and their persistent antagonism to the gospel, he was constrained as a prophet of God to declare the divine judgment against them. "The wrath," he says, "is come upon . . . [this people] to the uttermost" (1 Thess 2:16*b*). More than any people on earth, Israel has been shown mercy; more than any people on earth, Israel has forsaken its own mercy.

The sacred record does not hide the secret motive and source of all the opposition of the Jews. It is written against them without modification: Envy! "When the Jews saw the multitudes, they were filled with envy, and spake against those things which were spoken by Paul, contradicting and blaspheming" (Acts 13:45). So runs the story in Antioch, and when we come to Lystra we see the envious Jews from Antioch joining with the unbelieving Jews from Iconium to press the persecution to the utmost.

The history of Israel is badly pockmarked with this ugly disfigurement. In the patriarchal family the monster lifted its head, and envy sold Joseph into slavery in Egypt. Again the plague broke out in the priestly household, and Aaron and Miriam expressed the envy of their hearts in bitter complaints against Moses. Do you see those white spots of leprosy on Miriam's brow? They are but the bursting out of the inner leprosy of envy. We leap the centuries and stand in Pilate's judgment hall. The record reads, "For he knew that the chief priests had delivered him for envy" (Mark 15:10). Jewish envy will sell a brother into Egyptian bondage. Jewish envy will malign God's minister of the Law. Jewish envy will deliver the Son of God to death. And now Jewish envy will dog the steps of the great apostle to silence the testimony of the gospel.

But is Gentile envy less venomous than Jewish envy? And let me ask it in whispers: is Christian envy less foul than either Jewish or Gentile envy? Not that envy is ever Christian, but it too often dwells in the hearts of Christians, and there it is uglier and fouler and blacker and more hellish than anywhere else, for it crucifies the Son of God afresh and puts Him to open shame; it denies the faith that we profess, it retards the Kingdom we claim to promote, it rends our brethren whom we should love and cherish in the Lord. Whenever did a servant of the Lord have signal success that others through envy did not begin to speak against him and his work?

Oh envy! Let me declare thy judgment. War and famine and pestilence have slain their thousands, but thou hast slain thy ten thousands. Thou hast increased the burdens of men who nobly toil, thou hast brought to desolation temples and palaces of splendid achievement, thou hast made bitter the sweet fountains of love and life; thou hast made us a race of hypocrites who lie when we commend and assume false virtue when we condemn. Thou hast made a stench of the human heart. Begone, thou foul fiend, that mockest our fair

Christ and makest spoil of the saints! In the name of Him whom thou didst nail to the cross, begone from this heart of mine, and hold thy revels among the devils of the pit where thou belongest!

Notice the variety and the progression of the trials. From Antioch the apostles were expelled, in Iconium they were plotted against, and in Lystra, Paul was actually stoned and left for dead. God's school of suffering is progressive. He weighs every trial in the balances of His perfect wisdom, and never imposes burdens on us beyond our point of advancement. Paul was not ready for the stoning at Antioch, but by the time he came to Lystra he was fully prepared for the extremest measures of the enemy. The hardships of today toughen us for the greater demands of tomorrow. The army does not take a man out of a sedentary occupation and immediately expose him to arduous maneuvers under actual battle conditions. It puts him through toughening processes, progressively fits him for the extreme fatigues of battle, then sends him out to face the hardships and dangers of war. So our heavenly Father tempers "his rough wind in the day of the east wind" (Isa 27:8) according to our progress in endurance.

"Out of them all the Lord delivered me" (2 Tim 3:11), says Paul to Timothy. We can see that that is true with respect to Antioch and Iconium, but is it true of Lystra? Why, he was actually stoned and left for dead. Some believe that he was really dead; in either case, God wrought miraculously for him that day. First of all, grace was given to endure the stones. Then, if he really was stoned to death, what an unforgettable experience to walk as one raised from the dead by the power of God! Or if he were not quite dead, but far enough gone to make those Jews think that he was altogether gone, then again a miracle of God raised him up. For one in such case would ordinarily require long nursing to recover from such a severe wounding, almost certainly including concussion; but Paul was instantaneously healed, and went on as if nothing had happened, except that that touch of divine power made him a humbler, more trustful, more consecrated man all the rest of his days on earth. So we are made perfect through sufferings. Fear not! "Out of them all the Lord delivered me."

"Then after that saith he to his disciples, Let us go into Judea again. His disciples say unto him, Master, the Jews of late sought to stone thee; and goest thou thither again? Jesus answered, Are there

not twelve hours in the day?" (John 11:9). Now Paul had not read
these words in John's gospel, for John's gospel was not yet written;
but Paul had learned their lesson nevertheless, the more so from his
series of experiences in Antioch, Iconium, and Lystra. He knew now
that he was immortal till the clock of his life struck twelve. When
therefore they had preached the gospel at Derbe and taught many
disciples, Paul said unto Barnabas, Let us go again unto Lystra and
Iconium and Antioch and confirm the saints there. Barnabas said,
Paul, the Jews of late stoned thee in Lystra, and sought to stone us
in Iconium, and expelled us from Antioch; and goest thou thither
again? Paul answered, Are there not twelve hours in the day? Then
said Barnabas unto their companions, Let us also go, that we may die
with him. But it was not time to die—it was not yet twelve o'clock.
That is the heroism of faith.

25

FREE FROM THE LAW

Acts 15:1-29

In this chapter we trace three stages of development:

1. The differences (vv. 1-5)
2. The discussion (vv. 6-21)
3. The decision (vv. 22-29)

DIFFERENCES are no great evil. What a maddening monotony this universe would be had not God made one star differ from another in glory, one mountain differ from another in contour, one flower differ from another in color, one face differ from another in expression, one soul differ from another in genius, one mind differ from another in mode of thought! Where personality is cast in individual molds, where there are varied backgrounds of tradition and training, where a thousand shades of influence beat on the soul, we are bound to meet differences of approach, outlook, and opinion.

Differences are the great mark of freedom. Democracy is the system which defends men's rights to differ. Authoritarianism denies that right, and gives us Fascism in politics and Romanism in religion. Condemn differences, and you must resign all human freedom. Our big concern is, what we shall do with our differences, and what we shall allow our differences to do with us. We may exalt our differences into standards and tests of fellowship, so making every shade of thought the basis of a new sect and division. When we do that we narrow ourselves down to the measure of our own opinion, we are driven into the narrows and into the shallows, while by way of reaction we become puffed up, hard, unteacnable. On the other hand, we may turn our differences to mutual advantage and enrichment, making them an

161

occasion of deeper, more prayerful search after the mind of the Spirit, and of more sympathy and largeness of heart. Our differences then become ministers of growth, helpers of our perfection in Christ, while in the process many of the differences themselves dissolve, or fade into insignificance.

The difference that arose between the men from Judea and the native Christians of Antioch was quite natural and understandable. To the Palestinian Jew who had embraced the faith, the Lord Jesus was the Messiah of Israel, Christianity was Judaism brought to its completeness, salvation was the special heritage of the chosen nation, offered on sufferance to those who came under the shadow of Israel. That Gentiles should come into the blessings of salvation independently of the ancient Jewish order was to him unthinkable. He knew that Messiah was to be "a light to lighten the Gentiles" (Luke 2:32), but the lamp and the holder were Jewish. It was almost axiomatic with him that to become a Christian a Greek must become a Jew. He learned not the parable of the wineskins for himself, but was still trying to carry his new wine in the old skins. It can scarcely be wondered at that he tried to thrust his old wineskins on the Greek believers and make them drink Christian wine in Jewish cups.

To the Greek believer Jesus Christ was the Saviour of the world. That He was of the seed of Abraham, of the line of David, was to him interesting, but incidental. With all his sense of gratitude to the Jews who brought the glad tidings to his city, the believing citizen of Syrian Antioch felt himself under no obligation to the ritual Law of the Jews, circumcision, sacrifices, feasts, or fasts. Christ had come to him directly, as Son of Man and God's gift to the world, not mediated through the Jewish system. The suggestion, then, that he should submit to Jewish usages as requisite to any claim upon the redemption in Christ Jesus was to him both shocking and embarrassing.

One may readily see how critical was the danger that faced the church and the entire work of world evangelization when these two points of view clashed. The Greek was rejoicing in salvation "by grace . . . through faith . . . not of works" (Eph 2:8-9). The Jew, saved by the same grace and through the same faith, had not yet come to the vision of unmixed grace through unmixed faith, but thought of the salvation as coming to him as a Jew, and as having to be mediated to all through the channels of Jewish ritual. "Except ye be circumcised after the manner of Moses, ye cannot be saved" (Acts 15:1*b*). The question, therefore, is: Is salvation tied up to Judaism as its channel of mediation, or is it bestowed directly by Christ on all alike, in response to simple faith? More basic still: Is Christianity sacramentarian or evangelical? The controversy recounted in this chapter is critical, not only for the great emancipating answer given, but for indicating a cleavage which has divided Christendom ever since. For some did the right thing with their differences, and some did the wrong thing.

When we come to consider the discussion, it is of interest to note that while the delegation from Antioch was instructed to consult the apostles and elders at Jerusalem, these called the whole church together to take part in the deliberations and to have a voice in the decisions. No resemblance here to the councils of Rome, and much less to the ex cathedra dicta of the Roman pontiffs! Why did not Peter use the prerogatives of his primacy on such an opportune occasion?

After much airing of contrary opinions, the discussion was headed up in three statements; one by Peter, one by the leaders of the visiting delegation, and one by James.

Every phrase of Peter's brief statement is full of suggestion, but we must be content with a few highlights. He began by recalling an incident which had involved himself in a church trial—the incident of the carrying of the gospel to the house of the Roman Cornelius, for which he had to offer a defense on his return to Jerusalem. See how deftly he implicates the whole church in his now historic action. "God made choice among you" (Acts 15:7*b*, ASV), he declares, so relating his Gentile mission to the church at Jerusalem, of which he was a member, and whose representative he was by divine appointment to that task. Not only so, but the church had approved his action after the hearing. Peter was on firm ground.

He recalled, then, how God had gone to great lengths in dispensing grace to that Gentile household, had given signal witness of His full acceptance of them by bestowing the Holy Spirit with such tokens as proved the kinship of the event with Pentecost itself, had demanded no submission to the rites of Moses, but had honored the faith of these few Romans with every mark of vital salvation. That clearly indicated the direction in which God was moving, and it would be tempting God to seek to hinder the free operation of His grace and make demands on Gentile believers which God Himself apparently was not making, demands which indeed had proven a heavy and chafing yoke upon themselves and their fathers.

It was a great principle that Peter enunciated here. We may express it this way: Find the direction in which God is moving, and fall in line. The principle holds in the realm of nature. Nature moves in certain specific directions—we call them the laws of nature. If we go counter to these laws, put obstructions in the way, nature not only will not produce for us, but will turn and rend us. Interference is nature's pet peeve. Even your radio lets you know that. Likewise human interference in God's processes spells disaster. We are apt to be so jealous for our tradition, our program, our order, that we are either totally blinded to the thing God is doing, or we consent to His operations on condition that these things of ours be incorporated. Result, confusion and failure!

In these days of confusion and perplexity may God make seers of His own people, make us men of vision, men who perceive the direction in which He is moving! We need to catch a fresh glimpse of the ongoings of God today, in judgment, in salvation, in discipline, in world missions, in preparations for the great day of our Lord's returning. And then, may we be kept from tempting the Almighty with insistence on our cherished plans and programs, when it may be He has utterly rejected them! Circumcision was a great covenant seal in its day, but how utterly trifling it became in face of God's glorious purpose of grace for the whole world! Chiefly, then, let us beware of any intrusion upon God's pure, free grace in His dealings with men.

Paul and Barnabas mounted the rostrum. They rejoiced in Peter's fine prologue to their testimony. We are not given even a résumé of their address, but the purport of it certainly was this: "Men and brethren, Simon has told you how he perceived the direction of God in the house of Cornelius, and was powerless to resist. He has warned us not to attempt to put obstacles in the way of the Almighty. His counsel is good. But we have gone yet further. We too saw God's direction, and perceived His purpose to take out from among the Gentiles a people for His name. We not only did not seek to obstruct

God's way, but stepped out in the same direction as workers together with God, being called to this very thing. Now we are here to testify that this way of the Lord has been demonstrated to a certainty, for the same free grace which operated so convincingly in the house of Cornelius has wrought mightily unto salvation among the Gentiles wherever we have gone, in Antioch, in Cyprus, in Pisidia and in provincial Galatia. Not only have multitudes believed and given evidence of the miracle of regeneration, but God has given us abundant tokens of His working with us in signs of healing and of deliverance. We bring you witness from all these several places that this is how God is working among the Gentiles—without circumcision, without the sacrifices, without the works of the law."

So to Peter's laboratory case were added the multiplied field cases of the missionary party, and all spoke the same language. None could plead a special dispensation for Cornelius after that historic report. God's direction had been demonstrated beyond all doubt. See how much larger is the answer of the missionary apostles than that of Peter. Peter saw God's direction and said, "Don't obstruct! Don't thwart!" That is negative. Paul and Barnabas saw God's direction, and cried out with the thrill of a great passion:

> Oh, be swift, my soul, to answer Him!
> Be jubilant, my feet!
> Our God is marching on!
> Glory, glory! Hallelujah!
> Our God is marching on!

How are we related to the goings of God?

Surely it was time to rest the case. The opposition was silenced, and no doubt if it had been put to the vote at that point, there would have been an overwhelming majority in favor of the case for the Gentiles. But that gathering was not interested in a majority vote. For all their differences, and for all the vigor of these differences, that company of saints had assembled to find the mind of the Lord. The indications had become more and more clear, but one question remained to be answered: "What saith the Scriptures?" It was the contribution of James to present the argument from Scripture. I shall not attempt to expound the passage from the Old Testament and

James' application of it. He claims that this procedure of which they
have been hearing is in keeping with the words of *the prophets,* not
just one isolated text; so that the passage in Amos particularly referred
to is quoted freely, as representing the consistent message of all the
prophets. The expression used by James is beautiful. "To this *agree*
the words of the prophets" (Acts 15:15, italics added) , and from the
word translated "agree" we have our "symphony." The words of the
prophets are like a symphony, the voices of many instruments so at-
tuned and blended that they are one in the presentation of a great
theme, and the theme is this very procedure of God—grace toward the
Gentiles. So here is still another subject to study—grace in the Old
Testament. See, then, how those who met that day with very positive
differences were not searching for some proof text to buttress their
own opinion; they were seeking the symphony of Scripture, and they
found that it played a missionary number! Rather, it was singing a
missionary hymn:

> Far, far away, in heathen darkness dwelling,
> Millions of souls forever may be lost!
> Who, who will go, salvation's story telling,
> Looking to Jesus, heeding not the cost?
>
>   G. M. J.

The decision, for all its importance, need not detain us long, provided we heed its message. How did it emerge? Not—"It was moved
and seconded, and carried by a good majority," but—"It seemed good
to the Holy Spirit, and to us" (Acts 15:28, ASV) . Differences or no
differences, that assembly wanted the mind of the Lord, and when that
was made clear, it became the mind of the church. God will make His
will known to that kind of a church, but where factions gather to win
their point, the Spirit will be grieved and give a church up to its
carnal contentions, with consequent failure in testimony and barren-
ness in service. Our differences are no matter of concern. What we do
with our differences is the thing that counts.

The decision marked the triumph of free grace, and the emancipation of Gentile believers from the yoke of Mosaic ordinances, an
emancipation into which the believing Jews themselves later, and perhaps gradually, entered. With the exemptions, however, went several

demands, which the Holy Spirit and the church designated "necessary things" (Acts 15:28b). Their freedom was not to be misused and turned to license. The pollutions of idolatry were to be avoided, and afterward Paul expounded some high reasons for that. Fornication was to be shunned, and that this was no unnecessary exhortation is seen in Paul's letter to the Corinthian church. The abstinence from things strangled and from blood may be explained in several ways. It can be referred back to the dietary instructions given to Noah, long before Moses, or it can be thought of as an avoidance of undue offense to the Jewish communities throughout the Gentile world.

What is the significance of this decision for us now?

First of all, we can sing:

> Free from the law, oh, happy condition!
> Jesus has bled, and there is remission.
> Cursed by the law, and bruised by the fall,
> Christ has redeemed us, once for all!

Second, it means that God is saving men apart from the imposition of sacramental means. Those who make ordinances, or good works of any kind, a prerequisite of salvation, are the children of the Judaizers, seeking to frustrate the grace of God. Ordinances have their place, and far be it from me to minimize their place in the obedience of the individual and the witness of the church, but their place is not that of a requirement for salvation.

Again, the emancipated life is also a disciplined life. "Free from the law" (Rom 8:2b) does not mean loosed from all restraint. We are under the Law to Christ, we are bondslaves of His will. Grace is God's effectual means of having the righteousness of the Law fulfilled in us. Grace is walking in the constraint of the Spirit, not in the unbridled indulgence of the flesh. Grace means "giving no offense, neither to the Jew, nor to the Gentile, nor to the Church of God" (1 Cor 10:32, author's trans.). Grace means consideration for others, their rights, their sensibilities, their spiritual welfare. Grace means adherence to standards far higher than those imposed by the Mosaic system, for the realization of which grace has lifted us into such union with the Son of God that we may say, "It is no longer I that live, but Christ [that] liveth in me" (Gal 2:20, ASV).

This decision means that you, a Gentile sinner, may here and now, without circumcision, without baptism, without any long preparation, but right where you are and as you are, open your heart to Jesus Christ and receive freely, immediately, and forever, the pardon of your sins, the gift of eternal life, and the incoming of the Holy Spirit to dwell in your heart.

26

THE CALL OF THE REGIONS BEYOND

Acts 16:6-10

In this chapter we learn how:

1. God's checkmating disciplines the man of God
2. God's checkmating promotes the plan of God
3. God's checkmating unfolds the call of God

It was in Sault Ste. Marie that I learned the elements of the royal game of chess. My instructor was one of my deacons at whose home we always spent Christmas, which was the occasion of my annual attempt. You may imagine that I made little advance in the skills of the game, but my good deacon was patient with his perennial beginner. It was during those seasonal events that I became acquainted with the exquisite torture of being checkmated. That word "check!" became at times tormenting. It was a good way to sharpen me in the game, but it was tough going.

In the sterner business of life the apostle Paul was experiencing such a season of frustration. His purpose to revisit the churches had not worked out strictly according to plan. A driving restlessness had seized him, impelling him westward. Yet when he entered that new territory with a thirst to break new ground for Christ, a strange sense of restraint gripped him. The Holy Spirit said, "Check!" His feet still driven but his lips sealed, he went on, bewildered, to the northwest, till the northern province of Bithynia fastened its lure upon him. He was a debtor to the barbarians as well as to the Greeks, and here were barbarians indeed, in both the ancient and the modern senses of the word, in their gross darkness and clamant need. Then, as he hasted with eager step toward the new and inviting task which even now burned in his soul, the same Spirit of Jesus called aloud within him, "Check!" Frustrated, puzzled, and muzzled, the apostle continued his blind journey westward to the port of Troas. A very early tradition claims that on the way he visited Artemaia, the sacred town of the goddess Artemis, and Sir William Ramsay thinks it rather likely. If so, that check that was on him throughout the province of Asia must have been a sore trial to his burning heart in that citadel of heathendom. So the checkmated apostle arrived at Troas, still groping and perplexed.

God's man required the discipline of this checkmating. Paul was no reed shaken with the wind. The fact is he was right headstrong. You do not find the determination that faced the disappointed wrath of all Jewry, that stood up to the Judaizers, that took Peter to task before all at Antioch, that brooked no dictation from Barnabas, apart from a spirit that could be downright stubborn and self-willed. It is still a question whether Paul's refusal to have John Mark on the second journey was the strength of sound wisdom, obstinate resentment, or a bit of both. However high the motive, the fact remains that the journey began under the cloud of a contention in which Paul had shown little sympathy for the youth who had failed, and great determination to have his own way. That God overruled and brought double blessing is a mark of His wonderful grace, for He does not wait for perfection in order to use us; but the itinerary that began so badly was to see the disciplining of that strong spirit, that he might be fitted for the greater tasks and severer tests ahead.

Paul had once said, "What wilt thou have me to do?" (Acts 9:6), and there was no greater passion in his soul than to do the will of God. But it is possible for a man of strong will and high passion, for all his consecration, to plot his own course with a fixed determination which he mistakes for an unshakable purpose to do the service of God. We can in some measure perhaps enter into the utter amazement of the apostle as he was made conscious of the checkmating of the Holy Spirit. First, his impulse to preach in Asia is checked, checked, checked, the whole length of his journey across that great province; then his decision to enter Bithynia is checked, and now he is forced on to the coast with no explanation of his dilemma, no light for his darkness. At the end of that dreary, apparently fruitless journey he was a mellower, humbler man and apostle, and at Troas the lesson broke in upon his soul, that the impulses of the human spirit must yield to the orderings of the divine Spirit. He might have made that long journey in peace of mind and contentment of heart had he known this before; as it was, that was the most terrible journey he ever had, for he went in restlessness and heat of spirit. Have we not been where Paul was? Have we not also chafed and fretted for our chosen activity when we might have gone faster by waiting longer, and known peace instead of confusion? This is a great lesson for us who serve the Lord; let us learn it well: the impulses of the human spirit must yield to the orderings of the divine Spirit.

The work of God as well as the man of God needed this series of checkmating. "Known unto God are all his works from the . . . [foundation] of the world" (Acts 15:18) . The Lord of the harvest has his own program for the progress of the work, and His own order for the opening of the several theaters. He was interested in the evangelization of the provinces of Asia and Bithynia, and had planned for these needy territories. Paul was taking for granted that he should take them in stride, but God had other fields to open, and had His own preparations for the parts that He was now bypassing. A study of God's ways in missions will show that all the bypassing and encirclements and pincer movements which are so exploited by our military experts in war have been God's methods right along. The bypassing of Asia and Bithynia was part of God's strategy for the speedier spreading of the gospel. By a great encirclement He was about to bring within the impact of the gospel the whole center of the world's culture. This was the northern arm of an even wider pincers movement to lay the entire Mediterranean open to the message of life, the southern drive through Egypt being already under way. The fill in, or the mopping up, would come on the heels of the wider movements.

Yes, God has His grand strategy, and happy are we if we have some clear grasp of it. It is good to "brighten the corner where you are," but you can labor for the Master more intelligently if you know something about His plans. We shall have to wait upon Him to know our place in the overall strategy, and if He checkmates our plans at times, let us be content that He knows better than we do where we may most effectually serve the whole campaign. Not all of us will be chosen to lead the big movements. The army personnel is not all generals. But our service as privates will be more effective and thrilling if we see it as part of God's mighty operations. I am sure that Paul must have reviewed that whole experience years later, perhaps when he lay in prison in Rome, and thanked God for the checks that forced him into the majestic sweep of divine operations for the proclamation of the gospel in Philippi, Thessalonica, Athens, Corinth, and Rome. It was a hard experience, but it was worth it!

The call of God necessitated this season of stern discipline. It looked as if God was narrowing this man down, and pushing him into a corner. His world of ministry was being wrested from him, his horizons were closing in upon him. Little did he know that this was God's strange but required method of bringing him to look out on wider horizons, of giving him a bigger world, of thrusting him out into a larger place. That place of straightenment, Troas, was to be the observatory whence he would catch sight of the fields afar, the auditory where he would hear the great cry of the regions beyond, the wicket gate through which he would be given entrance to the vaster reaches of ministry.

"Come over into Macedonia, and help us" (Acts 16:9*b*), cried the man of his night vision. Now Paul did not think of the little span of water between him and Macedonia as the line between two continents. European and Asiatic distinctions were not yet. But if I understand Paul, that Macedonian and his heartrending call awakened still farther visions and echoed more distant cries in his soul. That day he saw Athens, the citadel of pagan culture; that day he saw Rome, the seat of imperial power; that day he saw Spain, the limit of the Mediterranean world. Did he that day see also Britain, the outposts of the world, and dream perhaps of unknown lands and continents still out there beyond the swells of the ocean? At any rate, that day the title "apostle to the Gentiles" took on larger meaning for Paul—it was henceforth a catholic title, the world was his expanded parish. The narrowing was for widening, the straitenment for enlargement.

This, too, is part of God's ways. It is God's answer to that fatal disposition in us that so long as we are at large it is well-nigh impossible for us to see God's larger purposes. Our world is big enough for us till it is snatched from us. Our engrossment in the free task hinders our vision of the wider reaches. During J. Hudson Taylor's first term of service in China, the Ningpo Mission was his sphere, and, while hoping that the great interior would also share the blessings of the gospel, he was satisfied to make the best of his little world. Then God gave him the "hidden years" in London, where he was pressed into a study of the whole field in order to write awakener articles for others. They proved just that for himself. "While in Ningpo, the pressure of claims immediately around him had been so great that Mr. Taylor had been unable to give much thought to the still greater needs further afield. But now—daily facing the map on the wall of his study and the open Bible whose promises were gripping his soul—he was as near the vast provinces of inland China as the places in which he had laboured near the coast."* It was there, then, backed into the corner of broken health and practical concealment, that the field widened immeasurably before his eyes, and the crisis came on the sands of Brighton when it was borne in on him that he himself must take up the immense task which he had been wishing on others. If God has been backing you into a corner by a whole sequence of checkmating of your own plans, look out from that corner beyond; your man of Macedonia may even now be standing on the shore of your new world of service, crying, "Come over and help us!"

That call of the regions beyond, which came to Paul that day, has reverberated down the corridors of the centuries, and claims a hearing from every one of us. We are far from the place where we can sit down and weep that there are no more worlds to conquer. "There remaineth yet very much . . . to be possessed" (Josh 13:1*b*) and the cry of the Christ-less multitudes rises from every continent to challenge our smugness and rebuke our sloth. I sometimes wonder if we have a right to so much spiritual luxury when the regions beyond still call, and the laborers are so few. During World War II, Mrs. Etta Shiber shared the risks of helping British soldiers to escape from France until she was caught by the Gestapo, and underwent the horrors of imprisonment in Nazi prisons in France. After her release (for she was exchanged for the notorious German spy Johanna Hoffmann), she recounted her experiences in *Paris Underground*. Her closing para-

*Dr. and Mrs. Howard Taylor, *Hudson Taylor's Spiritual Secret* (London: China Inland Mission, 1935), p. 78.

graph is searching as a patriotic clarion call, but it needs little imagination to translate it into the call of missions.

"The indifference I meet everywhere frightens me. I believe in
human solidarity, but so many live unconcerned with the pains of
their millions of brothers under the yoke! I believe in divine justice
—even in our materialistic world—but I know it works through the
instrumentality of human beings sufficiently in tune with it to strive
for its execution. And as I see how many there are who put their own
comfort above the efforts necessary to save millions of helpless beings,
I feel guilty myself—guilty for being here now, in a place of safety,
busied with matters of no importance, while this clash of the forces of
good and evil is shaking the world.

"Yes, I am troubled with a sense of guilt. Some who are alive today
may be shot tomorrow; and how can one rest knowing that he might
be able to contribute to saving precious lives, if he is not doing so?

"Is it only quieting my conscience if I say to myself that when God
desires that we should act, He shows us the way, tells us what to do—
lest they die?"

Let it burn home. That some of us have to remain on the home
front does not mean that the cry of Macedonia has no application to
us. Even as in a national war effort there ought to be a more equitable
distribution of the sacrifice, so in the greater task of missions. The
evangelization of the world is our concern, and if some of our brethren
go to the far-flung fields of spiritual battle, it is ours to toil for them
in the power factory of prayer, and to "back their attack" with our
means to the ultimate of the need.

Who was the man of Macedonia? Dr. Tom Lambie, home on fur-
lough after one term in Ethiopia, was faced with an alluring offer to
associate with his uncle in a lucrative practice in Philadelphia, and
soon to succeed to the entire practice. He could surely serve the Lord
as an influential professional man as well as by burying himself in
Africa! He wrestled with the matter, till one night a dream, so vivid
that it seemed more than a dream, decided him. A foul, leprous hand
arose out of the heart of Africa and a voice said, "Take that hand!"
While he shrank back, the voice repeated, "Take that hand!" Finally
he went forward, and though nauseated, even in his dream, took the
diseased hand in his, and immediately it was in his grasp the lovely

pierced hand of the Lord Jesus. Who was the man of Macedonia? I am not interested in any of the speculations, even of so great a man as Sir William Ramsay, as to its being Luke, or any other. It was the Lord, the Son of Man, who has identified Himself with the need of this poor, sin-stricken world. It was the Son of Man, who is not only the Man of Galilee, but the Man of Macedonia, and the Man of Ethiopia, clothing Himself with the needs of our race, and crying to us from every place where sin and want abound, crying to His own redeemed ones who are made rich in His grace, "Come over and help us!" Would you go for Him?

It may be that someone reading these lines has been cornered by the Lord. He has checkmated you in plan for plan. But the corner into which He has forced you is your tower of vision, and your Lord is asking for your life for the wider reaches. What is your answer?

> I was not ever thus, nor prayed that Thou
>   Should'st lead me on;
> I loved to choose and see my path, but now
>   Lead Thou me on!

So His restraints are as much part of His leading as His constraints.

27

THE ASSAULT ON EUROPE

Acts 16:11-34

In this chapter we view:

1. A beachhead secured
2. A counterattack instigated
3. An offensive launched

AFTER THE STRONG RESTRAINTS of that journey across the province of Asia, and the vivid call to Macedonia, Paul must have landed at Neapolis and made his way to the colony of Philippi full of expectation that great things were about to transpire. Actually, the beginnings of the European conquest were decidedly disappointing if the apostolic company looked for something spectacular. There was no strong synagogue in this military center to give them a big start, as was the case in Pisidian Antioch. A little group of women by the riverside was their first congregation. Here is an indication that Paul had clean overcome his rabbinic prejudices and drunk deep of the spirit of his Lord, who did not scorn to teach a woman by Jacob's well, unfolding to her the mysteries of the gospel.

But there was something compensating even in this situation. The woman who stood out above all the others in this group of worshipers was a native of that very Asia which so weighed on Paul's heart while he journeyed through with sealed lips, and she doubtless carried the story back to her hometown, Thyatira, and became in some measure the apostle's representative. Lydia was a keen woman of business, representing one of the famous dyeing concerns of Thyatira, the center of the manufacture of purple cloth. Whether her "household" consisted of a family, or of business associates and servants, is still an open question, so the incident offers little support to the exponents of either infant baptism or exclusively believers' baptism.

Gentile by birth, Lydia was a God-fearing woman, having been attracted by the pure monotheism of Judaism. Rejecting, then, the pagan conceptions and practices, she had come to trust under the wings of the God of Israel, and associated with the few Jews of Philippi, consorting with the women who met for prayer by the river just outside the city.

Here, then, was a woman of character, a woman of ability, a woman of means, a woman of deep piety, but above all a woman "whose heart the Lord opened" (Acts 16:14). Without the last, Lydia the seller of purple would not have been the first convert of Paul's European mission, would never have been a convert at all. Too often we build our expectancy of results on the natural temperament and attitude of our hearers, so that we are greatly disappointed when the most likely do not respond, and surprised when the least likely accept the message. But here again we see the sovereign work of God in opening the hearts of His chosen ones to the gospel. A farmer in northern Ontario had three sons. Two of them were quiet, stay-at-home boys who gave their godly father no anxiety, so that he was quite sure they would in due season be converted. The third boy was something of a high flier, vivacious and dashing. He left home for the city, and gave his father much alarm by his careless ways. One evening, just to please the young lady with whom he was keeping company, he attended an evangelistic meeting, where the Lord opened his heart, so that he attended unto the things which were spoken by the evangelist. And when an invitation to accept Christ was given, he marched down the aisle with the step of a guardsman. Before long he was attending Bible college, then university, and is today an aggressive, evangelical pastor in one of Ontario's northern cities. I have no knowledge of the two "likely" ones ever having taken a clear stand for Christ. Neither the likely nor the unlikely will ever come except the Lord open their hearts.

This does not mean that we are to despise the human factor in conversion. Human personality is an instrument which God is pleased to use in the work of redemption, and some are made "a new sharp threshing instrument having teeth" (Isa 41:15). There was something

about Paul and Silas and Timothy and Luke which carried conviction
and stirred the interest of this unusual woman; and there was something about this woman that gave what she said and did weight in the
eyes of those about her. She was a key person, and when she embraced
the faith of the Lord Jesus, her action favorably inclined the members
of her household to the gospel, until their hearts also were opened,
and all were baptized together.

This is one of the three cases of household salvation and baptism
related in the book of Acts, but this stands unique as being a woman's
household. Cornelius, Lydia, and the Philippian jailer were sufficiently held in honor in their own homes to make their influence
potent and vital. If one's influence does not count for much at home,
it is not likely to carry far abroad; but if one has gained the esteem
of his own kindred, he will be respected in the wider circle and be a
useful man. How much does your testimony count for at home?

The apostolic band not only won their first converts in Lydia and
her household, but secured new and comfortable headquarters. Now
there were at least four men in the party, yet Lydia pressed them to
accept the hospitality of her home, as the two Emmaus disciples pressed
the risen but unknown Lord to shelter with them that wonderful
evening. What a comfort it must have been to that gospel team to
leave their hired lodgings and enter a real home, where they found
love and understanding and gratitude and fellowship and prayer, and
a hundred little home touches that only such a hostess as Lydia could
provide! Many a woman is going to receive rich reward for providing
a real haven for God's ministers. If the Lord will give me opportunity,
there are some I want to speak for on that day.

So a beachhead was won in Europe for the gospel—the heart and
home of a woman. It seemed a very small and narrow corner for
deploying forces that were to overrun all Europe, forces which would
not be content with storming this colony of Rome, but would capture
proud Rome itself. But it was a secure beachhead, which would
quickly expand, despite opposition, till Paul would be writing from
the chief bastian of Rome "to all the saints in Christ Jesus which are
in Philippi, with the bishops and deacons" (Phil 1:1).

The counterattack followed quickly. The beachhead had been won
without immediate contact with the enemy forces, but the presence

of an established gospel testimony was not to go unchallenged. Setting the demonized girl on the trail of the apostles was at once a lure and a challenge. It planted demonic powers squarely in the path of the apostolic band. The true witness of the girl was the more subtle. Either the apostles must accept it and so enter league with the demon, or else they must refuse it and come to open conflict with hell.

Some have been deceived by such tactics into the bondage of spiritism. When the spirits touch on Christianity, it is generally with a fatal lack or a deadly perversion, but I have heard of spirit messages giving a true testimony with regard to the gospel, to the confusion of good people. We had better not judge the source by individual utterances, but like our Lord refuse the witness of demons, however true. As Dr. Campbell Morgan has tersely said, "We are to refuse the patronage of hell."

That is what Paul and his company did. Knowing right well that his act would stir hell to open antagonism, the apostle, being exceedingly vexed, "turned and said to the spirit, I command thee in the name of Jesus Christ to come out of her" (Acts 16:18). The powerful name of Jesus prevailed, and the poor girl, till now doubly a slave, a slave to the demonic power, and a slave to greedy devils of men who made gain of her pitiful condition, was set free. Here now was a trophy of a different sort from Lydia. Christ brought the high-souled woman to the end of her quest for God, and satisfied her deepest longing. The same Christ loosed the poor pythoness from her bondage, lifted her from her degradation, redeemed her personality. The same Saviour meets the need of all kinds of sinners. We used to have a little acrostic in Sunday school on the name of Jesus: Jesus Exactly Suits Us Sinners. Whether we be cultured sinners or vicious sinners, learned sinners or ignorant sinners, religious sinners or impious sinners, moral sinners or degraded sinners, we need Jesus, and He is all we need.

An old coat of arms carries the motto, *Nemo me impune lacessit* (No one hurts me with impunity). I think that is the motto of the devils, for they certainly hit back when they are hurt. When Paul invaded the realm of evil spirits that day, he might have expected the explosion which they were actually making ready. If the apostle would not weaken the witness of the gospel by accepting the testimony of the demonized girl, and if, to silence that rejected testimony he entered the lists with the demons themselves, he must be prepared to feel the fury of their anger. I heard a minister declare a few days ago that every time he preached a series of sermons which he has prepared on "The Biography of Satan," some serious illness or other adversity came to his home. It is no child's play to "wrestle . . . against principalities, against powers, against the rulers of the darkness of this world" (Eph 6:12). We had better know how to stand in the triumph of Christ Jesus our Lord if we make bold to do so.

The adversary uses men, and he did so on this occasion. The emancipated girl lost her power of divination, and with it her ability to make money for her greedy masters. Yes, there are some powers we may lose when we are delivered. A missionary told a group of us recently about a young native who had a remarkable ability to handle poisonous reptiles without hurt. He seemed to be a born snake charmer. The Lord opened his heart to the gospel, and he received the Saviour. A few days later a deadly snake entered the missionary's compound. The missionary, instead of killing the snake immediately, thought he would like to see this young man handle it, so he called him. The youth made a few passes over the reptile, then stooped down to take it up. Suddenly he drew back, looked at the missionary and said, "White man, I cannot." The missionary then knew that it was no natural gift which the youth had had, but the empowering of an evil spirit.

The girl's masters were furious that their wicked profits were at an end. What matter to them that a soul was delivered from the clutches of sin, that a life was redeemed, a personality restored? They were like the Jews of Gadara who wanted no Saviour at the cost of their swine.

These men of Philippi became, therefore, the vessels and instruments of the wrath of hell, in the attempt to silence the testimony that would not be compromised. So if the conversion of Lydia secured a home for the apostolic group, the salvation of the demonized girl meant for two of their number the lash, the inner prison, and the stocks.

All this did not seem to bear out the vision. "Come over and help us," the man of Macedonia had cried; and when Paul landed in Macedonia in response to the call, the Macedonians did not welcome him, did not sit at his feet drinking in the message. They cold-shouldered him so long as he did not interfere with them; then as soon as he touched their wicked gains, they beat him up and threw him in jail.

So the need of the unevangelized world calls imperiously for our help; but do not think that when you go out in obedience to the call you will find the heathen ready to fall on your neck in unrestrained gratitude, and to give up their idols as soon as they hear of Christ. They will look on you with suspicion or indifference or at best curiosity. They want neither you nor your Christ, and when your message breaks in on their evil practices, threatens their doubtful profits, condemns their sin, or claims some few of their number, you will hear the hiss of the serpent, the snarl of the wolf. What will you say then? Will you begin to question your call, doubt your leading, become discouraged, and wish to turn back? Better not to go at all than that! That was what John Mark did the first time, but Paul never. The clearest leading may be the most discouraging task, and many a servant of God, robbed of every comfort in circumstances and events, has been held steady and faithful and assured by the unshakable sense of divine call. So it was with Charles Abel, who toiled among the natives of New Guinea for nine years before witnessing one conversion.

The enemy's attempt to wipe out the gospel beachhead in Europe was quickly brought to nought.

> Stone walls do not a prison make,
> Nor iron bars a cage.

Those two free souls, Paul and Silas, whose bodies were in chains and stocks, answered the assault with prayer and songs of praise, even at the midnight hour. He "giveth songs in the night" (Job 35:10). Till the other prisoners—no, it does not say "other" prisoners, for these two, for all their stripes and chains and guards, were not prisoners; we shall never be prisoners so long as we can pray and praise!—the prisoners stopped their swearing and their moaning to hearken. "And the smoke of the incense, which came with the prayers of the saints, ascended up before God out of the angel's hand. And the angel took the censer, and filled it with fire of the altar, and cast it into the earth: and there . . . [was] . . . an earthquake" (Rev 8:4-5). That was heaven's answer to the prayers of Paul and Silas. It was heaven's artillery answering the adversary. And before the day broke, not only were the apostles out of jail, but the jailer and all his house were the Lord's rejoicing captives. The enemy forces were a most crestfallen and humiliated group, and this mighty clarion had been sounded forth on the gospel trumpet for all Philippi and all Europe and all Asia and all Africa and all America and all the islands of the sea and for you and for me: "Believe on the Lord Jesus Christ, and thou shalt be saved, and thy house!" (Acts 16:31).

28

PAUL AND ATHENS LOOK AT EACH OTHER

Acts 17:16-21

In this chapter we examine:

1. What Paul saw in Athens
2. What Athens saw in Paul

PAUL BEHELD THE CITY. I was talking a few days ago to a Christian lady who for many years conducted tours to Europe. In course of our conversation I made bold to ask her about the discipline of her parties. She replied that she kept them so busy seeing things all day that when night came they wanted nothing but to go to bed. It was a good recipe for discipline, but in such circumstances one does not do the kind of seeing that Paul did in that great tourist center, Athens. One may be glutted with sights, and behold nothing.

The ruins of what the apostle saw in the city of renown may still be seen, and even in their decay the statues and buildings of Athens command the admiration of all who have an eye for grace and beauty. Now Paul was no boor, yet the three thousand exquisitely wrought public statues did not send him into an ecstasy of admiration. For where the tourist of our day sees only architecture and sculpture, grace, and art, the apostle penetrated to the awful reality within, and "beheld the city full of idols" (Acts 17:16, ASV). Renan has scoffed at Paul's ignorance in thinking of these statues in terms of idolatry, but as A. T. Robertson keenly remarks, "Paul knew paganism better than Renan."

Not only did Athens have its great temples to Artemis, Demeter, and Athene, but altars were erected to many other gods, including abstract ideas as mercy, philanthropy, shame, rumor, and energy. So were the gods multiplied that Petronius declared that in Athens it was easier to find a god than a man. The chief center of the world's learning, with all its proud tradition and treasure of art and philosophy, was a hotbed of base and debasing idolatry. Philosophy can neither impart the knowledge of the true God, nor deliver from the bondage of false gods.

The Athens that Paul visited was a city of novelty seekers. "All the Athenians and strangers which were there spent their time in nothing else, but either to tell, or to hear some new thing" (Acts 17:21). The restless and insatiable curiosity of the Athenians has been noted by many ancient Greek writers, and H. V. Morton finds the same character today, despite the dilution of all kinds of Balkan blood. In his *In the Steps of St. Paul,* this vivid writer says, "Was it not Demosthenes who pictured the Greeks bustling about the agora, asking, 'Is there anything new?' or 'What is the latest news?' If you sit at a cafe table under the pepper trees in Constitution Square today, you will hear each man, as he sits down at a neighboring table, say to his friends:

" 'Well, and what is the latest news? Is there a recent development?'

"Heads in black felt hats are obscured by one of the numerous newspapers, which is immediately flung aside when a boy comes along crying, so truly and delightfully, *'Ephemerides!'* with the latest crop of political discussion under his arm."*

That cry, "Ephemerides!" is typical. It means, "lasting for a day." It was said in prewar days that every Athenian read ten newspapers a day! So it was in Paul's day. A thing was old as soon as it was heard, and the ears itched for something novel. Any man could get a hearing who could strike a new note, but he could not hope for a heeding!

The Athenians are not alone in this craze for the novel. America can run a close second, and even in our Christian circles we are in danger of losing our moorings in this constant demand for new thrills in religion. The old truths must be administered in homeopathic doses, well sugared with something hyperemotional or super-

*Henry C. V. Morton, *In the Steps of St. Paul* (New York: Dodd, Mead, 1936), p. 263. Quoted by permission.

sensational. The competitive element, which has entered so many spheres of Christian activity and ministry, has opened the sluice gates for floods of printed matter, screaming forth the new thrills that await those who will attend this or that meeting, conference, rally, or club. Has the Athenian thirst for novelty so completely mastered us that all dignity must be thrown to the winds and our Christian faith fed on endless sensation?

What kind of man did Athens find in Paul? We know a man by his reactions. How, then, did Paul react to the multiplied images, statues, altars, and temples? "Now while Paul waited . . . at Athens, his spirit was provoked within him as he beheld the city full of idols" (Acts 17:16, ASV). The King James Version rendering "stirred" is inadequate here. It would be no exaggeration of the Greek to use its own word and say, "his spirit was thrown into a paroxysm." It was no paroxysm of bad temper, but a surge of holy sorrow and deep anger that shook his very spirit. A superficial look at the grace of the artistry would have reacted in superficial emotions of admiration, but the deep, contemplative penetration into the inner reality came back to rend his own inmost being with overwhelming passion.

Two considerations were the cause of this profound shaking of spirit. Paul saw in all this idolatry the dishonor of God and the degradation of man. For all the beauty of those images, they cried aloud the sin of the Greeks in common with barbarians who "changed the glory of the incorruptible God for the likeness of an image of corruptible man, and of birds, and fourfooted beasts, and creeping things" (Rom 1:23, ASV). The Greeks had given more grace of form to their images, but the dishonor to God was just as real; and Paul, jealous for the honor of the invisible God, whose everlasting power and divinity were clearly written into all things created, burned with holy indignation.

Then, too, he saw in this idolatry the debasing of the highest quality in man, that quality which most nearly relates him to God— his capacity for God. What a perversion, that man's faculty of worship should be dissipated and degraded in these sensual exercises, till instead of being raised Godward the worshipers were reaping the harvest of their idolatry in the pollution of the whole being. "Wherefore God gave them up in the lusts of their hearts unto uncleanness, that their bodies should be dishonored among themselves: for that they exchanged the truth of God for a lie, and worshipped and served the creature rather than the Creator, who is blessed for ever" (Rom 1:24-25, ASV). It was this dishonor of God with the consequent degradation of man that disturbed the spirit of the apostle as he beheld the city.

I wonder do we share in any measure Paul's paroxysm of sorrow and godly anger when we behold the modern idolatries and degradations of our own cities! The little city of Quebec is a great tourist center. It is also a center of Roman Catholic idolatry. I remember how the crowds used to be led around by guides to the many Roman churches and shrines, where the sensualities of idolatrous worship were much in evidence. Some few were stirred with deep and hot indignation at this perversion of Christian worship, but most seemed to be well pleased because they were seeing the sights. But there are other idolatries and other degradations beside those of Rome. Are not all our cities full of idolatries, shrines to the god of pleasure, the god of lust, the god of greed? Jesus looked out over the city of Jerusalem, and wept. Paul beheld the city of Athens, and was thrown into a paroxysm of spirit. Can we look out upon our own cities, and be unmoved?

A spirit so moved will find vent in witness. The synagogue was the natural place to reach the Jews, and we can well follow the apostle's presentation there from other examples of his preaching to his own kindred after the flesh. His approach to the Greeks of Athens was very different. The synagogue did not give access to Gentiles as in other parts, so Paul went out to the agora and adopted the very method of approach followed by the great Socrates four hundred and fifty years before in that same city, in that same marketplace. Every "chance" meeting was an opportunity to introduce Christ. He would seldom lack a listener, or a group of listeners, in that market where talk was the chief commodity.

The schools of philosophy soon fell to discussing the new teacher, and they were divided between scorn and curiosity. "What will this babbler say?" (Acts 17:18b), sneered some. It was no very complimentary remark. This term translated "babbler" means a seed-picker, referring first to the birds on the streets picking up grains, then to a poor wastrel who picked up the scraps of food from garbage piles, then to a quack philosopher who had picked up a few phrases and imposed them upon the ignorant with high-sounding rhetoric. There were others who suspected Paul of the very crime of which Socrates was accused—and for which he was made to drink the cup of hemlock—setting forth new gods. They thought he was introducing two separate gods—Jesus, and the resurrection. No charge was laid against him, however, for the Athens of Paul's day was not so jealous for the religious status quo as the Athens of Socrates, but they invited him to an official hearing, perhaps to determine whether he should be licensed to teach, as Ramsey suggests, but more likely to satisfy their curiosity. Thus Paul found himself in one of the most difficult, and morally in one of the most dangerous, situations of his life. Will he fail?

29

DID PAUL FAIL AT ATHENS?

Acts 17:22—18:1

1 Corinthians 2:1-5

In this chapter we consider:

1. Paul's attack on idolatry
2. Paul's call to repentance
3. Paul's renewal of purpose

PAUL IS STANDING in the very center of the world's culture, in an atmosphere at once of proud learning and base idolatry. He must penetrate the armor of philosophy to attack the idolatry and open a breach for a breakthrough of the gospel. His tone is conciliatory, his manner courteous, but his message is fearless and uncompromising. That is a rare combination which we who profess to contend for the faith may well seek to cultivate.

In the first place, Paul did not call the Athenians "too superstitious" (Acts 17:22), as rendered by the King James Version, but observed that they were "more religious than the average." The word he used denotes a religious fear of spirit beings or divinities, and may refer to grosser form of superstition, or may signify simply religious devotion. The context here, with its measured tone, demands the latter use. The ground of Paul's observation was that among the many altars erected to many gods he had come across one inscribed "To AN UNKNOWN GOD" (17:23b, ASV). More than six hundred years before, Epimenides, the poet-prophet of Crete, had visited Athens upon invitation to deliver it from plague, since none of the gods they applied to answered them. The counsel of Epimenides was that they offer a sheep "to the befitting god," whoever he might be. The plague stayed, according to the story. This may well be the beginning of Athens' devotion to the unknown god. "Whom therefore ye worship while not knowing Him, Him I set forth to you" (17:23c, author's trans.), said the apostle, at once arousing a profound interest and answering the suspicion that he was setting forth new gods.

Now he comes to grips with idolatry, dealing it two mighty blows: one, the argument from the nature of God, and the other, the argument from the nature of man. He presents a conception of God so vast, so all-inclusive in its reach, that it not only dwarfs other gods, but leaves no room for them in the field. Without saying in so many words, "There is only one God, and your thirty thousand gods are no gods at all," he proclaims God in such cosmic, universal terms that there can be no second to Him. The whole system, the very idea, of sensual worship, including temples, offerings, and the service of men's hands, becomes ludicrous in the presence of so vast a thought of the Lord of heaven and earth. Try to catch the transcendent glory of the apostle's thought of God, which is his answer to all idolatry. "God that made the world and all things therein, seeing that he is Lord of heaven and earth, dwelleth not in temples made with hands; neither is worshipped with men's hands, as though he needed any thing, seeing he giveth to all life, and breath, and all things" (Acts 17:24-25).

Now God is bigger and greater and more glorious than any thought of Him: bigger and greater and more glorious than even an apostolic conception and statement of Him. We need to train our thoughts to large and lofty conceptions of God. Why so much irreverence, so much neglect, so much putting self before God? Why are the Word of God and the house of God and the will of God treated so lightly? Because we have not given ourselves to high thoughts and lofty conceptions of God. Here is the counsel of Paternus to his son: "First of all, my child, think magnificently of God. Magnify His providence: adore His power: frequent His service; and pray to Him frequently and instantly. Bear Him always in your mind: teach your thoughts to reverence Him in every place, for there is no place where He is not. Therefore, my child, fear and worship and love God; first, and last, think magnificently of God." That will answer many problems.

The nature of man argues against idolatry as strongly as the nature of God. "In him we live, and move, and have our being; as certain also of your own poets have said, For we are also his offspring. Forasmuch then as we are the offspring of God, we ought not to think that the Godhead is like unto gold, silver, or stone, graven by art and man's device" (Acts 17:28-29). We degrade ourselves, and belie our high origin, when we stoop to idolatry, when we bow to things less than ourselves and make gods of things on the brute level.

There is a doctrine of divine fatherhood and universal brotherhood that we rightly refuse, but let us not therefore repudiate the grand truth that man is the son of God in the sense that he came directly from the Creator's hands and was formed in the image and likeness of God. A remembrance of our native dignity makes all the more tragic the havoc of sin. A sow wallowing in the mire is not a dainty sight, but a man wallowing in the gutter in his own drunken vomit is a sight to make angels weep and the whole human race put on mourning. That man, created with a capacity for God, to walk with God, should be found bowing down to idols and groveling in the mire of sin, is an unspeakable tragedy. A lofty conception of God and a high sense of our own dignity will at once humble us and give us a holy abhorrence of sin.

The gospel comes from such a God to such a creature with an imperious demand: Repent! John came pointing out the Lamb of God with this word on his lips—Repent! Our Lord came among us with this same call—Repent! Peter cast the gospel net for our Pentecostal age with the same cry—Repent! Paul shouted it from the center of the world's philosophy and culture—Repent! With the coming of a Saviour the times of ignorance are over; with the opening of a way of salvation, God's overlooking of sin is no more. Bethlehem, Calvary, and Olivet cry out—Repent!

We have been wont, I fear, to make the gospel too easy. We have rightly insisted that the gospel is good news to be believed, but we have too much forgotten that believing that Good News is the deepest, most revolutionary act of which the human soul is capable. It involves a repudiation of all one's past, a reversal of one's whole attitude with respect to sin, God, the world, and himself, a complete change of outlook, purpose, and aim. It is impossible to exercise saving faith without a real turning from and renunciation of that from which we are to be saved, namely, our sin. Nor is it possible to believe the Good News in the sense of personal appropriation without turning to God with a humble, fixed purpose to love, serve, and obey Him. You may have given a mental assent to the gospel because your ears have echoed with its sweet sound from your childhood, and you may be able to give all the answers concerning the finished work of Christ, but "except ye repent, ye shall all likewise perish" (Luke 13:3). It is true that Paul said nothing of repentance to the jailer in Philippi in answer to his question, "What must I do to be saved?" (Acts 16:30), because, as Dr. Ironside has well expressed it, "The man's whole attitude bespoke the repentance already produced in his soul." It is true also that repentance is a gift from God, as every godly exercise of the soul is wrought by His grace, but that does not lessen our responsibility. We must not allow our Calvinism to become lopsided and to deafen us to the commands of God. We can trust God to be faithful in the bestowal of the gift. It is ours to heed the command and obey. May the Holy Spirit ring it in your heart: "God . . . commandeth all men every where to repent!" (Acts 17:30).

Paul gave the Athenians a tremendous reason for repentance without delay: "Because he hath appointed a day, in the which he will judge the world in righteousness by that man whom he hath ordained" (17:31a). Repent, for judgment is ahead; the Judge is appointed, the day is set! Yet these Athenians went on trifling with their philosophical speculations and indulging their senseless idolatries; and modern Americans go on trifling with their crazes and indulging their lusts. God is so urgent, and we are so heedless! If we believe that God raised our Lord Jesus from the dead, we are accepting not only a fact of history, but we are accepting that fact which is the divine token and assurance to all men that judgment is on the way! "Turn ye, turn ye, . . . for why will ye die?" (Ezek 33:11). "Repent ye, and believe the gospel" (Mark 1:15).

Did Paul fail in Athens? No! But the Athenians did. To the Greeks the gospel of Jesus Christ, with its cross and resurrection, repentance and forgiveness, was foolishness. Some were open scoffers, some politely talked of another interview; but all were haughty, superior, scornful. The wisdom of man can be terribly foolish. Yet a few believed, and discovered that the gospel is "the power of God unto salvation" (Rom 1:16). What Christ and His gospel mean to a man determines both his character and his destiny.

The humiliation at Athens moved Paul to a review of his whole situation. He reexamined his message and his presentation of it, and weighed the issue of it all. Should he make changes? Should he develop the philosophical approach now that he was in the Greek world? Should he trim his sails at Corinth until he had wormed his way in? But the more he thought of it, the more his heart burned within him. He had known a paroxysm of holy zeal in Athens, and he knew that the sight of Corinth would stir his soul again. He knew there was only one answer to the unspeakable degradation and corruption of that most corrupt and degrading city. Therefore, though it should mean still deeper humiliation, more intense suffering, he would not allow the thought of any dilution of his message, but decided on an even greater abandonment to the unvarnished proclamation of the one supreme, all-embracing message, "Jesus Christ, and him crucified" (1 Cor 2:2).

30

PAUL IN CORINTH

ACTS 18:1-18

In this chapter we consider:

1. The pressure of the testimony
2. The encouragement in the testimony
3. The opposition to the testimony

WHEN PAUL REACHED CORINTH, he stepped into an atmosphere very different from that of Athens. It was a new city, built by Julius Caesar in 46 B.C., on the site of the old, which had been razed to the ground by Lucius Mummius just a century before. New Corinth had quickly leaped to the front rank of the world's commercial centers, and contained great wealth. This city of nouveaux riches assumed an air of culture, but it was superficial, in striking contrast to the learned refinement of Athens. Beneath the veneer of culture was an abandonment to immoral practices and voluptuousness which made the city a byword in all Greece. To say that a man "lived like a Corinthian" was to mark him as utterly degraded. The temple of Aphrodite, with all its magnificence, supported a thousand ministers of vice.

Such was the city into which Paul entered with his steadfast purpose to know nothing among them, "save Jesus Christ, and him crucified" (1 Cor 2:2). Here in Corinth he witnessed an abysmal profligacy which must have been his "inspiration" for that dreadful picture of human depravity which he painted in the first chapter of his Roman letter. The longer he remained there, the heavier the burden of it all became, till, with the arrival of Timothy and Silas from Macedonia, he was "pressed by the Word" (Acts 18:5, author's

193

trans.). The idolatry of Athens had thrown him into a paroxysm of grief and anger; now the degradation of Corinth laid an insupportable pressure upon him to give that saving Word of "Jesus Christ, and him crucified," to the needy multitude. The weekly ministry in the synagogue, with the balanced, calculated arguments concerning the Kingdom of God and Jesus Christ, was chafing his spirit. He longed to reach out and cry aloud to the perishing throngs.

> Oft when the Word is on me to deliver,
>   Lifts the illusion, and the truth lies bare;
> Desert or throng, the city or the river
>   Melts in a lucid paradise of air.
>
> Only like souls I see the men thereunder,
>   Bound who should conquer, slaves who should be kings,
> Hearing their one hope with an empty wonder,
>   Sadly contented with a show of things.
>
> Then with a rush, th' intolerable craving
>   Shivers throughout me, like a trumpet call,
> Oh, to save these, to perish for their saving,
>   Die for their life, be offered for them all!

That was Paul in Corinth. Would God it were I in my place, and you in yours!

With this pressure upon him, and the "intolerable craving" to break through to the Gentiles, the apostle determined to bring to an issue his testimony to the Jews. This stirred the slumbering opposition, till they began to blaspheme. Then Paul made the inevitable break with the synagogue, and launched his campaign to reach the city. But when he opened his Gentile center in the home of the Roman proselyte, Justus, he brought with him Crispus, the chief ruler of the synagogue, and all his house, whom Paul baptized with his own hands. Still "there is a remnant according to the election of grace" (Rom 11:5), and Paul will return again and again to his Jewish brethren to find them.

"I was with you in weakness, and in fear, and in much trembling" (1 Cor 2:3). So wrote the intrepid apostle, as we regard him, to these same Corinthians. What threw him into this state? Actually, this is the only right feeling for a servant of God, so long as it is balanced by such trust in God as Paul had. "When Ephraim spake trembling, he exalted himself in Israel; but when he offended in Baal, he died" (Hos 13:1). If our task does not seem too big for us, so that we cry out, "Who is sufficient for these things?" (2 Cor 2:16*b*), we have no right to the answer, "Our sufficiency is from God; who also made us sufficient as ministers of a new covenant" (2 Cor 3:5*b*-6*a*).

The Corinthian situation seemed to intensify Paul's fears. His experience at Athens had shaken him more than all persecution. Then he came alone to Corinth, that is, without human companion. Who would not tremble to enter a great heathen city alone on the mission of salvation? The coming of Silas and Timothy doubtless buoyed his courage, but he soon knew that he was laboring under the cloud of Jewish resentment and intrigue. He had had experience of the envy of the Jews, and well he knew that the great successes which the gospel was achieving among the Gentiles were not passing unnoticed by those at whom he had shaken his raiment.

"Then spake the Lord to Paul in the night by a vision, Be not afraid, but speak, and hold not thy peace: for I am with thee, and no man shall set on thee to hurt thee: for I have much people in this city" (Acts 18:9-10). Gracious encouragement! The Lord approved that passion to tell forth the message, even "in weakness, and in fear, and in much trembling" (1 Cor 2:3), and gave the double assurance of protection from hurt, and of large fruitage.

There was double purpose in this word of encouragement. First it was to meet Paul's personal condition. Frankly, I believe he was fighting an attack of "juniperitis," and, like Elijah, needed a lift. This word from the Lord was more to him than angel's food and a hiking vacation. Then it was to hold Paul in Corinth, where God had much work for him to do, when he was inclined to return to Macedonia. Having thus a clear indication of God's immediate will, an assurance of divine protection against any attempted hurt, and the promise of large returns for his labor, the apostle gave himself with yet greater abandon to his apostolic task, much more settled in mind and heart. He "sat down," the Greek text tells us, for eighteen months, "teaching the word of God among them" (Acts 18:11). The passion to deliver his message was now coupled with an unhurried, unperturbed spirit which lent great strength to his ministry.

These two are not always found in combination. Frequently men
of great zeal find it difficult to "sit down." They are feverish in their
tasks, and must needs be dashing hither and thither to satisfy the
feeling of being busy for the Lord. On the other hand, men of settled
habit are often hard to stir. Their tendency is to discourage too much
warmth. They are great plodders, but with difficulty do they rise to
great heights of inspiration and holy passion. Paul was at the peak of
spiritual efficiency and power when his heart was aflame and quiet at
the same time. He was "pressed with the Word," and he "sat down."
Magnificent grace!

With the coming of a new proconsul, the Jews of Corinth thought
their opportunity had come to wreak their vengeance and rid the city
of this "pestilent fellow," Paul. Time had not abated their wrath, but
one circumstance after another had added gall to bitterness. Paul's
message offended them to begin with. Athens and Corinth were always related in the apostle's mind, and these two cities doubtless
loomed large in his vision when he wrote to the Corinthian church:
"For the Jews require a sign, and the Greeks seek after wisdom: but
we preach Christ crucified, unto the Jews a stumblingblock, and unto the Greeks foolishness" (1 Cor 1:22-23).

Sir William Ramsay says: "It must be acknowledged that Paul had
not a very conciliatory way with the Jews when he became angry."
The time for conciliatory manners was past when they began to
blaspheme; so, satisfied that he had fully declared the witness to the
Jewish community, "he shook his raiment, and said unto them, Your
blood be upon your own heads; I am clean: from henceforth I will go
unto the Gentiles" (Acts 18:6). The Jews were triply offended at
that. The shaking of the skirt of the robe was far from complimentary;
the first word amounted to the imposition of a curse; the last word was
wormwood. Later it was this very mention of the Gentiles which sent
the Jerusalem mob into an hysteria of anger.

The location of the new Christian teaching center would certainly
not meet with Jewish approval. The home of Justus "joined hard to
the synagogue" (18:7*b*). Whether the buildings actually had a common wall, or whether only the lots on which the buildings stood were
contiguous, matters little. They had a common boundary, is the sense
of the word. How would your congregation feel if a preacher who

had occupied your pulpit for some weeks opened a school of heresy next door to the church? That is exactly how the unbelieving Jews felt, only more so! For they were fanatical in their rejection of the gospel, considering it utterly offensive.

To make matters worse, Crispus, the chief ruler of the synagogue, and his whole household, went out with Paul. "It would be like the pastor of a church of one denomination joining another next door," says Dr. Robertson, and that is almost an understatement.

It did not mitigate the Jewish antipathy when the Gentiles began flocking to the Christian banner. They would not have the message for themselves, and they opposed others having it. "Woe unto you, scribes and Pharisees, hypocrites! for ye shut up the kingdom of heaven against men: for ye neither go in yourselves, neither suffer ye them that are entering to go in" (Matt 23:13).

All in all, the Corinthian Jews were thoroughly exasperated, and took occasion of Gallio's arrival to press their complaint. They thought that the new proconsul would naturally be seeking the favor of the populace, and would readily grant the unanimous petition of the strong Jewish colony. They misjudged their man, however, for Gallio, elder brother of Seneca, shared his more illustrious brother's passion for Roman justice, and refused to have part in "a question of words and names, and of your [the Jewish] law" (Acts 18:15). Moreover, when the Grecian mob turned on the Jews and beat Sosthenes, the new chief ruler of the synagogue—who doubtless had led the riot against Paul—Gallio reckoned that the turbulent, ever complaining Jews needed a little scourging, and "cared for none of those things" (18:17b).

Thus Paul, fortified by a proconsular act which clearly indicated the Roman policy of religious freedom, was able to carry on the good work in Corinth "yet a good while" (18:18a). The word of the Lord was made good, and this was one of the few centers which Paul left in peace. He had been begged by the authorities to leave Philippi after being beaten and imprisoned; he had been sent away from Thessalonica with the Jews hunting for him; he had been hurried from Berea with the Jews still on his trail; he had left Athens with the laughter of scorn echoing in his desolate soul. In Corinth it was different. The assuring word of the Lord was fulfilled in the policy of the new proconsul, and his enemies were impotent to hinder. The much harassed apostle was being given a little easing of the yoke. "He knoweth our frame; he remembereth that we are dust" (Psalm 103:14). "He stayeth his rough wind in the day of the east wind" (Isa 27:8).

> Sometimes a light surprises
>   The Christian while he sings:
> It is the Lord who rises
>   With healing in His wings.
> When comforts are declining,
>   He grants the soul again
> A season of clear shining
>   To cheer it after rain.

So, whether in the furnace of affliction and persecution, or whether by the sheltering mercies of God, the gospel is preached, the church is built, the Kingdom of God is brought nigh. And whether the servant be exposed to the full blast of the tempest, or sheltered from the rage of the adversary, the word still holds: "I am with you alway, even unto the end of the age" (Matt 28:20, ASV margin).

31

"RECEIVE YE THE HOLY GHOST"

ACTS 18:24—19:7

In this chapter we consider:

1. The discovery of a deficiency
2. The diagnosis of a deficiency
3. The cause of a deficiency
4. The cure of a deficiency

THE WHITE PENNIES that were issued some time ago were confusing to begin with. The first one that came into my possession I offered for a dime. To the casual glance it seemed the size and color, but the shop-keeper refused it! Some time later I was in a drugstore, and made purchases to the amount of forty-six cents. I threw down on the glass counter a quarter, which rang heavily, two dimes, which rang shrilly, and a white penny, which did not ring at all, but fell with a little dead thud. It is the ring that counts!

Paul arrived in Ephesus for his second visit, the first having been but a passing call. There he met a group of men, about twelve in number, who passed for disciples. They mingled with the disciples, they made profession of discipleship, outwardly their lives resembled disciples. But there was a lack in them which the discerning, Spirit-filled apostle could not fail to sense. The ring was not there. They reacted dully to spiritual things; they wanted vitality.

The great apostle was not being hypercritical or Pharisaical or "holier than thou" when he noted this deficiency. There was no more self-abasing saint in the early church than this same Paul, who honestly felt himself "the least of all saints" (Eph 3:8), and the chief of sinners. Nor are we necessarily supercilious and self-exalting when we

feel a lack of spiritual comradeship with those who claim the Christian
name but are strangers to the realm of the Spirit. Any attempt at
spiritual conversation hits back at us as foreign to present company.
Their interests are in the sphere of the material, the carnal, the temporal. They lack appreciation of the holy things, they are without
understanding of the Word of God, they want that distinctive mark
of the spiritual man, the aroma of Christ. They may be amiable,
kindly, warmhearted people, with enough "religion" to make them
respectable, but not enough to make them conspicuous.

Until a few years ago a bird was just a bird to me. Then I decided
I ought to know enough about birds to distinguish at least between a
wren and a robin! So I got me a pair of field glasses and some bird
books. I never made a serious study of ornithology, but did learn to
identify the more common birds, and occasionally spotted some less
common ones. The other day, being on the New Jersey coast, I went
out with my field glasses in the hope of seeing something of interest.
An intelligent-looking gentleman, returning from a fishing expedition, greeted me, and launched into a conversation which left me completely sunk. Although not a professional naturalist, he had made a
life study of birds and plants. He spoke utterly beyond my reach of
the birds now in migration which we could expect to see and of different species of hibiscus which he had found in the district, till I
inwardly writhed in an anguish of ignorance. He must have discerned
that, although I had the field glasses and other outward appearances of
the naturalist, I was hopelessly deficient even in the basic principles.
Now if he despised my ignorance, he was an intellectual Pharisee, but
if he simply took note of my ignorance, and was somewhat disappointed that he had not met someone who could talk his language, he
was a gentleman. So the truly spiritual will quickly discern deficiency,
not to despise and condemn, but to help. So it was with Paul and
those Ephesian disciples.

Unlike my naturalist friend, Paul set about a cure of the situation
which he found.

A good physician does not prescribe until he has diagnosed. Correct diagnosis is a very large part of the physician's art. In many cases
it is the difference between life and death. What doctor would order
an appendectomy simply because I complained of a pain? He would

want to know where the pain was, what kind of pain it was, whether it was accompanied by nausea, what my bowel condition had been, whether I had a temperature. He would examine by palpation the intestinal region; he would take a blood count. Diagnosis calls for great care, and if so in physical diseases, how much more in spiritual ills! Now Paul was not only quick to sense the defect in this little group of Ephesians, but skillful in analyzing it. Two questions only, and the whole situation lay open before him.

His first query was, "Did ye receive the Holy Spirit when ye believed?" (Acts 19:2a, ASV). The question of the apostle is not, as the King James Version would suggest, whether at some time subsequent to their believing they had, as a second experience, received the Holy Spirit, but whether, at the time of their believing, they had become recipients of the Holy Spirit. In other words, to echo Dr. G. Campbell Morgan, he was not inquiring regarding a second blessing, but regarding the nature of their first blessing. The whole point of the question was that if they had believed in the full evangelical sense, they should have received the Holy Spirit and be showing evidences of it. It was the lack of those evidences that puzzled the apostle. Would he be equally puzzled if he met us?

The answer indicated that Paul was on the right track in his questioning. They said, with commendable frankness, "On the contrary, we did not even hear whether the Holy Spirit is" (19:2b, author's trans.). That is it quite literally rendered, but the American Standard Version adds a word as a suggested rounding out of the sense: "We did not so much as hear whether the Holy Spirit was *given*" (19:2b, ASV, italics added). That was a very wise, and I believe a true, suggestion of the revisers. As we shall see in a moment, those Ephesian disciples had received the teaching of John the Baptist. This being so, ignorant as they were of the full gospel, they could not be ignorant of the existence of the Holy Spirit, for part of John's teaching about the coming One was that "He shall baptize you with the Holy Ghost" (Matt 3:11). Expectation of the Holy Spirit's coming in connection with the ministry of the Messiah was a portion of the body of truth entrusted to the disciples of the fiery successor of Elijah. The problem of the Ephesian believers, then, was not "whether there be any Holy Ghost," but "has He come?" "Has He been given?" They did not know that "the promise of the Father" (Acts 1:4) had been fulfilled; they did not know that the Son had been glorified and had sent the Spirit in His name; therefore, they did not know the rivers of living water gushing forth from their inmost beings.

The apostle's next question is somewhat surprising: "Unto what then were ye baptized?" (Acts 19:3a). He did not ask them if they had been baptized. He took for granted that, being disciples, being believers, they had submitted to baptism. He would not be able to take that for granted today, when many assume that baptism is not necessary at all. Behind the apostle's question is a suspicion that there must have been something irregular about their baptism. He could not imagine anyone receiving true Christian baptism and yet being in the condition of those twelve, so lacking in evidences of the Holy Spirit and so ignorant of His ministry. And, indeed, we have a right to expect, as Paul did, that those who receive baptism will give evidences of the work of the Holy Spirit in their hearts. It is a travesty to receive the token and not show the fruit.

"Unto John's baptism" (19:3b), replied the Ephesian disciples. That explained everything. But now we must go back. Since Paul's first visit, another preacher had come to town, Apollos by name, a Jew of Alexandria, "an eloquent man, and mighty in the scriptures ... instructed in the way of the Lord" (Acts 18:24-25). But for all his eloquence of speech, and all his instruction in righteousness, and all his skill in the Scriptures, he was behind hand in his message, "knowing only the baptism of John" (18:25b). Now all his fervor and diligence and boldness, in which he was a good copy of his Elijah-like teacher, could not make up for the lack of the true evangel. He had no accomplished atonement to offer, no resurrection triumph, no living Advocate at God's right hand, no indwelling Holy Spirit, no victory in the power of a risen Lord. Repentance he demanded, with baptism to seal it: righteousness he proclaimed, insisting on high ethical standards. But it was only the preparatory repentance, only the preparatory righteousness that he knew and preached; for "the way of God" (18:26b) in which he was instructed was "the way of the Lord" as Isaiah and John the Baptist knew it—something to be prepared, as it is written, "Prepare ye the way of the Lord, make his paths straight" (Matt 3:3b).

We shall not dwell on the superlatively beautiful incident of Priscilla and Aquila and their instruction of the young preacher. I suggest that you read Alexander Whyte's essay on Apollos in volume five of his *Bible Characters*. It is difficult to know whether to admire more the gracious, godly, faithful couple who took the learned, eloquent, but defective young preacher to their hearts and taught him with so much wisdom and sweetness; or the young preacher of such noted talents who was humble enough to receive instruction from two members of his congregation who boasted no more learned occupation than that of tentmakers. Happy is the young minister who has in his congregation some man or woman of deep learning and long experience in the ways of the Lord, and thrice happy if he is humble enough to sit quite frankly at the feet of such an instructor.

All that is a digression—I hope a profitable one. The immediate point here is that a minister can carry his hearers no further than he has gone himself. An Apollos may be learned, skillful, eloquent, fervent, diligent, fearless, but if he have not a whole gospel, he cannot lead his people into the "fulness of the blessing of the gospel" (Rom 15:29). If he knows only the baptism of John, his people will know only the baptism of John, unless a Priscilla or an Aquila or a Paul come along to help them out of their deficiency into the sufficiency of Christ. Those Ephesians had made preparation for Christ, but they were not enjoying participation in Christ. They were sincere and earnest believers so far as they had been instructed, but ministerial deficiency had left them in that less than halfway state.

Is it possible for men and women to be in like condition today? That will find its answer in another question. Are there ministers today with a defective message? Yes, only too many, and with less excuse than Apollos had. In more pulpits than one cares to think, an ethical message is proclaimed, but no divine Saviour is offered, no crucified, risen, exalted, interceding, indwelling Christ; no divine satisfaction is presented in the death of our Lord, no regenerating work of the Holy Spirit, no supernatural salvation. If Christ is preached, it is as an ideal, an example, master in some vague, impersonal sense.

What can be expected of people so robbed of the message of the gospel? They sincerely embrace what is delivered to them, thinking it is Christianity. They are quite sure they are believers. They are exemplary in their moral conduct, faithful in their "religious" duties, but lacking an adequate conception of spiritual things, so that they have none of the distinctive marks of those who are indwelt and controlled by the Holy Spirit. A spendid couple in just such case recently moved to our town and began attending our services. They had been active in their former church, but immediately felt there was something radically different in our group. They began to study the Bible, privately and in study circles, with great eagerness, till they realized that they had never been born again, for all the righteousness and religious activity of their lives. They were not without their struggles, especially concerning some of the abstinences which they observed in our people, but they could not escape the reality of Christ in their godly neighbors; till finally they made the great decision to accept the Lord Jesus as their own Saviour. Immediately the marks of Christ began to appear, and the most spiritual of our congregation sense that new affinity, that new oneness of spirit. The apostle would not require to ask them now, "Did ye receive the Holy Spirit when ye believed?" They have truly believed, and they have truly received. Be sure that you are not left floundering at a halfway point, with a baptism of good intentions instead of a baptism of personal faith in a living Saviour who loved you, and gave Himself for you.

We are not given the full text of Paul's instructions to those deficient disciples, but enough is recorded to show clearly that he led their minds and hearts to Christ Jesus. He gave them the gospel of a finished work, a complete provision, a full salvation. That is how to repair the defects in the faith of badly taught people. The Holy Spirit wrought on their hearts to make room for Jesus, and then entered to control their newly yielded lives and to form Christ in them. The token of their submission to the newly acquired truth and the newly received Saviour was a second baptism, this time in the name of the Lord Jesus.

"Should I be baptized again?" That query has frequently come from men and women who, after years of false, because uninstructed, profession have come to a living knowledge of the Lord Jesus. The case may be somewhat different from that of the Ephesians, for their first baptism was confessedly the baptism of John, while these have received a baptism professedly Christian. Nevertheless, I doubt the validity of an ordinance administered apart from personal, living faith. Therefore, while I cannot lay down a law of procedure, I should point to this incident and encourage a following of the impulse of the renewed heart. "And let it be, when these signs are come unto thee, that thou do as occasion serve thee; for God is with thee" (1 Sam 10:7).

Must one have the imposition of hands to receive the Holy Spirit? Not so long as the story of Cornelius and his Roman household remains in the Book. The Holy Spirit is not bound to one method or two or three, nor does His using a certain method today bind Him ever to use it again. He is "the Lord, the Spirit," and it is His prerogative to use what instruments He will in manifesting His presence. The Samaritans received the Holy Spirit by the imposition of apostolic hands after baptism, apparently without the accompanying sign of tongues. The household of Cornelius received the Holy Spirit before baptism, without the laying on of hands, but with the sign of tongues. The Ephesians received the Holy Spirit after baptism, in connection with the laying on of the hands of Paul, and with the manifestation of tongues and prophesying. The reasons in detail may be beyond our scrutiny, but such variety of operation forbids our laying down dogmas that thus and thus must be the coming of the Holy Spirit upon a believer. Only let Him exert His sovereign control in our lives, and the fruit of the Spirit will not be wanting in us.

32

TRIUMPH IN EPHESUS

ACTS 19:8-41

In this chapter we examine:

1. The extent of the triumph
2. The means of the triumph
3. The peak of the triumph

PAUL WILL ALWAYS REMEMBER Ephesus. He will remember it as a place of immense opportunity and intense opposition, a place of unremitting toil and unexcelled triumph. Ephesus to him will always be the place of blood, sweat, and tears—the blood of conflict with wild beasts, the sweat of labor for the sustenance of himself and his party, the tears of travail shed night and day in the passion of ministry.

Corinthian degradation was a byword in Greece, but Corinth would have had many rivals for that doubtful distinction in Asia. In Ephesus the worship of Artemis opened the sluice gates of vice, so that the city was inundated with a flood tide of iniquity. Deception, fraud, trickery, chicanery flourished in the precincts of the magnificent temple, and the occult arts were practiced universally. Renegade Jews joined in the easy market for quick profits. Into this Vanity Fair came the apostle, and before long we are reading this record of victory: "So mightily grew the word of God and prevailed" (Acts 19:20).

The geographical extent of this triumph reached far beyond the city limits. "All they which dwelt in Asia heard the word of the Lord Jesus, both Jews and Greeks" (19:10). The Asia referred to is, of course, that southwest section of what we know as Asia Minor, which constituted a Roman consulate. The seven churches to which the apostle John wrote the Apocalypse were in this territory, Ephesus being one of the seven. Now it was through this very Asia that Paul had passed on his westward journey three years before, muzzled and perplexed, longing to break in upon the darkness with the true light, but forbidden by the Holy Spirit. Since that heartsore journey he had never ceased to pray for this spiritually desolate region, and now the fruit of those prayers, as well as of the more recent preaching and teaching, was being reaped. The Word had spilled over from the Ephesian cup till even Demetrius said in his complaint to the silversmiths, "Not . . . [only] at Ephesus, but almost throughout all Asia, this Paul hath persuaded and turned away much people" (Acts 19: 26).

The measure of the triumph is seen not only in its geographical reach, but in its effect upon the popular religion, as reflected in the panic of the silversmiths who made shrines, images, charms, and the rest. When the industry of sin is in jeopardy, we know that the gospel is making deep inroads into the enemy's territory. During the great revival in Wales, the boarding up of liquor houses and theaters and dance halls was a common occurrence. All mighty movements of the Holy Spirit have cut deep swathes in the profits of iniquity.

When the record says, "*So* with power the word of the Lord grew and overcame" (19:20, author's trans.), we must ask for the antecedents of that "so." By what means was this expansion effected?

In answer, we first focus our attention on one man and his ministry. Dr. G. Campbell Morgan excellently depicts the apostle in Ephesus doing the work of tentmaker, Christian apologist and teacher, devoted pastor, and missionary statesman. In that heathen center where religion meant money, this herald of the cross would receive no gift, but toiled for a living that he might make the gospel free to all. So supported, we see him go, as was his rule, "to the Jew first" (Rom 1:16). The inevitable breach came, and "he departed from them, and separated the disciples, disputing daily in the school of one Tyrannus" (Acts 19:9b). Any synagogue which denied the Lord Jesus and refused His message thereby became a synagogue of Satan, and was no place for the disciples of Christ. So today, a church which turns away from the word of the truth of the gospel can no longer be "church" to those who love our Lord Jesus in sincerity. It is indeed a serious matter to divide a church, and only an issue which is vital to Christian doctrine and practice can justify such a step, but "what fellowship hath righteousness with unrighteousness? and what communion hath light with darkness? And what concord hath Christ with Belial? or what part hath he that believeth with an infidel?" (2 Cor 6:14-15). When the lines are so drawn, someone ought to be ready to separate the disciples. When Luther separated the disciples from a papacy that refused to be reformed, then the Word of the Lord grew and prevailed. When the Wesleys separated the disciples from a state church which would not rise to its responsibilities, then the Word of the Lord grew and prevailed. When Zinzendorf separated the disciples from a dead deism, then the Word of the Lord grew and prevailed. There are occasions when separation is the only way to victory. There have, alas, been many separations which had no justification, effected only to indulge the whims and tempers of carnal men. The Word of the Lord does not gain its victories through these.

This man who separated the disciples for the sake of the Word was God's instrument in special miracles for the confirmation of that Word. Here God condescended to exhibit His might in a manner suited to men and women who had long been held in the bondage of superstition and trickery. He allowed Paul's sweat cloths and aprons, which he used in his daily manual toil, to be the "carriers" of His power. It is distinctly stated that these were "special miracles" (Acts 19:11), and it would be folly for any to attempt to imitate the method.

I have been greatly moved many times by evidences of this condescension of our glorious God, stooping to the weaknesses of men. Some years ago, in a Canadian village where I was conducting evangelistic meetings, several of the "town characters" were converted. One of them was an old woman, called Nell Pete, who had for many years been a helpless drug addict, till her mind was quite dark. The Lord lightened her darkness, and she rejoiced in salvation. The drug, however, proved too strong for her own feeble resistance, and she became greatly troubled. One day as she climbed the hill toward the shack which was her solitary home, the voice of the Lord was made audible to her: "Nell, do you really want to be freed from the drug, for My sake?" She answered simply, "Yes, Lord!" Then it was that the Lord wrought so wonderfully and condescendingly. He bade her go to the drugstore and ask for a certain compound, telling her also how to take it. Nell did as she was told, and in several days was entirely and permanently free from the craving. She related this in all simplicity to the pastor, a man not given to accepting and rehearsing stories, and he gave the account to me as entirely authentic. I realize that this is not God's usual method, but He stooped to the state of that poor old weakened sinner. Oh the tenderness of our God! In like manner He wrought special miracles to meet the special situation in Ephesus. "*So* the word grew and overcame."

The wizards and sorcerers of Ephesus could not but acknowledge the superior power that wrought in Paul. With their weirdest and most elaborate incantations they could not effect what this stranger, this preacher of strange doctrines, seemed to accomplish with consummate ease. Some of the wandering Jews who dealt in sorcery and witchcraft, so contrary to their ancient Law, decided to imitate Paul's technique and borrow the name which he invoked. Little did they know that the name of Jesus is terrible in destruction for those who believe not, as it is wonderful in healing for those who know Him. The name of Jesus on the lips of these exorcists was as dynamite in the hands of mischievous, careless children. As Alexander Maclaren has so aptly said, "They spoke His name tentatively, as an experiment," in an attempt to improve their skill in wizardry. Their blasphemy turned back upon themselves. "Jesus we acknowledge, and Paul we know, but you! Who are you?" (Acts 19:15, author's trans.). And "they fled out of that house naked and wounded" (19:16*b*). The mimicry had failed. "*So* with power the word of the Lord grew and overcame" by the confounding of blasphemous imitators.

That was a cruel blow for necromancy and the black arts in Ephesus. Now many who had become believers had not yet abandoned all their evil practices, especially in this so fascinating and alluring realm of spiritism. This demonstration of the great gulf between the faith in Christ and the practice of sorcery sent a mighty wave of conviction of sin through the church. Like the judgment upon Ananias and Sapphira, it produced a holy fear, resulting in open confession and a public burning of the iniquitous books, to the value of fifty thousand silver drachmae. This was not an auricular confession, such as the Roman church demands, but an open confession, with open destruction of the tools of their sin. What a burning, what a cleansing! And that purifying of the church gave new impetus to the onward sweep of the gospel, as it always has, and always will. Where sin is condoned, the gospel is hindered, because the Holy Spirit is grieved. Where sin is condemned and forsaken, the power of God is manifested.

By the unflagging devotion of one man, toiling, teaching, weeping; by the condescension of God in miracles of an uncommon sort; by the rebuke of blasphemous imitators; by the purifying of the church: *"So mightily the word of the Lord grew and prevailed."*

"A great door and effectual is opened unto me, and there are many adversaries" (1 Cor 16:9). Thus did Paul himself describe his Ephesian ministry. We have seen how he entered the "great door and effectual." The operation of the adversaries calls for attention. There are hints in some of the letters that Paul endured much more in Ephesus than is recorded by Luke in this chapter. The verse we have just quoted from the first Corinthian letter would itself suggest continuous action on the part of the opposition. In this second letter to the Corinthians, written just after leaving Ephesus, Paul gives this enlightening description of his sojourn there: "For we would not, brethren, have you ignorant of our trouble which came to us in Asia, that we were pressed out of measure, above strength, insomuch that we despaired even of life: but we had the sentence of death in ourselves, that we should not trust in ourselves, but in God which raiseth the dead: who delivered us from so great a death, and doth deliver: in whom we trust that he will yet deliver us" (2 Cor 1:8-10). Over against his actually despairing of his life and yet being delivered from "so great a death," we have this written from Ephesus itself: "If after the manner of men I have fought with beasts at Ephesus, what advantageth it me, if the dead rise not?" (1 Cor 15:32). Personally, I am not prepared, in the face of these statements of the extremity of the apostle's sufferings in Ephesus, to turn this reference to the arena into a figure of speech and apply it to the Ephesian riot, in which Paul had no part. The early church seems to have held it as common knowledge that Paul was miraculously saved from the lion, and Hippolytus uses that as an argument for the credibility of Daniel's salvation in the lions' den. "If we believe," he says, "that when Paul was condemned to the beasts the lion that was set upon him lay down at his feet and licked him, how shall we not believe that which happened in the case of Daniel?" We do not lean too heavily on tradition, especially in its detail, but when a general tradition has the support of such statements as Paul himself has given us, I am inclined to accept it. The evidence, at any rate, all goes to show that the apostle had one of his severest times of testing in that most fruitful field, Ephesus.

The opposition reached a climax during one of the Artemisian festivals, when great throngs had gathered at Ephesus from all over the province. Till now, the Jews had been the leaders and the schemers and the sponsors of the antagonism against Paul and his message, but now the Gentiles come forward on their own account. This may be regarded as the beginning of the pagan persecutions. It started with the silversmiths, whose commerce in silver shrines was showing a serious shrinkage, not only in Ephesus, but throughout Asia. Demetrius certainly reveals the true inspiration of their attack in his speech to his fellow craftsmen. Our wealth—our trade! These are the things that are at stake. The honor and the glory of Diana are a secondary matter, indeed are only the pretext for action, not the reason. They will piously shout for their goddess, but their only care is their profits. The silversmiths of Ephesus have their children among us today. The liquor interests are loud in their "protection" of our "personal liberty," while they engage in wholesale enslaving and debasing of the population. The hypocrites are no more interested in our moral freedom than the moon is interested in cheese. On the contrary, they are bent on making men slaves, for therein lies the security of their wicked gains. They feed on blood money.

The unbelieving Jews did not lose their heads in the confusion. They saw in this sudden turn an opportunity to further their own designs against Paul and secure themselves. They chose Alexander as their spokesman. (Was he the coppersmith who did Paul much harm, and against whom Paul warned Timothy?) They managed to have their man recognized and brought to the rostrum of the theater. There their little scheme ended, for the mob was not interested in listening to a Jew. Only the appearing of the town clerk succeeded in quieting the howling multitude, and doubtless he came just in time to save Aristarchus and Gaius, Paul's companions, from lynching. The tide of danger that rose so suddenly and threateningly subsided as quickly, as the town clerk gently reproved the populace for their unwarranted uproar, and threw a cloak of official protection around the messengers of Christ.

The climax of victory had been reached. That bit of official protection started a new and sadder phase in the history of that so well-born church. The church breathed easily and began to lay aside her armor. The watchers slept. The wolves entered. Self-seekers fleeced the flock. Love grew cold. The candle went out. The candlestick was removed.

So it was when Constantine spread a patronizing hand over the church. It then plunged headlong into an apostasy that remains with us today. "The Church persecuted has always been the Church pure, and therefore the Church powerful. The Church patronized has always been the Church in peril, and very often the Church paralyzed. I am not afraid of Demetrius. Let him have his meeting of craftsmen, and let them in their unutterable folly shout a lie twenty-five thousand strong. The truth goes quietly on. But when the town clerk begins to take care of us, then God deliver us from the peril."*

*Dr. G. Campbell Morgan, *The Acts of the Apostles* (New York: Revell, 1924).

PART FOUR

The March on Rome

33

A NEW IMPERATIVE

In this chapter we trace:

1. The nature of the divine "must"
2. The unfolding of the divine "must"
3. The hazards of the divine "must"

I SUPPOSE *The Battle of the Books* is one of the classics of English literature. I should like to see someone of talent write a companion volume, "The Revolt of Words." If words of high significance were able to take up arms in their own defense, we should witness a battle royal against the trivial uses to which they are daily put. Among the leaders in the revolt would be this great word "must," the monarch of the imperative mode. A word that moves with regal dignity among lofty moral conceptions, that carries its scepter into the high counsels of God and into the profound regions of the human soul, must be ill at ease in the trumperies of fancy and craze and pleasure. To apply the "must" to the seeing of the latest show, the wearing of the newest fad, the hearing of the latest song hit, is to speak an untruth, and to degrade a word which in its rightful place is girded with power and supreme authority. "Must" is the imperative in the superlative degree, it is the word that conveys the absolute authority of the Most High God to the soul.

When Paul said, "I must also see Rome" (Acts 19:21b), he was not using the "must" of the tourist or the pleasure seeker. "See Naples and die," travelers used to say. It was not in such a sense that Paul felt the urge to see Rome. The imperative lay not on his fancy but on his

215

spirit, in line with that other imperative which dogged him all his apostolic days: "Necessity is laid upon me; yea, woe is unto me, if I preach not the gospel!" (1 Cor 9:16). It was the "must" of the missionary. It was the same "must" which lay upon our Lord, when, as He fulfilled His course, "He must needs go through Samaria" (John 4:4).

The will of God is the imperative for every man. The sinner is the man who has refused that high and holy demand; but because every man must have a "must" of some kind in his life, he crowns some low thing with the diadem of the imperative. The child of God is one who has accepted the will of God as the grand imperative of his being, so that whatever is in line of the fulfillment of "that good, and acceptable, and perfect, will of God" (Rom 12:2*b*) is the "must" for him.

Paul embraced the will of God as the imperative of his life that day outside Damascus, when, with the light which blinded his eyes searching his soul, he cried out, "Lord, what wilt thou have me to do?" (Acts 9:6). In Damascus itself, and more vividly at later stages, he realized that the will of God for him was the preaching of the gospel, and that became the binding, driving, unremitting "must" of all his days. Then there was the process of discovering the range of ministry, the plan of operation, the order of undertaking. These in turn, as recognized, became the more immediate "must." Do you see then where this life in the imperative mode begins? By accepting the unseen, unknown will of God. Then we go forth to prove that will in all its unfoldings.

"I must also see Rome." So said the apostle, because Rome had swung into his vision as part of the revealed will of God for him. Nothing would divert him from that purpose now. Beloved, those "musts" of God in the soul are veritable tyrants. They are utterly unbending, they are frightfully imperious, but they are glorious. A very dear friend of mine, who recently returned to India, went out at first with a mission whose primary purpose had been to reach the tribes of the Indian jungles for Christ. He believed that God's will for him was to minister to those aborigines. They constituted the "must" of his life. As time went on it became more and more apparent that the mission had forgotten its original purpose, and refused to be reminded of it, satisfied to be a comfortable institution in a big center, with schools, orphanages, and leper asylum. My friend faithfully labored in his mission assignment, but the "must" of the tribes lay upon him heavily. He made effort after effort to stir up the mission leaders to their obligation, but they turned a deaf ear. The imperative would not lift from his soul; he found no exemption on the ground of the action of the mission. "The calling and election of God are without repentance" (Rom 11:29, author's trans.). Finally the "must" of God made its fearful demands upon this man and upon this man's wife, till, severing their relation with the mission, they broke into the jungle and pioneered for seven years among the tribespeople. That is not the end of the story. Those were years of proving the faithfulness of God, and God vindicated the faithfulness of His servants. The mission passed into the hands of men who were ready to go forward with God, and this obedient witness returned to India as field director to lead that same but rejuvenated and regenerated mission into the great work which he himself had pioneered. The only white man who speaks the language, he is now in a position to direct a great new field; and if the present trend of events materializes, I expect to see there a work that will command the attention of the Christian world. The "must" of God is terrible in its demand, glorious in its issue.

See in what different manners and to the accompaniment of what divers circumstances these "musts" of God burst upon the soul. We have already followed Paul along his via dolorosa through Asia, longing to break the silence and give those devotees of Diana the gospel of Christ, but restrained, to his own perplexity and amazement, until he came to Troas and saw in the night visions the man of Macedonia crying out, "Come over into Macedonia, and help us" (Acts 16:9). On that occasion God led His servant into a corner to bring him face to face with the next necessity of the divine will. Now God has given Paul the desire that was before denied him, and that very Asia through which he had traveled in heaviness of spirit has been the scene of his greatest triumphs over a period of about two and a half years. When he is right at the peak of these triumphs the farther field breaks in upon his view, and the new imperative seizes his soul, till he cries out, "I must also see Rome."

Most of us would have said rather, "Here is a work to satisfy a man for a lifetime. I can do no better anywhere than right here." Or if we did speak as Paul spoke, we should have had friends enough to convince us of our folly, and to argue that God's blessing on the work was the sure sign that we ought to remain. So we might have stayed on at Ephesus till the zenith was past, the farther vision vanished, and the dull ordinary had seized upon us. Mme. Marcella Semrich, one of the most versatile singers in opera and concert in the last two decades of last century, and the first of this, whose voice was favorably compared with Mme. Patti's, astonished the musical world by her retirement in 1909. In explanation she gave as her reason: "I wish to make my adieux while the sun is still high in the heavens—that is all. For me there shall be no pity." That is good worldly wisdom, and "the children of this world are in their generation [often] wiser than the children of light" (Luke 16:8). He is an object of pity indeed who has missed God's farther field by jealous clinging to a prosperous present which thereafter withers into the sear of autumn and the blight of winter.

Ephesus had been for Paul a place of opposition and danger. Perhaps, then, the thought of Rome may have suggested to him an escape from the constant pressure and unceasing peril in Asia. As a Roman citizen he would be right under the immediate protection of the emperor! Not at all! Paul was not running away from danger; he was running into it. He knew right well that if Asia had beaten him with whips, Rome would chastise him with scorpions. He knew that if Rome was the most strategic of all centers for the establishment of Christianity, it would prove the most formidable bastion to be wrested from the enemy. Rome taken for Christ meant the Roman roads turned into highways for our God, so that those arteries which carried the power of Rome to the ends of the earth would carry the lifeblood of the gospel. That would not be without a price. So Paul's Roman "must" meant, not an alleviation of danger, but an aggravation of it. This hero of the cross was not satisfied to show his scars. He was ready for new and fiercer battles.

Do you carry battle scars? And does your Rome, the "must" of God that now lies upon your soul, call you to new battles, new dangers, new wounds? What is your answer? Here was Paul's answer, in face of all that might come, even death itself: "I am debtor. . . . So . . . I am ready" (Rom 1:14-15) . "O God, to us may grace be given to follow in his train!"

34

A MINISTER'S FAREWELL

ACTS 20:17-38

In this chapter we consider:
1. The matter of Paul's witness
2. The manner of Paul's witness

PAUL HAD A GREAT MIND, and a great heart, too. Fortunately the heart was never divorced from the mind. The severest doctrinal passages in the apostolic utterances have the throb of the great heart as well as the strength of the great mind. It is to be expected, then, that when he comes to a farewell message like this, the mighty heart will leap to the foreground. Some of us have been in Paul's situation, and would rather not have it very often; most have been in the place of the Ephesian elders, reluctantly bidding farewell to a cherished pastor. Therefore we are all in a position to enter with some measure of understanding into this tender address of the apostle to the leaders of the Ephesian church.

Here was one minister, who, reviewing a specific term and sphere of service, was able to say, in all truth, "I have done my best," and on the basis of having done his best, to make this lofty claim, "I am pure from the blood of all men" (Acts 20:26). I was once invited to preach anniversary sermons in a certain church. One of the announcements that morning was the minister's resignation. In course of his statement he rather "lit into" his flock for their lack of appreciation and response, and closed with these words of the apostle Paul. The atmosphere was cold enough till then, but then it became frigid—a poor atmosphere for an anniversary sermon. The comments of the people afterward were a far cry from the scene on the sands of Miletus;

indeed, I was thoroughly embarrassed, and wished myself a thousand miles from the place. Actually, the manner in which some of the deacons asked me after the service if I would be available made me shudder. It was too much like a man bereaved of his wife proposing to another before the funeral of the first. What made the difference? We shall try to discover.

The apostle Paul vindicated his ministry on two pleas—the matter of his witness and the manner of it. As to the matter, he said, "I kept back nothing that was profitable" (Acts 20:20), and again, "I have not shunned to declare unto you all the counsel of God" (20:27). Nothing that was profitable withheld, all the counsel of God declared: these two statements cover the complete loyalty of the man to his message. Now that is a big claim, yet Paul was able to make it after no more than three years' ministry in Ephesus. Even after fifty years of ministry I would not dare to make either claim. Surely there are many profitable things that I have not even touched on; some of them I should hesitate to approach. And I am certain I have not given all the counsel of God; I do not know it all to give it.

Yet that is the standard of Christian witness, and today I impose upon myself anew, as I lay upon every minister of the Word, this criterion of ministry: nothing profitable withheld, the whole counsel declared. Whatever discipline of study that may involve, whatever travail of soul, whatever trembling before God and before the people, we may admit nothing less than that as the goal of our preaching.

Now I have every reason to believe that my ministerial friend, whose resignation was so chilly, was as faithful in the matter of his witness as he knew how to be. And inasmuch as he faithfully delivered his soul of the saving message of God, he could up to that point affirm, "I am pure from the blood of all men." Yet why was there not the warm assent to his claim that so manifestly met Paul's declaration? I think it lay in the *manner* of the witness.

Paul could say, "I have not only given you the true matter, but I have delivered it in the right manner." When I was attending university in Glasgow, a group of us aspiring preachers who knew all about it came to the amazing decision that in preaching the matter was everything, the manner nothing. We were quite sure, of course, that our matter was weighty and telling enough to overwhelm the gravest and most critical of Scottish congregations! Some of us have learned a little since then, and among other things, this, that however good the matter, it leans very heavily on the manner of its delivery for its effect on the hearers. Yet I find that still, with all the speech courses available, too many carry to the ministry of the Word an utter lack of training in the art of public address, some even despising such training as an interference with the work of the Holy Spirit!

But when I speak of the manner of Paul's witness, I am not thinking of his diction, voice, pulpit decorum, and the like. The fact is, he was not in the same class as Apollos for sheer oratory. No, the manner of Paul's witness was this—humility, tears, temptations. Listen to his passionate appeal: "Ye know, from the first day that I came into Asia, after what manner I have been with you at all seasons, serving the Lord with all humility of mind, and with many tears, and temptations" (Acts 20:18-19). There, beloved, is where my resigning friend had failed, till even in his act of resignation there was no note of humility, no sob of hardly restrained tears, no brotherly feeling as from a man of like temptations with ourselves. And exactly for that reason there was no response of brokenness, of grief, of sympathy. There is a rigid correctness, a faithfulness to the letter, which kills—kills sympathy, kills love, kills tenderness. "For scarcely for a righteous man will one die: yet peradventure for a good man some would even dare to die" (Rom 5:7). My friend was the righteous man; Paul was the good man. My friend had the matter; Paul had the manner with it.

"Be not highminded" (1 Tim 6:17), exhorted the apostle, and he obeyed the Holy Spirit's injunction himself. I sat on an ordination council once where the candidate was splendidly accurate in his answers, but so blatantly superior, so daring and assuming, that I could not give my voice to his being set apart to the ministry of Him who said, "I am meek and lowly in heart" (Matt 11:29), or to share the ministry of the apostle who served "with all humility of mind" (Acts 20:19).

Our Scottish ecclesiastical lore carries the tale of a young minister, newly graduated from theological college, and candidating for a pulpit to which he was entirely confident he would be called. He mounted the winding stairs of the high pulpit with an air of assurance, but the penetrating gaze of so many frankly critical eyes thoroughly wilted him. Time for the sermon found him in a regular panic, till he descended a very crestfallen young man. The sexton (who in Scottish churches is a personage of considerable dignity!) met the youthful preacher at the foot of the pulpit steps with the kindly but reproving words: "Laddie, if ye had ga'ed up as ye cam' doon, ye wad ha'e cam' doon as ye ga'ed up." "Whosoever exalteth himself shall be abased; and he that humbleth himself shall be exalted" (Luke 14:11).

St. Augustine has given us this on the primacy of humility among the graces: "As the rhetorician being asked what was the first thing in the rules of eloquence, he answered, Delivery. What was the second? Delivery. What was the third? Still he answered, Delivery. So if you ask me concerning the graces of the Christian character, I would answer firstly, secondly, and thirdly, and forever, Humility."

But it is when I come to these tears of the great apostle that I am smitten to the ground. "Remember," he says, "that by the space of three years I ceased not to warn every one night and day with tears" (Acts 20:31). I stand in awe of that, I hang my head in shame at that. If God stores up our tears in His bottle, as the psalmist so picturesquely declares, they must be among God's precious things. Those tears of penitence, those tears of fellowship in the sufferings of Christ, those tears over saints and over sinners, those tears of love for the Saviour: how they will witness in that day when the records are opened! And how the absence of them will witness against us!

Some will have none of this thought of ministerial tears. It is too much emotion, they say. Then they must drive out the godly Murray McCheyne of Dundee, whose sexton, years after the minister's death, taught an English cleric the manner of McCheyne in the pulpit; and when he had got him reading a favorite passage of the departed saint, stopped him, and said, "Na, na, he didna read it like that! Ye maun greet while ye read it." And if you will not have tears, you must drive out blessed John Tauler of Strassbourg, whose first attempt to preach after his submission to the dealings of the Holy Spirit was drowned in a flood of tears that would not be stayed. And if you will not have tears, you must drive out Paul, and obliterate his three glorious years of tears and triumphs in Ephesus. And if you will not have tears, you will reject the Lord and His piteous weeping over Jerusalem. I say to my own heart, and to yours, if we had more tears, we should have more revival.

Then the apostle ministered out of a multitude of temptations, whose sharpness he knew right well, so that he came to the people with a great confession of understanding. He was no colorless saint; he had blood in him that knew passion; and as a sinner who knew also the might of the Saviour, he came with the message of deliverance to fellow sinners. Says Joseph Parker on this passage, "An untempted minister will never do us any good; an untried man will talk over our heads. My great preacher must be a man who has carried heavier chains than I have strength to bear, who has fought with lions the very shadow of which would be too much for me to look upon." And while we think of the value of ministerial temptations, let us remember that "we have not an high priest which cannot be touched with the feeling of our infirmities; but was in all points tempted like as we are, yet without sin" (Heb 4:45).

Now let us not confuse ministerial temptation with ministerial sin. A minister who knows temptation as an occasion of overcoming grace is a man of high value in the Kingdom of God, by whatever channel the temptations come. Paul's came to him in Ephesus through the antagonism of his fellow Jews. John Wesley's chief temptation apparently came to him through his wife, an insanely jealous woman and a fearful tyrant. I do not suggest that a young preacher should marry a shrew as a means of grace! We had better keep praying, "Lead us not into temptation, but deliver us from evil" (Matt 6:13). Nevertheless, temptation, of whatever sort and amount the Lord allows, turned to victory, will give a touch of kinship to our ministry that nothing else can. But I say again, do not confuse temptation and sin. If ministerial temptation brings a quality of worth to the witness, ministerial sin will blight and damn the witness. We may at times resent the "double standard" sometimes set up for ministers and laymen, but we may as well face the fact that the more public our profession, the severer demands will be made upon us. "Let every one that nameth the name of Christ depart from iniquity" (2 Tim 2:19b). Those who minister Christ will be scrutinized with closer eyes than others. Let me give you an example.

Some time ago I was at high school commencement exercises because of twin nieces who were graduating. The father of these girls has the smoking habit, and it is quite taken for granted in the home. Outside the auditorium, after the exercises, a clergyman, wearing the "dog collar," stood near, smoking a cigarette. Our nieces' mother drew my attention to him and said, "I think it is terrible to see a minister smoking." Now it will avail nothing to say, "We have as good a right to do this or that as anybody else," or to give it another turn, "They have no more right to do it than we have." We had better accept the challenge, and in face of all the temptations that beset us, pray with Murray McCheyne, "Lord, make me as holy as it is possible for a redeemed sinner to be." We ought to be that anyhow, whether we be ministers or no, and if we are called to be ministers, all the more so.

So, my brethren, if we, in the matter of our witness, withhold nothing profitable, but declare all the counsel of God, and in our manner of witness are humble in mind, have ready tear ducts at least in our hearts, and are compassionate as those who know the sting of temptation, yet are triumphant in Christ, we shall be in the true apostolic succession. May the Lord grant it to us all!

35

PAUL RECALLS AN ARGUMENT

ACTS 22:17-22

In this chapter we learn:

1. How Paul perceived the will of God
2. How Paul protested the will of God
3. How Paul pursued the will of God

DID PAUL DO WRONG in going up to Jerusalem? The Holy Spirit had kept telling him all the way from Achaia and Macedonia that "bonds and afflictions" (Acts 20:23) awaited him in the holy city, but the warnings of the Spirit did not seem to signify to him a prohibition. When he came to Tyre, however, the disciples there "said to Paul *through the Spirit,* that he should not go up to Jerusalem" (21:4, italics added). At Caesarea the prophet Agabus announced again the bonds that awaited him, till his own companions joined the disciples of that place in attempts to deter him from proceeding farther. His reply was a declaration of his willingness to die in Jerusalem for the name of the Lord Jesus.

Certainly things did not go well in Jerusalem, not just that the bonds and afflictions came as foretold, but that they found Paul in rather a compromised position. He had scarcely time to draw breath in the city before the elders of the church were pressing him into participation in Jewish ordinances, from which he had already claimed emancipation. We have no doubt that Paul engaged in this Jewish ritual in keeping with his own high principle, "I am made all things to all men, that I might . . . [win] some" (1 Cor 9:22b), but he did it under pressure of men who were definitely compromising with the Judaizers and were seeking to avoid trouble which they were

226

afraid would arise with the coming of Paul, the champion of the new "free from the law" (Rom 8:2) covenant. So it was not while he was reasoning in the synagogues that Jesus is the Christ, nor while he was preaching in the court of the Temple "Jesus Christ, and him crucified" (1 Cor 2:2), that Paul met his bonds and afflictions, but while he was engaged in ritual offerings of the Old Testament.

I very much hesitate to sit in judgment on the great apostle. If he did err (even through some degree of pride and willfulness, there is a measure of comfort, though not of license, for us in our errors, as also in the manifest overruling of the Lord. And there certainly is a warning to us that we should walk carefully and humbly and obediently if we would avoid compromise and gain our best ends. For the elders did not secure the peace they sought, neither did Paul win the Jews to Christ.

So the apostle was seized in the Temple, and would have fared badly indeed had not the Roman power stepped in. Reaching the stairs of the castle, he asked permission to address the Jewish crowd. Leave being granted, he spoke to them in the Aramaic tongue. He offered a defense of the gospel, and of his own part in its ministry as apostle to the Gentiles. His method was that of a personal testimony, and it is part of that testimony that demands our special attention now.

Paul recited his first meeting with the Lord, and followed his story down to his return to Jerusalem, whence he had set out with authority from the chief priests to blot out the very name that was now the sweetest music to his soul. He had received preliminary orders from the Lord through Ananias in Damascus, but it was meet that he should receive his definite commission in the very place where he had accepted his former orders of so contrary a sort. Then he had been given command to kill and to destroy; now the ministry of life and peace was being committed to him.

Damascus and Arabia lay behind him, and Paul no doubt was conscious of the urge to enter upon some definite line of work in the gospel. With this burden on his heart he went to prayer in the Temple, and as he thus sought the Lord for definite leading, he was lifted out of himself that the impressions which the Holy Spirit would make on his heart might be the deeper and clearer. For indeed the demand which the Lord was about to make was so contrary to all that was in the mind of the apostle, that it was necessary to use extreme measures in order to bring the message home. So it is with ourselves. We become so set in our own plans and programs that the Lord cannot turn us to His will in the ordinary course of leading. Then He stirs up our nest, or smashes our plans, or brings us into the wilderness, or in some way jolts us out of our sufficiency and assurance, and in the ecstasy of wonder and grief and soreness He makes known His mind. The Lord uses that sort of ecstasy more than the kind that Paul knew in the Temple or Peter on the housetop, but the purpose is the same.

Then came the revelation: "Make haste, and get thee quickly out of Jerusalem: for they will not receive thy testimony concerning me" (Acts 22:18). Just as Paul was contemplating a long, fruitful ministry in this place where he had played a leading role in the persecution of the saints, the command was given to leave. It was an urgent command, too. See how the idea of haste is repeated: "Make haste . . . get out quickly!" The reason for the haste is given: where Paul thought his testimony would be of greatest value, the Lord declared it would be futile. It might even be disastrous.

Resistance immediately leaped up in the heart of the apostle to this command of the Lord. Paul was a Jew, and no less a Jew for being a Christian. His passion for the salvation of his own people more than matched his former rage against Christ. He knew their blindness, their zeal, their bondage, and longed to share with them the light and life and liberty which he had found in Christ. In his Roman letter he expressed the yearning of his soul: "I say the truth in Christ, I lie not, my conscience also bearing me witness in the Holy Ghost, that I have great heaviness and continual sorrow in my heart. For I could wish . . . myself . . . accursed from Christ for my brethren, my kinsmen according to the flesh: who are Israelites; to whom pertaineth the adoption, and the glory, and the covenants, and the giving of the law, and the service of God, and the promises; whose are the fathers, and of whom as concerning the flesh Christ came, who is over all, God blessed for ever" (Rom 9:1-5). To see them missing what was so close to them, what in a sense was their first right, and to see the hardness and the blindness settling on them more and more, created an anguish in the soul of Paul that well-nigh overcame him. How could he leave Jerusalem to its darkness and its doom without first delivering his soul unto his own people? Could God ignore such holy fervor, such high motivation?

We may do a wrong thing with a right motive, and the right motive will never justify the wrong action. Resisting the will of God is never right, whatever the motive. Even intrinsic rightness in the action to which our high purpose prompts us cannot be urged against the will of God. Motive, then, is not the determining factor in a Christian's actions. Our first question is: What is the will of God? After that the motive is the determining factor in the quality of the action.

Paul had his argument ready to support his resistance of God's will. He was sure that his amazing conversion would command a hearing for him. Had he not been the most zealous of the opponents of Christ, an outstanding champion of the traditions of the elders? His scholarship, his prestige, his rapid advance to Sanhedral rank had all made his name a byword. Jerusalem could not but listen to him.

For once Paul failed to read the Jewish mind, for his thinking was colored by the complete change in himself. Little did he think that the reaction of the Jerusalem Jews would be the opposite of what he pictured. His former high position among them, so far from influencing these fanatics toward Christ, inflamed their rage and hatred all the more.

We make the same mistake in our thinking today. We reckon that the conversion of a few prominent Catholics, for instance, would open the way for a great exodus from that church. Not at all! There is enough fanaticism in Romanism to make the wrath proportionate to the position of the one converted. One of the most successful personal workers in the circle of my acquaintance, a converted Romanist, told me that when she has to speak to a Catholic, she does not tell him that she was once of that faith, for instead of helping, it hinders. The reaction always is "You were not a good Catholic." The converted Catholic is regarded as a traitor, and his testimony is distrusted accordingly. This is emphatically so in Quebec, where the race question enters, so that a French Catholic who becomes an evangelical believer is branded as a double traitor—to his church and to the French race. Paul, in the first flush of his love for Christ, failed to see that just because he had so recently been so prominently one of them, the Jews would be doubly prejudiced against his witness. He was only learning now, while making his defense years later, that Jerusalem had never forgiven him.

It is so foolish to resist the will of God. For one thing, the will of God will not change by our resistance. Sometimes parents retract on pressure from their children. The children soon learn then who is boss, and the will of the parent, having been demonstrated to be a changeable quantity, is disregarded. I do not suggest that parents should be stubborn when circumstances indicate that a certain command or prohibition was wrong, but a child should know that mother and father mean what they say. Too often a parent's "no" is but the prelude to an "all right," and a "do this" signifies "run off and do as you please." How can children learn to obey God when parental authority is so uncertain?

The will of God is resolute. Note the Lord's answer, to Paul's demur, "Depart: for I will send thee far hence unto the Gentiles" (Acts 22:21). I think that "depart" is too soft. "Begone!" would indicate the sharpness of the command. I believe it was the Duke of Wellington (the "Iron Duke" he was called) who said curtly to a subordinate officer who tried to argue with him, "I am not asking for an opinion, I am giving an order." That is just what God said to Paul that day, and how we need that answer! God is not asking for our opinion; He is demanding our obedience.

How often sinners answer God's demands with an "I think." One says, "I think that if a fellow lives a good life and does nobody any harm, he will get into heaven all right." Another says, "I don't think a merciful God would throw any poor sinner into hell." Beloved, God is not asking our opinion on His justice or His mercy or His way of salvation. He is issuing an order, "Repent . . . and believe the gospel" (Mark 1:15). The will of God is sovereign, so it will be the part of wisdom to accept His terms and obey His demands.

The will of God is always better, aye, best. It is "good, and acceptable, and perfect" (Rom 12:2). Of course we can see how much better was the will of God for Paul than his own plans to stay in Jeru-

salem. His apostolic work probably would have ended before it began. Those wide-ranging triumphs of the gospel would not have been
his. He would not have been the champion of Gentile freedom, nor
the father of the Galatian, Asian, Macedonian, and Achaian churches,
nor the inspired writer of these great letters to the Corinthians, the
Galatians, the Romans, the Ephesians, the Thessalonians, the Philippians, and the Colossians. And if he had escaped Stephen's fate, I am
sure he would have had a hard time with Peter and James. They
would not have understood each other. God knows best, and we court
sorrow and disaster when we resist His will.

Paul soon abandoned his resistance, and learned that, while the
way of the Lord is not always easy, yet its rewards are great beyond
measure. For one thing, what he gave up in favor of the will of God
was given again to him, for his ardent desire to testify in Jerusalem
was granted—not in such circumstances as he would have chosen, but
in conditions which would burn his message unforgettably into the
minds of the Jews. They never could forget that eager little man
preaching from the castle steps, delivering his soul of his great message.

Then Paul was rewarded with the opportunity of proclaiming
Christ in the imperial center, Rome. The encouragement that God
gave him as he lay in prison in Jerusalem was: "Be of good cheer,
Paul: for as thou hast testified of me in Jerusalem, so must thou bear
witness also at Rome" (Acts 23:11). And so he did, receiving all that
came to him in his own hired house over a period of two years,
"preaching the kingdom of God, and teaching those things which concern the Lord Jesus Christ, with all confidence, no man forbidding"
(28:31). And during all that time it was he, not Caesar, who was
fashioning the course of the world's history.

My brethren, we shall do a far bigger job by receiving dictation
from our Lord than by the fulfillment of our own biggest ambitions
and dreams. "The world passeth away, and the lust thereof: but he
that doeth the will of God abideth for ever" (1 John 2:17).

> Thou, sweet beloved Will of God,
> My anchor ground, my fortress hill,
> The Spirit's silent fair abode,
> In Thee I hide me and am still.

O Will, that willest good alone,
Lead Thou the way, Thou guidest best;
A silent child, I follow on,
And trusting, lean upon Thy Breast.

36

THE ANSWER OF THREE JUDGES

ACTS 24:25; 26:24, 28

In this chapter we look at:

1. Felix and his answer of procrastination
2. Festus and his answer of ignorance
3. Agrippa and his answer of scorn

ACTUALLY it was not Paul that was on trial, but his judges. For no man is ever a hearer of the message of God without thereby being brought to trial. Felix, Festus, and Agrippa may think they are determining what shall be done with the servant of the Lord, but they are rather determining what shall be done with themselves.

It is no light thing for you to attend the Lord's house on the Lord's Day and listen to discourses from the Word of God. You may imagine that the matter is ended when you have passed judgment on the preacher and the sermon. You are mistaken. Your opinion of the sermon is a very insignificant matter. What is of real concern is that you are answerable to God for what you hear, and your answer, the answer of your heart and life, constitutes your judgment and determines your eternal future. May the Lord save you from giving the answer of these three men!

"And as . . . [Paul] reasoned of righteousness, temperance, and judgment to come, Felix trembled" (Acts 24:25a). Right good cause he had to tremble; for not only was his life a cesspool of iniquity and intemperance, but he had a man before him as fearless as Elijah before Ahab and John the Baptist before Herod, to tell him of his sins and warn him of the judgment to come. That Paul was a prisoner, and that he was addressing the one whose word could release him, weighed nothing with the faithful apostle. He had no concern for himself, but great concern for the souls of his judge and his judge's Jewish wife, Drusilla.

This was an "off the record" interview. The official hearing had been given, and Felix had been deeply stirred, so that he determined to hold a special audience at which his wife could be present with him, to inquire "concerning the faith in Christ Jesus" (Acts 24:24, ASV). Here, then, was definite interest, which must have aroused Paul's hopes for real conversion. But religious interest is one thing, conviction of sin is another. Many a one has an interest in the Christian religion who does not know himself a lost sinner. Many there are who should like to be known as Christians, but who are not prepared to give up their sin.

John Bunyan, in his classic work, *Pilgrim's Progress,* pictures for us the departure of Christian from the City of Destruction. Prominently featured in the portrait is the burden on his back, representing the load of sin which weighs heavily upon him, and to be rid of which he is willing to endure all the hardships of the pilgrim journey a thousand times over. Two neighbors, Obstinate and Pliable, pursue the departing pilgrim with intent to dissuade him from his purpose; but one of the two, Pliable, finds Christian's description of the heavenly country so pleasing that he resolves to accompany him. So on the return of Obstinate, the two set out together. There is, however, a notable difference between the two. Pliable has no burden, no sense of sin weighing him down. His interest in religion springs from no realization of need. We are not surprised, then, that he acts so true to his name when the two of them encounter their first obstacle, the Slough of Despond, while Christian presses on to the place of deliverance, Calvary.

Our Lord always went straight to the heart of the sin question. As soon as the Samaritan woman expressed her desire for the living water, He brought her face to face with her sin. Likewise, when Paul perceived Felix's interest in the Christian faith, he set out to bring the man's sin to light. He showed what the Lord required of men, and the judgment reserved for those who failed in those requirements. In a word, Paul gave Felix a good dose of the Law in preparation for the gospel. "The law was our pedagogue to bring us to Christ" (Gal

3:24), wrote Paul, with special reference to Israel, but with perfect application to every one of us. I well remember how the thunders of the Law roared in my young heart, and its sharp lightnings flashed around me, and I ran for refuge to the Saviour. I knew that God demanded what I had not given, and shook before the judgment to come, until I saw my sin and judgment transferred to One upon the cross. Then I learned to sing:

> Now my heart condemns me not,
> Pure before the law I stand;
> He who cleansed me from all spot
> Satisfied its last demand.

"Felix trembled." I know what that means, for so did I, although I did not have the long, loathesome category of iniquity to tremble over that Felix had. In that hour of revelation, when the Holy Spirit gave him a foretaste of hell, the very throne on which he sat must have shaken under him. There is no more terrible thing on earth than an awakened conscience. An old writer gives us this:

> O conscience! who can stand against thy power!
> Endure thy gripes and agonies one hour!
> Stone, gout, strappado, rocks, whatever is
> Dreadful to sense are only toys to this:
> No pleasures, riches, honors, friends can tell
> How to give ease to thee, thou'rt like to hell!

But even an awakened conscience, with all its terror, is not irresistible. I have seen strong men stand trembling, their faces drawn and blanched, and great beads of cold sweat on their foreheads, just with conscience of sin, and I have seen them set their jaws and turn away. So did Felix. Felix trembled and said, "Go thy way" (Acts 24:25b). How stupid men can be! Awakened to a sense of sin and judgment, and salvation within their grasp, they will bid not only God's messenger, but the Holy Spirit Himself, go from them; till sometimes He does go, and the doomed soul goes its unconcerned way to a lost eternity!

See it in Felix. He had no thought of being finally lost He purposed someday to get right with God. "When I have a convenient time, I shall call for you" (Acts 24:25c, author's trans.), he said to

Paul, and to the Holy Spirit of God in Paul. Perhaps he thought that
another time he could "get religion" without such dreadful stirrings
of conscience. But the Holy Spirit of God will not be mocked. He
does not come and go at the whim of the sinner. When He comes with
a stirring of conscience, He comes with the imperious demand that we
act now; and if we presume to say, "Not now, but another time," He
gives no promise that our other time will ever come. There is a
sovereignty and a finality about the Holy Spirit that ought to make
sinners fear to resist Him. And besides all that, spiritual laws make
every resistance more nearly fatal, till it is altogether too late.

When Felix turned from his big opportunity, and shook off the
terrors of his awakened conscience, his old sins began reasserting
themselves. He was a covetous soul, and regarded every event in the
light of its promise of money. He began to see possibilities of gifts
coming in for Paul's freedom, so he communed with Paul the oftener.
No more trembling, though! He could now listen to all that Paul had
to say, unmoved, and did not know that this was the symptom of
death. When the pain and fear of freezing give place to a sweet in-
sensibility and desire to sleep, then death is near. When the discom-
forts which the hearing of the gospel used to awaken no longer appear,
a man is far along the way of death. If the gospel does not now affect
you as it used to, beware! Shake your dull soul, and flee for your very
life to the Saviour before the last vestige of feeling goes and you become incapable of repentance, bereft of the Spirit!

It is difficult to imagine the man who once trembled before the
preaching of Paul becoming so calloused, so unconcerned, as to play
the political trick of leaving Paul bound, to obtain favor of the Jews,
and avert the disaster which threatened him for his misrule. But once
a man refuses the salvation which the gospel offers, his moral sense is
found to suffer eclipse, as he sinks deeper and deeper into death, "dead
in trespasses and sins" (Eph 2:1). How then can I plead with you
if the gracious Spirit of God has wrought an awakening in your soul,
that you will follow that awakening to the cross of Christ, and see the
Lamb of God bearing away your sins with the sin of the world!

We can dismiss Festus with a word. His was the answer of ignorant
rudeness. There was, to say the least, a total lack of good manners in
his loud interruption of Paul's address, and little courtesy in what he

said. Quite customarily the world's veneer of good breeding has been forgotten in its treatment of Jesus Christ and His messengers. We must not covet better treatment from the world than our Lord received; and the more like the Master we are, the more likely are we to suffer with Him. "Marvel not . . . if the world hate you" (1 John 3:13). "If the world hate you, ye know that it hated me before it hated you" (John 15:18).

Paul, then, was a partaker of Christ's revilings when Festus cried out, "Thou art mad, Paul; thy much learning has turned thee to madness!" (Acts 26:24, author's trans.). Did not our Lord's very "friends," His own brethren after the flesh, say the same of Him when they saw His zeal; while His enemies added further venom to their judgment, "Said we not well that Thou hast a devil, and art mad?" (John 8:48, author's trans.).

Now Festus condemned himself, and showed exactly where he stood in relation to God when he laid the things Paul was saying to madness. For what saith the Scriptures? "The word of the cross is to them that are perishing foolishness; but unto us who are [being] saved it is the power of God" (1 Cor 1:18, ASV margin). Festus, then, was a perishing soul to whom the word of the cross was foolishness. Even so, if you are saying in your heart, "This Christianity is a lot of nonsense!"—by that you are branding yourself as a perishing soul. Nay, it is the sinner who is mad, for he is running in the ways of death and forsaking his own mercy.

We shall leave Festus to his rudeness, for I want to have a word with you about Agrippa and his answer to the gospel. Right here we strike an example of the Greek New Testament spoiling many a good sermon. For many a good, solemn, and faithful sermon has been preached on the words, "Almost thou persuadest me to be a Christian" (Acts 26:28)). They have been messages of truth, too, much needed truth, truth that cannot be too much emphasized; only they have been hung on the wrong peg. The divines who gave us the King James Version over three hundred years ago did a great piece of work, but they did not quite catch Agrippa's meaning here. The Greek will hardly bear their translation, so while I think our evangelistic preachers are quite justified in their sermons on "Almost Persuaded," I am more than almost persuaded that in Bible exposition we must get back to the original sense of the passage. It is rather significant that in his great appeal hymn, "Almost Persuaded," P. P. Bliss harks back to Felix, not to Agrippa, and in that he is accurate.

"Almost persuaded" now to believe;
"Almost persuaded" Christ to receive;
Seems now some soul to say,
"Go, Spirit, go Thy way;
Some more convenient day
On Thee I'll call."

Agrippa did not say that he was nearly convinced, but scornfully told Paul that he was not as easily persuaded as the apostle seemed to think. Admittedly it is a difficult phrase to translate accurately, but if we put ourselves into the situation we shall gather the spirit of Agrippa's statement.

Paul has just negatived the loud interruption of Festus; then, seeing that he is getting nowhere with the Roman, he addresses himself to Agrippa, part Jew by birth and all Jew by tradition. He appeals, then, to the Jew. "King Agrippa, believest thou the prophets?" (Acts 26:27a). Then, with consummate courtesy, "I know that thou believest" (26:27b). Agrippa saw whereto Paul was leading him—to a confession of Jesus as the Christ, which would mean taking his part with the despised Christians; which would mean also forsaking his sin, including the incestuous woman who sat by him. I have no doubt that, so far as argument goes, he *was* almost persuaded. But when he recalled the price of being a Christian, the price in forsaking sin, the price in renouncing this world, the price in sacrifice and scorn and humility and ostracism, he recoiled, hated himself momentarily for allowing this prisoner-preacher to affect him so, and covered his confusion with bitter, biting words of sarcasm: "With little (argument) thou goest about to persuade me to become a Christian? You will find that it takes more than a little to land *me*."

It is noticeable that so long as Paul expounded, Agrippa listened, courteous and interested, but as soon as the apostle made the home thrust, and attempted personal application, he bristled and spat out his venom. There are many Agrippas today, quite interested in Bible exposition and gospel preaching, but ready to snap back as soon as Nathan says, "Thou art the man" (2 Sam 12:7), or a Paul inquires, "Believest thou?" I have had more than one man say to me, "You are becoming rather personal, aren't you?" Our trouble is that we are not more personal with this most personal thing in the world. The gospel is not for mass consumption, but for personal acceptance. The most universal things are, after all, the most personal. What is more universal than love? Yet love making is tremendously personal, is it not? Bayart Taylor has this in one of his poems:

> Each one thought a different name,
> But all sang "Annie Laurie."

Now God says "whosoever" instead of "Annie Laurie," and each one is asked to supply the individual name, his own name.

Listen to Paul's gracious answer to Agrippa's scorn: "Whether by little or by much (argument), I would to God that not only you, but all here, were even as I am, except for this chain" (Acts 26:29, author's trans.). As much as to say, "Agrippa, I would be willing to stand here and reason with you till doomsday if by that you would give your consent to Christ and know the glorious spiritual liberty that I enjoy in Him." But Agrippa would have none of it, and turned back to his sin and his damnation.

Some of you have had much reasoning, much persuasion, and you are not yet saved. I beseech you, go not the way of Felix, the way of procrastination; go not the way of Festus, the way of ignorance; go not the way of Agrippa, the way of the scorner. Give you the answer of consent to the Lord Jesus, and pass this day from death into life, from darkness into light, from bondage into freedom. May the Lord give you grace so to do!

37

THE ESSENCE OF APOSTOLIC
TESTIMONY

Acts 26:22-23

In this chapter we are reminded:

1. That apostolic testimony rests on the Scriptures
2. That apostolic testimony centers in Christ

WHAT A BOASTER is this man Paul! If he is not boasting about the mercy of God to such a sinner, then he is boasting of the grace bestowed upon some group of saints of whom he is especially proud; or he is boasting about what many would mention only in apologetic whispers, the cross of Christ; or he is boasting about the help he has obtained from God.

This last is the theme of his boast before Agrippa and Festus. He has just been describing the tight place in which he found himself in Jerusalem, when it looked as if the days of his witnessing were over. "But," he boasts, "here I stand, still witnessing: and you, Agrippa and Festus, must recognize that I never could have escaped the clutches of the Jews apart from divine intervention. The chief captain and his soldiers were but God's implement of help. They had no special love for me nor purpose to help me, but I had an ally in God Himself, and He afforded me the sort of help that comes from Him only. Till here I am, large as life despite this chain, carrying on my witnessing for Him, and privileged to do so before you big fellows as well as to the small fry around you. You must surely see that God is in all this business, and that ought to make you pay the more attention to my message."

Now I have not offered this as a literal translation of what Paul said that day, but I declare that I have not exaggerated the sense of it by a hair's breadth. It is all there, if we are not too prosaic to catch the overtones and the undertones of his remarkable words. They tell us that that is what frequency modulation is doing for us in the sphere of radio. If you could hear a piece played from an old record on an old-time gramophone, and then hear the same piece brought in on the FM, I am sure you would discern a marked difference in richness and fullness of tone! So we want to get the full tone of our great Bible passages, not the bare words, and I like to catch the overtone of boasting and the undertone of humility in this statement of the apostle. As it is written, "He that glorieth, let him glory in the Lord" (1 Cor 1:31).

But it is the substance of the testimony we are chiefly concerned with; and first we notice that apostolic testimony rests on the Scriptures. I testify "to small and great," declares Paul, "saying nothing beyond those things which the prophets and Moses spoke" (Acts 26:22, author's trans.). Here, then, is a rule for all who desire to be in the apostolic succession. I know some who claim to be in the apostolic succession and yet pay no attention to this so apostolic regulation. The Roman church, for instance, claims the apostolic prerogative, but refuses the apostolic rule, not only going beyond Scripture in its dogmas and practices, but giving tradition and papal bulls and the canons of councils precedence over the very Word of God. Many fanatical sects are guilty of like transgression, while modernism does not profess to be guided by the Holy Scriptures, but rather by modern developments in philosophical thought.

Not all orthodox preaching is Bible preaching. Dr. Day, in his biography of D. L. Moody, traces the development of the man and his preaching. This great evangelist had to learn what Bible preaching was, and then he had to learn how to do it. He learned the hard way, too. Henry Moorehouse saw the defect in Moody's preaching in England in 1867, and followed him to America to tell him bluntly, "You're on the wrong track," and then to demonstrate what he meant in the notable meetings which he conducted in the Moody Church. The pill was hard for Moody to swallow, but he swallowed it, and disciplined himself to Bible study and Bible preaching until he be-

came a model for others to copy. Apostolic preaching is not taking a
text and preaching from it, but it is sticking to the Bible. "To the law
and to the testimony: if they speak not according to this word, it is
because there is no light in them" (Isa 8:20). "The prophet that hath
a dream, let him tell a dream; and he that hath my word, let him speak
my word faithfully. What is the chaff to the wheat? saith the LORD"
(Jer 23:28).

Now we strike a difficulty. A soldier in an A.S.T.P. unit came to me
one day with this problem. Paul says in this place that he had been
preaching nothing beyond what Moses and the prophets declared, but
in the epistles he tells us of certain mysteries which he received by
revelation, and which were not known in former generations. The
soldier thought that this revelation must have been made to Paul between the time he addressed Agrippa and the time that he made
known the mysteries, so that there was a change in Paul's preaching.
I do not think my friend knew that there is a whole school of interpretation based on this problem. It is not my purpose to discuss that
school, but to draw attention to the fact that Paul began speaking
about "mysteries" before he addressed Agrippa. The epistle to the
Romans was written before this time, and contains this remarkable
ascription: "Now to him that is of power to stablish you according to
my gospel, and the preaching of Jesus Christ, according to the revelation of the mystery, which was kept secret since the world began, but
now is made manifest, and by the scriptures of the prophets, according
to the commandment of the everlasting God, made known to all nations for the obedience of faith: to God only wise, be glory through
Jesus Christ for ever. Amen" (Rom 16:25-27).

Here we have the gospel which Paul calls "my gospel," and here is
the mystery "kept secret since the world began, but now is made
manifest." That is what Paul has been preaching, yet he says to
Agrippa, "I have testified nothing beyond what Moses and the
prophets spoke." All of which means that for all the secrecy and all
the hiddenness of Paul's gospel, the mystery included, it was all implicit in the Old Testament all the time. So in our Roman passage Paul is quite bold to affirm that the mystery is made known to all
nations "by the Scriptures of the prophets." The Old Testament had
carried the whole secret of the New Testament in its bosom, and none

knew it, not even the prophets themselves, till He of whom it spake came and died and rose and ascended and sent forth the Spirit and the jewel fell out. It fell into the hands of God's specially trained expert, Paul, who held it up to the admiring view of all who have eyes to see. The Puritan divine was right when he said, "The New is in the Old enfolded, the Old is in the New unfolded." We might say it without the jingle: "The New Testament is implicit in the Old, the Old is explicit in the New.

The second outstanding feature of the apostolic testimony is that it centers entirely in the Lord Jesus Christ. Some preachers, I know, would consider themselves terribly hampered if they confined themselves to Jesus Christ as their sole topic. They must needs make wide excursions into other realms to make up sermons for fifty-two Sundays per year minus vacation Sundays. As for me, I confess I can never get enough of preaching Christ. He is so inexhaustible, and the amount of material not yet preached seems to grow rather than diminish. "In the volume of the book it is written of me" (Heb 10:7) , He declares. In half of a century I have only shaken off the first ripe figs of observation, and even at that have not preached through the whole volume. In heaven our conversation and our songs will all center on the Lamb in the midst of the throne. If you cannot stand much of Jesus now, I do not know how you will ever get along up there!

The substance of Paul's witness is presented in the form of a proposition for discussion: "whether the Christ were liable to suffering, and whether, as the first of the resurrection of the dead, he would announce light to the people and to the nations" (Acts 26:23, author's trans.) . It was Paul's intention to proceed now to demonstrate from the Old Testament Scriptures that these things were so. That is why he appealed to Agrippa's faith in the prophets. The astute ruler saw whereto Paul's question was leading, and was sure enough that he would have no answer to the apostle's trenchant reasoning. He was unwilling to be treed, so refused to listen to Paul's discussion of the proposition. However, if the proposition had to go undemonstrated that day, it serves excellently to indicate the foci of the apostolic witness: Christ crucified, and Christ risen.

'Whether the Christ were liable to suffer" was a question much debated by the Jews, and generally admitted by them. In the course of his dialogue with Justin Martyr, Trypho the Jew makes the admission, but is offended by the cross. "Whether Christ should be so shamefully crucified, this we are in doubt about. For whosoever is crucified is said in the law to be accursed, so I am exceedingly incredulous on this point. It is quite clear, indeed, that the Scriptures announce that Christ had to suffer; but we wish to learn if you can prove it to us whether it was by the suffering cursed in the law." Again he said to Justin, "Bring us on, then, by the Scriptures, that we may also be persuaded by you; for we know that He should suffer and be led as a sheep. But prove to us whether He must be crucified and die so disgracefully and so dishonorably by the death cursed in the law. For we cannot bring ourselves to think of this."

Truly did Paul say that the cross was to the Jews a stumbling block! I should have liked to hear the apostle answer Trypho. I think he would have done better than Justin Martyr. The cursed cross was Paul's chiefest boast. "Christ hath redeemed us from the curse of the law, being made a curse for us: as it is written, Cursed is every one that hangeth on a tree" (Gal 3:13). It was not enough that the Christ should suffer. Before He could be a Redeemer, He must endure the suffering which the Law designated as a curse; He must become obedient not only unto death, but to the death of the cross. "As Moses lifted up the serpent in the wilderness, even so must the Son of man be lifted up," if the rest were to be true, "that whosoever believeth in him should not perish, but have eternal life" (John 3:14-15).

Yes, beloved, the Christ was liable to suffer. He was bound over to it before the world was. He is "the Lamb slain from the foundation of the world" (Rev 13:8*b*). And just because He hung on the tree of death, He bids us come and partake of the tree of life. The tree of death has become the tree of life.

But if His cross were the end, it would be the end indeed. All that we declare about the meaning and purpose of the death of Christ would be mockery if He still lay in the sealed tomb. "If Christ be not raised, your faith is vain; ye are yet in your sins. Then they also which are fallen asleep in Christ are perished . . . we are of all men most miserable" (1 Cor 15:17-19). We require the other focus of the apostolic witness, and blessed be God, it is as true as the first, even as it demonstrates and seals the truth of the first. "Now is Christ risen from the dead, and become the firstfruits of them that slept" (15:20).

Paul wanted to demonstrate from Scripture to Agrippa that it was as the first to be raised that Christ was to bring light. When he would remind the Corinthians of the essential facts of the gospel, he defined it thus: "That Christ died for our sins according to the scriptures; and that he was buried, and that he rose again the third day according to the scriptures" (1 Cor 15:3-4). That He was to rise is a good part of the argument that He did rise, though by no means all of it: and that He arose "according to the scriptures" points Him out as the One "of whom Moses in the law, and the prophets, did write" (John 1:45), even the Lord's Anointed, the Christ: His rising, too, gives assurance that the professed purpose of His death is true, and that indeed there is life in His name. We should love to have the full text of these apostolic arguments, from Peter's at Pentecost to Paul's before Caesar himself; but divine wisdom has withheld that we ourselves might search the Scriptures and grow thereby.

Neither can we stop now on the historical evidence for the resurrection itself. Paul gives us quite a list of eyewitnesses, even to the five hundred together, most of whom were still alive when he was writing his treatise on the resurrection to the Corinthians. In his address before Agrippa, he stresses that Christ was the first to rise from the dead. We immediately think of the Old Testament miracles of reclamation from death, and our Lord's own breaking in upon death to raise the child from her deathbed, the youth from his bier, and Lazarus from his tomb. But these all returned to death. Theirs was only a reprieve, a return for a season to the mortal state. Christ's resurrection was of a different sort: "Christ being raised from the dead dieth no more; death hath no more dominion over him" (Rom 6:9). Of this resurrection He is the firstfruits, the first begotten, the Pioneer and Captain. By this resurrection we have our birth into a living and inextinguishable hope. In this resurrection we rise to eternal victory.

Paul was a missionary, and the missionary vision was never dim before him. He needed only the slightest pretext to break away on the universal sweep of the gospel. He was, of course, a Hebrew, and he yearned for the unveiling of the darkened eyes of his own people. But he was also apostle of the Gentiles, and rejoiced in the true light which now shone for all nations. So it came to pass that he could never think of the gospel except in terms of the people and the Gentiles, and these made up the world.

Paul, and then Carey with his maps all around him, thinking Christ, thinking Christ crucified and risen, thinking Christ crucified and risen for the whole world. Here is an ancient and honorable fraternity indeed, in which every Christian might well covet life membership. I covet neither a knightship nor a commandership in the Order of the Bath, the Order of the Garter, nor any of them, but I wish my Lord and King would knight me into the holy order of Paul and Carey, sacred to the task of making Christ known in all the world.

38

CONTRARY WINDS AND CONTRARY OPINIONS

ACTS 27:1-15

In this chapter we consider three contrasts:

1. The wisdom of revelation versus the folly of opinion
2. The promise of sin versus the wages of sin
3. The way of the transgressor versus the path of the just

ONE CANNOT READ these chapters in Acts even cursorily, without sensing the dominance of Paul. In every situation he plays a superlative role. This is the more striking in view of the brief indications we have of the handicaps under which the apostle labored. Writing to the Corinthians he acknowledges the meanness of his outward appearance, as one sensitive regarding it, and refers to their remarks about him which have cut him to the quick: "his letters, say they, are weighty and powerful; but his bodily presence is weak, and his speech contemptible" (2 Cor 10:10). Despite all this, he is never long in any given situation till he is master of it, and becomes the commanding figure in every scene in which he appears. While fully recognizing the native force in this so handicapped personality, we cannot but see that the secret of all this dominance lay not in himself, but in that tremendous fact which he stated thus to the Galatians: "It is no longer I that live, but Christ liveth in me" (Gal 2:20, ASV). Nothing will so fortify and enrich one's personal presence and overcome defects of personality as this—Christ in you!

The incident now before us is an emphatic example of this truth. Paul is aboard ship, not only with these deficiencies of appearance that made one writer dub him "an ugly little Jew," but he is there as a prisoner, a further reason for being kept out of sight. Yet he becomes the one person of value among all the 276 souls aboard. He fills the canvas of the picture, while the others serve simply as lines of focus on the apostle. When he first steps to the foreground, he is snubbed, but soon his supremacy is recognized by all.

"Sirs, I perceive that this voyage will be with hurt and much damage, not only of the lading and ship, but also of our lives" (Acts 27:10). The apostle Paul does not here lay claim to special revelation; but as a man in tune with God, he knew what it was to have his powers of perception quickened by the Holy Spirit. It is true that he had more experience of the sea than the average Jew cared to have (for they were not a nation of sea lovers), and his former tastes of shipwreck would give him caution, but he could not claim acquaintance with navigational problems equaling that of the veterans of the sea who handled the ship. Nevertheless, he had a keenness of perception far beyond what his knowledge of the sea would warrant, because God the Holy Spirit was his Teacher and Guide.

The man who lives in "the secret of the Lord" has always the "jump" on the one who has to depend on natural skills alone. The psalmist realized this advantage. Listen to his godly boast: "Thou through thy commandments hast made me wiser than mine enemies: for they are ever with me. I have more understanding than all my teachers: for thy testimonies are my meditation. I understand more than the ancients, because I keep thy precepts" (Psalm 119:98-100). George Washington Carver in science and R. G. LeTourneau in business can testify of the Lord's help, enabling them to perceive things as if by intuition in answer to prayer. In an address in New York, the great colored scientist said: "God is going to reveal things to us that He never revealed before if we put our hand in His. No books ever go into my laboratory. The thing that I am to do and the way of doing it come to me. I never have to grope for methods; the method is revealed to me at the moment I am inspired to create something new. Without God to draw aside the curtain I would be helpless."

LeTourneau relates an experience in the days when his business was small. An important product was in the shop calling for completion the following day, but it lacked a vital part, the power control unit, which had not yet been designed. As he sat down at his board that evening, Le Tourneau remembered that he had committed himself to accompany a gospel team to a mission. His first thought was to excuse himself and attend to this urgent matter of business. The "still, small voice," however, reminded him of his promise and the priority of the Lord's business. He went to the mission meeting. Returning home he felt weary in mind, and became rather anxious at the prospect of tackling this piece of work with energy at low tide. Nevertheless, he went to his drafting board, and looked to the Lord for help. In ten minutes the design flashed into his mind as if it had been the finished article. The product was completed the next day, with a power control unit which later put similar machines produced by much bigger competitors out of the running. The man in touch with God has superior discernment.* We, too, can expect such help from God in our own spheres if we are walking with Him in the path of His will. I know a professor of Greek who keeps telling his students that the Holy Spirit will help them to learn this difficult language if they are doing it for the glory of Christ, and I know he is right.

The manner in which Paul came to a realization of the coming storm does not qualify the fact that his words constituted a warning from God, and it was incumbent on the centurion and the others to pay heed. There were, however, contrary counsels. There was the opinion of the experts, "the master and the owner of the ship" (Acts 27:11), who doubtless had seen many a season at sea. The popular opinion, too, was for going on, "because the haven was not commodious to winter in" (27:12). The experts said, Let's take the risk. The crowd said, Let's not be tied to this drab place for the winter. So the warning of God went unheeded, and the experts and the crowd won out. Or did they?

The situation here described surely has its counterpart in the attitude of men to the gospel. The gospel carries with it a note of solemn warning, seeking to convince men of the inevitable ruin at the end of their present course of sin. It cries out, "Turn ye, turn ye . . . for why will ye die?" (Ezek 33:11). It says: "Except ye repent, ye shall all likewise perish" (Luke 13:3). It adds to its offer of mercy and pardon and

*This incident is related by Albert W. Lorimer, *God Runs My Business* (New York: Revell, 1941).

life this grave admonition, "How shall we escape, if we neglect so great salvation?" (Heb 2:3). The gospel reveals, in addition, the place of refuge for sinners. It points to the Lord Jesus as the fair havens of the soul, where it is safe from the winter storms of judgment, bidding us come to Him and abide in Him.

But experts say, We know better. They will not have the Bible as the Word of God, nor Jesus as the Son of God, nor Calvary as the great atonement for sin, nor regeneration as the miracle of God in the soul. They will follow the way of human progress to the utopia of their dreams. Meanwhile the crowd resents the offense of the cross. They visualize a cramping of their social style in the incommodious fair havens of Christ, a diminishing of their round of pleasures, and a check on their selfish ambitions. It is not the popular thing to "go . . . unto him without the camp, bearing his reproach" (Heb 13:13).

Here was the poor centurion, then, caught in the contrary tides. The voice of God in the apostle said one thing; the expert voice and the popular voice said another. It was two to one, and he counted the voices instead of weighing them. That was a sorry day for the Roman officer, who bore the responsibility of the choice. There may be one reading this who is exactly where the centurion was that day. The voice of God rings in your soul, calling you by the gospel to receive Christ Jesus the Lord for your Saviour, warning you of the danger of delay and the doom at the end of your present way; but other voices call—the voice of doubt, the voice of pleasure, the voice of ambition. It seems like two to one, three to one, maybe ten to one against the gospel, but test the voices rather than count them. Perceive their shallow ring compared with the firm, sincere tone of the gospel message: and think, "What shall it profit a man, if he should gain the whole world, and lose his own soul?" (Mark 8:36).

The prosperity of the wicked is brief. So say the next two verses. "And when the south wind blew softly, supposing that they had obtained their purpose, loosing thence, they sailed close by Crete. But not long after there arose against it a tempestuous wind, called Euroclydon" (Acts 27:14).

That soft south wind is the devil's lure to draw on his victims until they are properly on the way of sin. The way of the transgressor is hard, but not at first. The sowing of the wild oats seems all to the soft accompaniment of the south wind. It is the reaping that comes with tempest and confusion and darkness. At first there is only the merriment, the dalliance, the voluptuousness, but at the end is the strappado, the sting, the payoff. Not only of strong drink, but of all sin, must it be said that "at the last it biteth like a serpent, and stingeth like an adder" (Prov 23:32) .

He won in a raffle; the gambling craze fastened upon him; debts increased; he gambled still more desperately; broken and ruined, he avenged himself, and walked to the gallows. He got a break, and made easy money; he took bigger chances, threw honesty to the wind, and went to penitentiary for embezzlement.

Beware of that soft south wind that promises prosperity in the way of sin. Somewhere along the line the Euroclydon waits to burst upon you with merciless fury and irreparable loss. "Be not deceived; God is not mocked: for whatsoever a man soweth, that shall he also reap" (Gal 6:7) .

There are five verbs in this chapter marking the stages of the story, and which aptly describe the youth who turns away from God. In verse 13 the ship is *loosed* from its moorings. In verse 15 the ship is *caught* in the tempest. In verse 17 the ship is *driven* by the wind. In verse 18 the ship is *lightened* of its cargo. In verse 41 the ship is *broken* on the rocks.

How many a youth has broken loose from the restraining influences of the gospel in home and church, thinking that freedom lay in going with the crowd in the way of pleasure, only to be caught in the whirl of excitement, driven by the storm of passion, lightened of former virtues, and at last broken on the rocks of everlasting destruction! Once the moorings are loosed, it is not so easy to recover. A schoolmate of mine used to answer my very frank warnings with a confident, "I won't go too far. I know where to stop." Only a fatal crash in France near the end of the First World War stopped his patronage of the Parisian houses of ill fame. A Christian who had been given deliverance from the tobacco habit was asked his opinion on the best way to stop smoking. His reply was: "The best way to stop smoking is never to begin." In the way of sin, the best place to stop is before you start. That act of loosing from God is a hard step to retrace. Then do not take it; but while the restraints of Christian influence are still upon you, make sure of your anchor ground. Tie up to God, definitely and forever, through faith in His beloved Son and in consecration to His will.

Sometimes the wicked seem to have the soft south wind for a long time, and the hard-pressed people of God are at times apt to look on them with a degree of envy. The other day a friend sent me a letter which had been written by a man in a sanitarium. He is thoroughly discouraged, by reason of this very thing. Here is what he says: "As for me, well there is nothing new, except I am losing faith in prayer. I have prayed for three years. I am still here. I can't find my way through. All those supposed to be heathens here get well in no time. They don't believe in Christ. I do. But what does it get me? I don't think it is fair. Do you?"

Now our friend is in good company. The psalmist Asaph found himself in perplexity over the prosperity of the wicked, and nearly became an apostate over it, till he saw the full picture in the light of eternity. See how Psalm 73 is just an enlargement of the words of the letter I have quoted (vv. 1-14). Then see the answer of the sinner's end (vv. 16-20). The rest of the psalm indicates the saint's rest in the faithfulness of God, the grace given for present trial, the satisfaction in God that outweighs the afflictions, and the bright beams of everlastingness which constitute the glorious prospect of the child of God.

Psalm 37 is to the same effect. Here it is David who warns against an attitude of envy toward the prosperous sinner, and exhorts to trust in the Lord, assured of a perfect adjustment in due season. There is a difference between the end of the wicked and the end of the upright; and it is the end that counts. But even so, for all the seeming ease of the wicked and trials of the just, "the way of transgressors is [still] hard" (Prov 13:15), while "the path of the just is as the shining light, that shineth more and more unto the perfect day" (4:18). I do not know when I pitied people more than an elderly couple, relatives of my mother-in-law, who had lived all their days in plenty, always putting on a brave front, but always in such mortal terror of death that it was a point of understanding among their friends not to speak of death in their presence. On the other hand, how many a tried saint have I seen rejoicing with "joy unspeakable and full of glory" (1 Pet 1:8), in face of the manifold temptations that were only preparing them for the "praise and honour and glory at the appearing of Jesus Christ" (1:7*b*).

The soft south wind of the sinner only lures him to his destruction, but the Euroclydon of the child of God reveals the faithfulness and power and deliverance of the heavenly Father.

> He knows! My heavenly Father surely knows
> The mortal limitations that oppress
> This earth-born frame; the dire distress
> Of surging griefs; the diabolic foes
> That hold the soul in grim encounter: every need
> He knows, and all my wants His mercies still exceed.
>
> He cares! I know my heavenly Father cares,
> And bids me cast on Him the pressing load
> Of dark, foreboding thought, 'Tis mine the road
> Of filial trust to tread, since He who bears,
> In hands omnipotent, the sparrow and the ages
> Makes me His care, and for my weel His might engages.
>
> He can! My Father's boundless grace can meet
> The high demands of full salvation: sure
> His succor in temptation, to endure
> His help sufficient, swift His rescuing feet.
> His promises are matched with equal powers: the score
> Of all my prayers this motto bears, "He can do more!"
>
> He will! Performance crowns the triple grace
> Of knowledge, care and power divine. What work
> Begun will be performed until the murk
> Of time dispels. Complete before His face
> I then shall stand, from pain and tribulation brought,
> While powers supernal loud acclaim, "What hath God wrought!"

39

BELIEVING GOD IN THE STORM

ACTS 27:21-37

In this chapter we see that:

1. The believing man holds the key
2. The believing man uses his head
3. The believing man cheers his fellows

OUR LADIES have no greater distress than to find that the color of some new material "runs" when it is washed. Most of our birds can boast of a plumage whose color is fast, but the poor turacou of Africa dashes from the treetops to the thickest foliage when the rains come, to preserve what it can of the "running" crimson on the secondaries of its wings. The faith of some is like the crimson of the turacou. It is fair-weather faith, much in evidence in the sunny and bright day, but miserably "washed out" in the day of affliction.

The disciples were very confident until the squall hit their boat. Then they did what the storm could not do; they awoke the Lord with their panic-inspired question, "Master, carest thou not that we perish?" (Mark 4:38). Of a different sort is the faith expressed in Psalm 46: "God is our refuge and strength, a very present help in trouble. Therefore will not we fear, though the earth be removed, and though the mountains be carried into the midst of the sea; though the waters thereof roar and be troubled, though the mountains shake with the swelling thereof" (vv. 1-3).

John Newton has expressed the all-weather faith in one of his best hymns:

> Begone, unbelief,
> My Saviour is near,

> And for my relief
> Will surely appear;
> By prayer let me wrestle,
> And He will perform;
> With Christ in the vessel,
> I smile at the storm.

Paul's was a faith which triumphed in all sorts of conditions. It was in the midst of a storm which threatened complete destruction that he stood up before all and said, "I believe God" (Acts 27:25). Fair-weather faith contrasts with robust all-weather faith. How much rough weather can your faith stand?

There is also a counterfeit faith which stands over against true faith—a faith centering in self, not in God. The kind of faith I refer to is well exemplified in one of the saddest poems I know—a poem which has become popular in religious circles, now set to music and sung by outstanding artists, but which is totally the reverse of Christian sentiment. I refer to Henley's "Invictus."

> Out of the night that covers me,
> Black as the pit from pole to pole,
> I thank whatever God may be
> For my unconquerable soul.
>
> In the fell clutch of circumstance
> I have not winced nor cried aloud;
> Under the bludgeonings of chance
> My head is bloody but unbowed.
>
> Beyond this place of wrath and tears
> Looms but the horror of the shade,
> And yet the menace of the years
> Finds and shall find me unafraid.
>
> It matters not how straight the gate,
> How charged with punishment the scroll,
> I am the Master of my fate,
> I am the Captain of my soul.

Dr. E. J. Pace has written an excellent parody on this poem as the Christian's reply, but Paul anticipated him by nineteen centuries, and gave the answer in three words, "I believe God." There is a majesty and a complete triumph in the apostle's simple statement altogether lacking in Henley's boastings—and it got him further! The faith that wins is a faith centered in God.

We ought to inquire into the nature of this belief which made Paul the master of a situation in which all others were thrown into panic and despair.

"I believe in God the Father Almighty, maker of heaven and earth." So runs the opening sentence of the Apostles' Creed, that ancient and splendid, while very brief, statement of evangelical truth. Multitudes repeat the statement every Sunday in church, but it is to be feared that to many it is only a splendid creed, a "body of divinity" to which they give intellectual assent. Paul's still briefer statement expressed not a creed, but a confidence. He believed in God in such fashion that he believed God. The recitation of the creed may signify nothing more than a belief in the existence of God, and James tells us that "the devils believe, and tremble" (James 2:19). Paul's declaration signified a complete confidence in the veracity and faithfulness of God. In the midst of all the tempest's threatenings, God had sent a message to His servant: "Fear not, Paul; thou must be brought before Caesar" (Acts 27:24a). That was enough. The apostle was satisfied that no storm that nature could produce, no opposition that hell could raise, would keep him from Rome after that word, and when the further promise was given, "God hath given thee all them that sail with thee" (27:24b), he was as sure of the safety of the whole ship's company as if he saw them already on dry land. "I believe God," he said, "that it shall be even as it was told me" (27:25). He so believed God that God's word was enough for him.

Paul's faith induced complete quietness of heart. In a recent issue of *The Christian Life* I came upon this "Gospel Thumb Tack"— "Quiet tension is not trust. It is simply compressed anxiety." Too often we think we are trusting when we are merely controlling our panic. True faith gives not only a calm exterior but a quiet heart. "Thou wilt keep him in perfect peace, whose mind is stayed on thee: because he trusteth in thee" (Isa 26:3).

Miss Amy Carmichael gives a beautiful illustration from nature of this kind of trust. The sunbird, one of the tiniest of birds, a native of India, builds a pendant nest, hanging it by four frail threads, gen-

erally from a spray of valaris. It is a delicate work of art, with its roof
and tiny porch, which a splash of water or a child's touch might destroy. Miss Carmichael tells how she saw a little sunbird building such
a nest just before the monsoon season, and felt that for once bird wisdom had failed; for how could such a delicate structure, in such an
exposed situation, weather the winds and the torrential rains? The
monsoon broke, and from her window she watched the nest swaying
with the branches in the wind. Then she perceived that the nest had
been so placed, that the leaves immediately above it formed little
gutters which carried the water away from the nest. There sat the
sunbird, with its tiny head resting on her little porch, and whenever a
drop of water fell on her long, curved beak, she sucked it in as if it
were nectar. The storms raged furiously, but the sunbird sat, quiet
and unafraid, hatching her tiny eggs.

We have a more substantial rest for head and heart than the sunbird's porch! We have the promises of God. Are they not enough?
However terrifying the storm,

> No waters can swallow the ship where lies
> The Master of ocean, and earth, and skies.

If we have Him aboard, we are safe, and if only we had as much confidence in our Almighty Lord as that little sunbird has in its frail nest,
we should certainly be experiencing "the peace of God, which passeth
all understanding" (Phil 4:7).

Believing God not only gives quietness of heart, but puts a song in
the heart and on the lips. The winter of 1944-45 was long and severe.
When we were beginning to long for spring, and instead the weather
was turning steadily colder, the morning would sometimes find me a
bit discouraged. One morning I was in just such a mood because of
the continuing cold, when all at once the clear, rousing song of the
cardinal redbird startled me, and rebuked me. I said to myself:
" 'Why art thou cast down, O my soul? And why art thou disquieted
within me?' (Psalm 42:11). If the cardinal can sing this cold morning, I ought to have a song, for the heavenly Father, who counts me of
more value than many redbirds, is caring for me."

What a difference between Paul and Jonah! Both men were sailing
the Mediterranean, both were in a storm, both were servants of God

thrown among heathen men. There the likeness ends and the contrast begins. The safety of Jonah's company depended on their getting rid of him, but Paul's presence was the security of his ship's company. What we mean to our fellows depends entirely on whether we are in the path of faith and obedience, or in the way of unbelief and willfulness. "Who is the Jonah?" Every time he is the man who is running away from the will of God. A Christian out of the will of God is bringing hurt to others; he is endangering the lives and souls of men. On the other hand, a Christian walking in obedience and trust brings blessings to those around him, although they may be ignorant of the reason. Potiphar and Pharaoh were blessed for Joseph's sake. Paul's presence secured the 276 souls which made up the ship's complement.

Dr. R. V. Bingham used to say, before he was promoted to glory, that if he were the president of a steamship line, he would make sure that he had missionaries on every ship, on every voyage, for there was no such insurance, even amid the perils of war, as having on board those servants of the Word, who were braving all dangers and hardships in the path of obedience to the will of God. The statement has been amply justified. The unbelieving world does not begin to know how much it owes to the few believing folk in its midst.

Another characteristic of true faith is remarkably exemplified in this incident. God's believing man used his head. Faith in God does not mean throwing common sense to the winds; on the contrary, faith gives direction to intelligence. The man of faith on board that doomed ship used his head far more, and to better effect, than the centurion or the captain or any of them.

First of all, when all were risking a dash from Fair Havens to Phenice, deceived by a brief spell of south wind, Paul urged caution, reminding them that it was "tempting Providence," as we would say, to strike out at that late season. His was the caution of faith; theirs the risk of unbelief. For, indeed, there is no such thing as the risk of faith. The man who does not believe God has no other recourse than to take risks; the man of faith follows certainties.

There are, indeed, times when God calls for unusual daring, but the path of faith is not the way of recklessness. The late Henry W. Frost, in his book *Effective Praying* relates an incident which taught the leaders of the China Inland Mission a deep lesson. The Toronto council had accepted three young ladies for the field, all from Iowa. It was late winter, and the council hesitated over sending the new appointees to the field at that time of year for they would arrive in China only shortly before the heat of summer. However, they decided to "put it up to God" on the basis of their passages and outfits. To this purpose the members of the mission prayed, and the answer was almost uncanny. A letter came from a young lady in an Iowa college stating that three colleges in that state—the home state of the three missionaries elect—had raised money to send three missionaries, preferably young ladies, to China; were such available? It looked like God's seal on sending them, even at this untimely season. Enthusiastically and confidently the three set out and arrived in China when spring was at its loveliest. It was not long, however, till the mistake was realized. The arrival of three new missionaries meant the keeping of the training school open during the summer, and instructors, already weary with the year's work, had to carry on when they ought to have been given rest. Moreover, the newcomers were not sufficiently acclimatized, and the oppressive heat brought them all down with severe illnesses, from the effects of which one of them never recovered. "Thus," says Mr. Frost, "the summer rest was lost both to the teachers and students, considerable physical harm was done to the young ladies, and the Mission had spent in vain a considerable sum of money." It was a costly lesson, but it taught the mission not to put out fleeces when the answer could be had by the use of common sense. Faith is venturesome indeed, but it also means caution. Our soldiers are nonetheless brave for being taught every art and device of self-preservation on the battlefield.

Paul used his head when he perceived the scheme of the ship's crew to make good their own escape from the wreck under pretense of casting anchors from the prow. He knew that they would need those men with their skill in handling the ship when the final crisis of abandoning the vessel arrived. Therefore, he appealed to the centurion to interfere with this act of desertion, and this kept the entire ship's company together.

God makes use of human skills. Faith, therefore, is not reckless of these instruments of God's help, but calls into play whatever may legitimately minister to the divine purposes. Faith is not fatalism.

The false faith of the Muslims and the Hindus is fatalism, and there is a hyper-Calvinism which tends in that direction, but the faith of the gospel is not a passive yielding to fate; instead, it is an active collaboration with the purposes of God. The faith of the farmer causes him to plow, harrow, and sow, not to desist from these. Faith is intelligent, active, cooperative. Faith uses its head.

Paul used his head a third time in this epic of faith, when he exhorted the men, weak with panic and hunger, to eat, setting a good example himself. They needed strength for the last ordeals of the shipwreck; and with divine assurances of the safety of every man aboard, he encouraged them all to this sensible act of taking nourishment. Faith does not expect God to make up for the neglect of the ordinary means of sustenance. Neglect and abuse of the body are not the work of faith, but the way of folly.

See how the man of faith lifts the morale of those around him. What a day of lifting up it was for enslaved Israel when Moses came with his message that God had heard their cries, had remembered His covenant to Abraham, and had come down to deliver them! So it was as life from the dead for those 276 men when Paul stood before them and said, "Cheer up! I believe God." And to this day, "How beautiful upon the mountains are the feet of him that bringeth good tidings . . . that saith unto Zion, Thy God reigneth!" (Isa 52:7). "Wherefore lift up the hands which hang down, and the feeble knees; and make straight paths for your feet, lest that which is lame be turned out of the way; but let it rather be healed" (Heb 12:12-13).

40

WINTER IN MALTA

ACTS 28:1-10

This passage teaches us that:

1. God's promises prevail against all threatenings
2. God's rewards are neither slow nor meager
3. God's angels bring their own recompense

THIS CHAPTER turned me to Sir William Dobbie's account of "The Miracle of Malta" in his excellent book, *A Very Present Help*. It is at least an interesting coincidence that this little island should come into prominence in the remarkable story of the beginnings of the gospel, and then again play so strategic a part in the colossal struggle of our day. Paul landed in Malta as a result of a devastating storm. Sir William landed there just before a more terrific and longer lasting storm burst upon the island. Through the presence of these two men of God, men of prayer and of trust, Malta witnessed the miraculous intervention of the Almighty.

Little could Paul know, as he went about his peaceful and happy occupations that winter, that one day a mighty soldier-saint would be there as the hero of "the most bombed spot on earth," as for two long years the "ghastly dew" of aerial bombardment rained on that fair island fortress at an average rate of three attacks per day! Over the span of nineteen centuries, and despite their different occupations and circumstances, these two men, the apostle and the soldier, are strangely linked, and especially in this, that they loosed the power of God on the same Mediterranean isle.

God had kept His promise. "God hath given thee all them that sail with thee" (Acts 27:24b), the angel had said, and neither the violence

261

of the storm, nor the attempted desertion of the sailors, nor the plotted treachery of the soldiers could damage a single hair of the head of one member of the ship's party. All 276 landed safely on Malta. You can bank on God's word, even when every circumstance would seem to give the lie to it. Timid unbelief has it this way: "God, but—!" True faith changes the order: "—but God!" A favorite chorus at the Canadian Keswick Conference has long been this:

> Faith, mighty faith, the promise sees,
>   And looks to God alone;
> Laughs at impossibilities,
>   And cries, It shall be done!

Paul found the promise true in his landing on Malta. General Dobbie found the promise true during the two years of his sojourn there as governor and defender. In the opening days of the siege Sir Edmund Ironside, chief of the imperial general staff, sent a telegram to Dobbie, referring him to Deuteronomy 3:22, which reads, "Ye shall not fear them: for the LORD your God he shall fight for you." In face of the hopelessly inadequate defenses of the island, and the vastly superior advantages which lay with the enemy, the Christian general accepted these ancient promises of God as for him, and the eminently successful defense of the island, upon which so much depended, was the answer of God's faithfulness. Whether God made the promise but yesterday, or two or four thousand years ago, matters not. His word stands forever. Malta bears its ancient and modern testimony to that blessed and cheering fact.

Yet another promise had God made to His servant Paul. The second night after his arrest in Jerusalem, "the Lord stood by him, and said, Be of good cheer, Paul: for as thou hast testified of me in Jerusalem, so must thou bear witness also at Rome" (Acts 23:11). How many times had the fulfillment of that promise seemed in jeopardy! The murderous plot of the oath-bound Jews, the delaying of Felix, the attempted compromise of Festus, the ill-fated voyage, the treachery of the ship's crew, and the soldiers' plan to kill all prisoners: these so far had been the adversary's efforts to nullify the promise of God and prevent Paul's arrival in Rome. All these having failed, a new danger, threatening God's word, appeared.

Paul, never a man to idle while others bestirred themselves, set about helping the natives in their kindly ministrations to the shipwrecked company. Gathering an armful of dried brush, he was about to throw it on the fire which had been kindled for drying and warming the shivering group, when a viper hidden in the brush, aroused from torpor by approach to the heat, fastened upon his hand. Although the verb used here does not necessarily carry the thought of actually biting, the whole context takes that for granted. I have not the slightest doubt that Paul was bitten by the poisonous creature, and that, lacking the means of immediate treatment now known to us, he would certainly have died in great pain and in a very short time, had not God wrought for him. But once again God remembered His word to His servant, and stayed the normal effects of the bite; and the servant remembered the word of his Lord, and with the same calm of faith which had marked his conduct in the pitch of the tempest, shook the beast off his hand into the fire, where it ended its venomous day. Once we have a word from the Lord, we dare not doubt it, though all the forces of nature, and all hell itself, conspire to overturn it.

> Though dark be my way,
>   Since He is my Guide,
> 'Tis mine to obey,
>   'Tis His to provide;
> Though cisterns be broken,
>   And creatures all fail,
> THE WORD HE HATH SPOKEN
> SHALL SURELY PREVAIL.

This deliverance also directed the attention of the islanders to Paul and his company, and the esteem which it won for them secured care and provision far beyond what might otherwise have been their lot. For three days they were the personal guests of the chief official of the island, Publius, while appropriate lodgings for the winter were being found for them. Besides that, the effect of the incident on the natives prepared them to listen to Paul's message with a degree of reverence and attention which benefactors would not ordinarily give to those beholden to them. We can be very sure that Paul quickly refuted the ascription of divinity, and turned it to good account in proclaiming the living and the true God, and His Son sent from heaven. So the attempt of the adversary to destroy God's word and silence His testimony failed, the steadfastness of God's promise received further demonstration, and the whole incident turned out to the furtherance of the gospel. That also is one of the ways of God.

God is no man's debtor. No one ever kindly entreats His people without recompense, for God operates on the principle, "Inasmuch as ye have done it unto one of the least of these . . . ye have done it unto me" (Matt 25:40). The widow of Zarephath shared the end of her little store with Elijah, the servant of God, and "the barrel of meal wasted not, neither did the cruse of oil fail, according to the word of the LORD" (1 Kings 17:16). The woman of Shunem offered hospitality to Elisha, and God rewarded her, first by taking away her sterility, and later by giving her back her son from the dead. The pages of history reveal a remarkable coincidence between the nations' treatment of God's people, Israel, even in their apostate condition, and the prosperity or declension of those nations. A little more attention to history, if nothing else, would have warned Nazi Germany of the end of its anti-Semitic program.

The inhabitants of Malta, then, did not go unrewarded for their kindly behavior toward Paul and his company, the household of Publius, which offered conspicuous bounty, being the first to realize the recompense. The father of Publius was suffering from an aggravated and dangerous form of dysentery. The arrival of Paul was indeed timely. Through prayer and the laying on of Paul's hands, the disease was checked and the patient immediately healed. Naturally, this brought requests from others, until Paul was conducting a ministry of healing which touched the whole island. Thus the common people, as well as the leading inhabitants, received their rich return for kindnesses shown to God's servants in the day of their need.

God is just the same today. He will never abide debtor to any man. We are constantly embarrassed by the bounty of His returns. On one occasion two itinerant missionaries called on us in Sault Sainte Marie on their way to lumber camps and other points of ministry in northern Ontario. Their stock of worldly goods was very meager, and their one suit of clothes each so worn that I did not see how they could endure the rigors of the journey. At the cost of almost all I had,

I fitted them out with new suits. They were not very stylish, costly garments, but durable, and not a bad fit! The men went on their way rejoicing. That very week, in most unexpected ways, I received back all that I had spent, in addition to the spiritual blessing which these sacrificing men of God brought to our home.

Hospitality is a grace enjoined on all the people of God. "Use hospitality one to another without grudging" (1 Pet 4:9), exhorts Peter, while Paul commands, "Distributing to the necessity of saints; given to hospitality" (Rom 12:13). John commends the like practice: "Beloved, thou doest faithfully whatsoever thou doest to the brethren, and to strangers" (3 John 5). The exhortation in the letter to the Hebrews stresses the duty and the blessing of hospitality to strangers: "Let brotherly love continue. Be not forgetful to entertain strangers: for thereby some have entertained angels unawares" (Heb 13:1-2).

Now they were not saints who received the marooned company with such kindliness, lavishing special bounties on Paul and his friends. Luke calls them "barbarians" (Acts 28:4), not, of course, in the sense which we now give to the word, but referring to the fact that they were non-Greeks, and did not speak the Greek language, but a native dialect. They were Phoenicians who had retained much of their own way of life, yielding but slowly to the infiltration of Greek culture. The fact to note for us is that here were non-Christians exhibiting a hospitality worthy of saints. I hope these ancient pagans of Malta do not outshine us, who have a long Christian heritage, in this beautiful virtue.

Then it is noteworthy that in this, as in many instances, God sent His recompense through the very ones who were the recipients of the islanders' kindness. Paul himself was their reward, in the gracious ministry which he exercised among them. I have no doubt that many of them found the Lord, in addition to the blessing of physical healing, and for many a year, as they gathered around evening fires, they would talk of that winter day when a whole ship's company landed safely from a wreck out of the worst and longest storm in the memory of their generation; and of that strange little man who shook the viper off his hand as if it were nothing more than a toad, and how he had brought to them physical and spiritual blessings far outweighing the little bounties they had bestowed on him and his friends.

Abraham and Manoah have entertained their angels unawares, but none more truly than those ignorant but bighearted Maltese, and great was the reward which these human angels of the Lord brought them.

We, too, have entertained angels, and as the years pass, we realize more and more what unspeakable enrichment has come into our lives through this intimate fellowship in the home with these beloved saints. For instance, every remembrance of Dr. E. Y. Fullerton's visit to us in Quebec City helps me to stand more erect and face my tasks with more strength of purpose. Just the thought of him is like a breath from the hills of God. Or I think of the week which that little giant spent with us in the north country—Dr. Max I. Reich, the Hebrew Christian whose passing to the Father's house has left a big vacancy here. What impetus the remembrance of him gives to my study of the Word of God! And Goforth of China! How his presence sanctified the home, and made Christ so real! These could be multiplied, and all to the same effect, that the angels of God bring their own reward with them.

I wonder is it so with you, and with me? Do we carry an aroma of Christ with us which imparts a benediction and a blessing wherever we go? Are those who kindly entreat us richly rewarded by something which we give all unconsciously? Are homes happier and holier for our presence in them? Do we leave behind us a sweet savor of Christ or the rancid atmosphere of the carnal man? O God, I cannot return in kind the many bounties which are bestowed on me, but let there be something of Christ flow from me into the lives of these my friends which will be rich and abiding recompense!

41

ROME AT LAST

ACTS 28:16-31

In this chapter we examine:

1. A preliminary conference
2. An official hearing
3. An unfinished story

JERUSALEM WAS WONT to be the great imperative of the Hebrews, as Mecca is still of the devout Muslim. Naples used to be the imperative of the traveler, but Rome fastened its imperious demand upon the great missionary-apostle. "I must...see Rome" (Acts 19:21), he had said years before. That "must" was at last realized. He was in Rome. Rome, the center, whose divers currents reached out to the perimeter of the world; Rome, the magnificent, the godless, with its luxury and its penury, its pride and its bestiality, its besotted citizenry and its menacing slavery; Rome, the mighty, enfeebled with its multiplied vices; Rome, the iron kingdom, already preparing for disintegration by reason of the admixture of clay. Into this Rome came Paul with a gospel, and a chain.

Superficially Paul came to Rome as a prisoner; essentially he came as an ambassador. He came as a citizen of Rome to submit his own case to the emperor, yet he came to herald another Kingdom before which Rome would yet bow the knee in submission.

For all his ardor as apostle to the Gentiles, and for all his privilege as a citizen of Rome, Paul was yet a Jew, and his first thought was for the host of his fellow Israelites who lived in Rome at the whim of the emperor, never certain what decree of oppression or banishment

267

might issue from the imperial throne. Therefore, when he was sufficiently settled, he called for a preliminary conference with the leaders of the Jewish colony.

When we consider all that Paul had suffered at the hands of the Jews, from Damascus and Jerusalem to Galatia, Asia, Macedonia, and Achaia; when we remember how his message had been rejected and opposed by them in every place, and how he had repeatedly turned from them to the more ready Gentiles; we can attribute his present action only to that unquenchable yearning which he had earlier expressed in his letter to the Roman believers, "I could wish . . . myself . . . accursed from Christ for my brethren, my kinsmen according to the flesh: who are Israelites" (Rom 9:3-4). I wonder was the love of God ever made perfect in another as in Paul!

Not only was his first thought and his first activity in Rome for his fellow Jews, but he took pains to assure them of his utter benevolence. It was because of their rage that he was bound with this chain, because of their determination to secure his death that he was forced to make his appeal to Caesar. Nevertheless, he urged no complaint against them, laid no accusation, harbored no rancor. He was still their friend, though they were his enemies. What a triumph of grace is here! If ever a man might have been excused from further dealings with Jews, it surely was Paul, who could besides have covered his turning away from them with his call to the Gentile apostolate. But all their stubbornness, all their foul plots, all their malicious attacks, could not destroy his "heart's desire and prayer to God for Israel . . . that they might be saved" (Rom 10:1). So he came back, again and again, to proclaim, to plead, refusing to give up. Oh that we had more of his spirit!

Paul began his ministry in Rome under a severe handicap. No, I do not refer to the fact that he was a prisoner. That is not always a hindrance. There are circumstances in which it is an honorable thing to be a prisoner. Outwardly, in self-interest, the Jews might have feigned opposition to Paul on account of his chain, but inwardly they would regard him in rather a heroic light. Nor do I mean his "thorn in the flesh" (2 Cor 12:7). The Lord had taken care of that, to make it an occasion of more abundant grace. The big handicap appeared in the answer of the Jews. It had nothing to do with the man Paul but the cause which he had espoused. "As for this sect, we know that it is everywhere spoken against" (Acts 28:22, author's trans.). Universal prejudice was Paul's big handicap, as it is of every man who seeks to make Christ known.

It is true that the gospel preacher has every man's conscience on his side, but men are not naturally following their consciences. Indeed, it is just because the gospel of Jesus Christ so perfectly sides with conscience that men fight it. If the gospel, with its wonderful offers, would cater also to men's self-interest or self-will or self-righteousness, it would be the most popular message in the world, crushing all rivals. But because it comes awakening the conscience to renewed attacks on those selfish principles by which men live, and threatening to lay low baser things which men love, men throw up a defensive prejudice against it. This is something more than sales resistance. A good salesman can convince most of us that we not only need his product, but that we desire it and must have it, and that at any price it is a rare bargain. The gospel, on the other hand, actually and alone meets man's supreme need, yet it involves such a radical upset in the sinner's outlook, and threatens such total revolution in his way of life, that it has to fight its way through opposition more bitter and determined than ever faced the most unwelcome legislation. We are dealing with the "evil heart of unbelief" (Heb 3:12). This is the reason the Holy Spirit was sent to "reprove the world of sin, and of righteousness, and of judgment" (John 16:8), because the unaided persuasions of the preacher would never overcome the prejudiced unbelief of the sinner, reinforced by the powers of darkness.

So the preliminary conference teaches us two things: the attitude of the gospel minister must be one of grace, and the attitude of the world to the gospel is one of prejudice.

The second scene brings before us the official hearing, for which the leading Jews came to Paul's lodging in sufficient numbers to crowd it. Here was one occasion when the preacher did not allow the clock to hurry him; he took all day for his sermon. It was expository preaching, too, not, however, confined to one passage, but ranging the whole vast area of "the law . . . and . . . the prophets" (Acts 28:23*d*). He laid the matter out to clear view, talking not in dark sayings and hidden mysteries, using no expressions of dubious or double meaning, but presenting the gospel in unmistakable terms, and that from the Scriptures.

Paul's exposition was in two movements, a thorough witnessing and a persuading. First he made it plain beyond question that his message was "the kingdom of God" (28:23b). Now that is exactly what every Jewish mind contemplated and every Jewish heart hoped for, however false the conception entertained. To make that his first emphasis was a masterstroke of wisdom on the part of the apostle, for it created common ground upon which he and his hearers met. It shifted the wind somewhat in his favor. Then he carefully, yet without hesitation, introduced the second division of his day-long exposition, "persuading them concerning Jesus" (28:23c). Right here is where the division took place. So long as the pupil of Gamaliel spoke of the Kingdom of God, the Jews were with him; as soon as the apostle of Jesus Christ began linking the despised, crucified Nazarene with that Kingdom, the atmosphere grew tense. The realm of controversy had been entered, and we can feel the emotional rise in the very change to the word, "persuading." There is passion there, coupled with strong reasonings and a setting forth of the testimony of all the Scriptures.

Are we permitted to wish that we had the text of that great statement? Perhaps it would spoil us to have it, its very fullness and completeness interfering with the discipline of searching the Scriptures for ourselves. I am sure the apostle would present the nature of the Kingdom of God, its spirituality, its universality, its insistence on righteousness. He would trace the idea of atonement as basic in its entire economy; he would develop the relation of the promised Messiah to this Kingdom, not only in the glory of a conquering Monarch, but in the role of a suffering Saviour. Then would he tell of Jesus, indicating the perfect parallel between all that He was and did and suffered, and all that the "volume of the book" (Heb 10:7) declared of the Messiah in His humiliation. Whereupon he would extend the offer of present salvation in His name, and hold out the promise of His coming again to fulfill the still awaiting body of prophecy. I should hesitate to encumber Paul with all the interpretations that have been adduced from his and other inspired writings, especially in the realm of prophecy, but some such general plan as I have indicated must surely have run through that wonderful day's discourse.

The clarity of the exposition, the force of the testimony, and the adequacy of the persuasions bore fruit, for some allowed their prejudices to be swept away, and believed. Others refused all the evidence, and were adamant in their unbelief. Now this was a representative group, come together for an official hearing. As such they refused the message, despite the belief of individuals. They would not, in their representative capacity, call together the Jewish colony of Rome and announce: "We have found him of whom Moses in the law, and the prophets, did write, Jesus of Nazareth" (John 1:45). Paul, therefore, was bound to follow his exposition with a denunciation, again taken from the prophets. This generation was like their fathers in having so perverted their faculties of hearing and seeing and understanding that they were incapable of being converted and healed. Sad, sad state, to which every man comes who persistently refuses the truth! "Be it known therefore unto you," cried the heartsore apostle to the wrangling, discordant group, "Be it known therefore unto you that to the Gentiles is sent this salvation of God" (Acts 28:28, author's trans.).

This is now the third time that Paul has made this statement, with slight variations—first in Antioch of Pisidia, then in Corinth, and now in Rome. I am not prepared to adduce or accept that either the first or the second or the third turning from the Jews to the Gentiles marks a new dispensation. Perhaps on the principle of "three times and out," we might say that with the Roman statement the distinctly Jewish era of the gospel closed, and the door of the Gentiles was fully opened. Yet I am persuaded that if, as is widely believed, Paul, loosed from prison, urged his restless way to Spain, and if he visited cities where were synagogues of the Jews, or places for prayer as in Philippi, he offered his first testimony there. For always he would argue: "Hath God cast away his people? God forbid. For I also am an Israelite, of the seed of Abraham, of the tribe of Benjamin. God hath not cast away his people which he foreknew . . . so then at this present time also there is a remnant according to the election of grace" (Rom 11:1-5). Wonderful, faithful Paul!

The historian, Luke, begins his second treatise to Theophilus with the unfinished work of Christ, and closes it with the unfinished work of the great apostle and of the church and of the Holy Spirit. The last sentence is a parable. "But he remained two whole years in his own hired house, and received all who came to him, heralding the kingdom of God, and teaching the things concerning the Lord Jesus Christ with all boldness, without hindrance" (Acts 28:30-31, author's trans.). Look at Paul in Rome and you see the church in the world. The world will lay its chains and restrictions upon the church, but the church is still bound to herald that Kingdom before which the world must fall, and to teach the things concerning the Lord Jesus Christ against every demand for a change of message. Let the church but be bold enough to press its task with energy and devotion, and that church will still be free, unhindered, despite all worldly restrictions. The measure of the church's hindrance in its task is the measure of its submission to the condition imposed by the world. Those who will be prisoners of none but Jesus Christ, bondslaves to none but their Lord, will be the Lord's free men, and their preaching and teaching will give multiplied evidence that "the word of God is not bound" (2 Tim 2:9).

So the book ends, but the story goes on. "Upon this rock will I build my church; and the gates of hell shall not prevail against it" (Matt 16:18).

> 'Mid toil and tribulation,
>   And tumult of her war,
> She waits the consummation
>   Of peace forevermore;
> Till with the vision glorious
>   Her longing eyes are blessed,
> And the great Church victorious
>   Shall be the Church at rest.
>
>   SAMUEL J. STONE

"After this I beheld, and, lo, a great multitude, which no man could number, of all nations, and kindreds, and people, and tongues, stood before the throne, and before the Lamb, clothed with white robes, and palms in their hands; and cried with a loud voice, saying, Salvation to our God which sitteth upon the throne, and unto the Lamb" (Rev 7:9-10).